'Everything is in flux – you cann[illegible] Heraclitus. It sounds a truism to [illegible] millenium has been preceded b[illegible] g concepts of the Christian ministry. Both [illegible] se outside tend to have different views of the work of the pastor [illegible] us generations. To the world at large, the Church is viewed simply as one social institution among others, and the minister is expected to take his place alongside social workers in coping with society's urgent demands. Within the church, elders and other office-bearers often feel that less control should be exercised by the minister, and that some of his responsibilities should be shared around, so that others, in effect, have a turn.

A great challenge as we enter a new millenium is how to alter the past mould of the Christian ministry where it clearly needs to be changed, without losing the immeasurable benefits of the past where its practice has been true to the biblical pattern. Unchanging truth is to be proclaimed to people in fast changing circumstances, people whose basic spiritual needs are no different from those before them. This can be achieved only as we re-establish the biblical principles of ministry and then try to re-apply them honestly to our contemporary situation. Peter White has endeavoured to do this with integrity. Although written from a Scottish Presbyterian perspective, the issues he tackles have marked, and sometimes painful, relevance to church leaders everywhere.

Derek Prime
Pastor Emeritus, Charlotte Baptist Chapel, Edinburgh

'I am very pleased to commend this unusually helpful book, in which from his pastor's heart Peter White reflects on long years of experience in parish ministry. Yet he does so in the light of his wide reading, his leadership of a theological college, and his constant and rigorous self-examination before the Lord.

The Effective Pastor will without question make pastors more effective, and pulses with the energy and commitment of one whose effectiveness in the Lord's service is beyond doubt.'

Nigel M. de S. Cameron
Dean of The Wilberforce Forum, Reston, Virginia;
Executive Chairman, The Centre for Bioethics and Public Policy, London

'Comprehensive. Deep. Contemporary. Practical. These are the words that come to mind on reading *The Effective Pastor*. It covers a wide scope, dealing comprehensively both with the pastor as a person and the nature of the pastoral task without falling into superficiality. It is deep because it lays secure spiritual foundations for ministry and shuns the cheap and superficial answers which abound today. Depth is also seen in its use of the insights of our great evangelical forefathers and in the wise use of personal experience of ministry. The book is also contemporary. It is not locked into the past but makes good use of contemporary management, psychological and sociological research. It is aware of the privileges and strains of ministry today rather than yesterday. Finally, it is thoroughly practical. Building on the good foundations, practical suggestions are made as to how one can grow in a pastoral gift and tackle things differently. All in all, it is a rare and delicious blend. It's worth drinking slowly and savouring every mouthful.'

Derek J. Tidball
Principal, London Bible College

'There has long been a need for a contemporary manual of biblical and practical instruction on the work of the ministry. Christian ministers, old and young alike, have needed material to which they could turn regularly and with confidence for wise counsel, encouragement and biblical direction in their high and immensely demanding calling.

The Effective Pastor recognises this need and meets it. It will be widely welcomed, eagerly read, and should stimulate thought and discussion about many aspects of pastoral work.

Peter White is well-equipped to author such a book. He brings to his task more than two decades of wide experience as a minister and the added experience and reflection of a former Bible College principal. Consequently there is much here which will not only serve to direct, stimulate and encourage younger ministers but also to reinvigorate and challenge experienced ministers to serve Christ better than ever. Many of us have felt that someone needed to write it; Peter White is to be congratulated on having the courage to be that someone.'

Sinclair B. Ferguson
Minister, St George's Tron Church, Glasgow

'We are constantly reminded of the urgency with which many pastors are looking for assistance. At the end of the twentieth century, the Christian minister is facing unique challenges of organization and a sad decline in passion. Peter White has provided a most helpful assistance to preachers in his new volume. Covering the urgently important issues of ministry, Peter White serves as an experienced guide and a thoughtful analyst of the Christian ministry. Rightly, he places central emphasis upon the preaching of the Word and the faithfulness of the minister as preacher. In this respect, the church is at the end of the twentieth century where it began in the first century. We face the glorious but challenging task to preach the Word, in season and out of season. Preachers are in Peter White's debt for his assistance.'

Albert Mohler
President, Southern Baptist Theological Seminary, Lousiville, Kentucky

GET THE TOOLS TO UPGRADE
YOUR MINISTRY

PETER WHITE

MENTOR

C. Peter White pastors Sandyford Henderson Memorial Church of Scotland in Glasgow.

For details of our titles visit us on our web site
http://www.christianfocus.com

ISBN 1 85792 120 8

First Published in 1998 by
Christian Focus Publications,
Geanies House, Fearn, Ross-shire,
IV20 1TW, Great Britain.
Updated edition with study guide printed 2002

Cover design by Alister Macinnes

Contents

To George Philip,
my minister and my predecessor at Sandyford,

model of such warmth in pastoring
and
such naturalness and passion in preaching.

PREFACE AND ACKNOWLEDGEMENTS

I shall never forget the words of a candidate for the Christian ministry the day he left College. 'Thank goodness that's over,' he said, 'now I can go back to being a Christian.' The comment reflects an approach to theological principle, personal faith and practical service which this book seeks to correct.

In approaching Christian service, three great pitfalls lie in wait for the unwary. The first is to deal directly in practicalities without due regard for good theology. The trouble is, programmes of activity offer themselves from every quarter. Like Don Quixote we find ourselves jumping on our horse and galloping off madly in every direction.

The second pitfall is to attempt Christian leadership without living faith and trust in the Holy Spirit, as though theology and skill make a Christian worker. No, ministry requires a spiritual life and integrity not absolutely demanded in any other work.

The third is theology whose only natural home is the lecture theatre. Like Salvador Dali's 'Christ of St John of the Cross' it remains several feet above ground level, unearthed, failing to touch the lives of those toiling below.

Christian leadership requires an integration of theological principle with the spirituality of the pastor and his exercise of Christian care. Such is the aim of *The Effective Pastor*. It is based on thirty-four years' experience of Christian service in several church and parachurch contexts, including eighteen years in parish ministry and six as Principal of a Bible college. During that time I lectured in pastoral theology and had the opportunity to reflect on the union between principle, person and praxis.

One benefit is that the book's content is supported by research evidence drawn from the behavioural sciences as well as the practice of ministry; and from letters and conference addresses not otherwise easily accessible. The footnotes suggest further reading for those wishing to examine issues in greater depth.

I am grateful to the following for their help in the preparation of this volume: Irene Crosthwaite for typing help; the Governing Body of Glasgow Bible College for three months' study leave; David Clarkson, Sinclair Ferguson and Noël Peacock for constructive criticism; the publishers, especially Malcolm Maclean, for their encouragement and patience; and my wife Liz for her eagle eye and feeling for the clarity of a passage.

C. Peter White

ABBREVIATIONS

INST Calvin, John. *Institutes of the Christian Religion*. McNeill edition, London (SCM) and Philadelphia (Westminster), 1967: Library of Christian Classics Vols XX and XXI.

NPNF *A Select Library of the Nicene and Post-Nicene Fathers of the Christian Church*, ed. Philip Schaff, 10 vols, 1885-99; Eerdmans reprint, Grand Rapids, Michigan, 1978-79.

NTS New Testament Studies

op. cit. In the work already quoted. Where there have been two works quoted from one author in a chapter, the work being referred to is identified by date; in the case of the same date, by the title in abbreviated form.

RP Baxter, Richard. *The Reformed Pastor*, 1656; ed. William Brown with an introduction by J.I. Packer, Edinburgh, Banner of Truth, 1974.

RPH Baxter, Richard. *The Reformed Pastor*, 1656; ed. James M. Houston with an introduction by R.C. Halverson, Basingstoke, Pickering and Inglis, 1983.

TDNT *Theological Dictionary of the New Testament*, ed. G. Kittell, trans. G.W. Bromiley, Grand Rapids, Eerdmans, 10 vols, 1964-1976.

In transliterating Greek words I have made no distinction between epsilon (short e) and eta (long e), nor between long and short o.

BEFORE GOD

CHAPTER ONE

OUR VISION

What are we *for*?

The people whom I formed for myself
that they might declare my praise (Isaiah 43:21).

The God of heaven will set up a kingdom that will never be
destroyed. It will endure for ever (Daniel 2:44).

I saw the holy city coming down out of heaven from God, prepared
as a bride beautifully dressed for her husband (Revelation 21:2).

In his book, *The Pastoral Nature of the Ministry*, Frank Wright records a telling incident from an early stage in his Christian work. 'At Monday morning's staff meeting we were organising parishioners from the comfort of our armchairs: someone to take over the Brownies, supervise the envelope scheme, help with the monthly Pram Service. "But what," asked my colleague, "am I supposed to be doing with the people I meet? What am I for?" '[1]

The failure to keep clearly in mind just what it is that we are engaged in can overtake any Christian worker. I shall never forget the shock of it happening to me on a very public occasion. The Glasgow 'September Weekend' is a local public holiday and for some years the favourite haunt of young people from the Glasgow area over that weekend was the town of Brodick on the Isle of Arran. The pubs were crowded, the camping sites full to overflowing and the celebrations as riotous but good-hearted as only Glaswegians can make them.

On one such weekend I was the joint leader of a Christian outreach to the town. Camp site visiting, open air preaching, tract distribution ... we did it all. The day after we arrived a camera crew from BBC Scotland turned up to record the events of the weekend, stuck a microphone in front of my face and asked what the Christians were about.

My mind froze. I hadn't a clue. Busy, I had been busy. I had bought food, found sleeping bags, borrowed (and dented) a glazier's van to carry all the equipment; and had become so involved that I had clean forgotten what it was all about, why we were doing it.

It was a real warning. The work can take over from the Lord. To retain the vision is important. It is especially important when we are discouraged and during the long dark times; but it is life-shaping at all times. Let us remember what it is that we are doing.

A bride for God's Son

What is Christian work ultimately about? Let us start at the beginning. God had no insufficiency that made him need to create a universe. But he is a trinity: one God, yet three persons who with total justification delight in and live for one another's honour. In the affection that the Father has for the Son he chose to make a companion for him, a people, the church: his 'bride', to glorify and enjoy him. The Son was thrilled.

> From heaven he came and sought her to be his holy bride;
> With his own blood he bought her, and for her sake he died.

God, then, is the subject of all existence and the object of ours. We exist to enjoy and glorify him. Why? Because of the stunning brightness of his holiness; because he is so perfect and admirable in himself; because he is *God*.

The glory of God

What is this glory of God that is our aim and his? The Old Testament word translated glory (*kabod*) has as its underlying thought the idea of weight or weightiness, and hence of value or worth. Since God is, his importance carries weight; he evokes respect.

But it is not only *that* he exists. Just think about him; about the 'glorious splendour of his majesty'.[2] He *is* wisdom and goodness, love and power. He is everywhere, yet without position; first and most recent, without time and beyond time; good, pure and righteous without qualification or limit; as the Shorter Catechism has it, 'infinite, eternal and unchangeable in his being, wisdom, power, holiness, justice, goodness and truth.'[3] He alone is self-existent; he knows everything; this is the glory of him in himself.

But we must add to that. The verse that speaks of his majesty goes on, 'and I will meditate on your wonderful works'. He holds us in existence by his mighty word of command. He rules the universe. And he has acted, at inconceivable cost to himself, as deliverer and Saviour. We see how glorious he is, in the person and work of Jesus Christ. All of these – creation, providence, grace and the person of Jesus Christ – are worthy, immense, splendid: they are expressions of his glory.

The result is a radiance that men and angels cannot see and still live.[4] When evidence of it filled the tabernacle in the Exodus wanderings, and at Solomon's dedication of the Jerusalem temple, men had to leave; it was unbearable:

> Then the cloud covered the Tent of Meeting, and the glory of the LORD filled the tabernacle. Moses could not enter the Tent of Meeting because the cloud had settled on it, and the glory of the LORD filled the tabernacle.
>
> The cloud filled the temple of the LORD. And the priests could not perform their service because of the cloud, for the glory of the LORD filled his temple.[5]

It is only right and proper, therefore, it is an irresistible imperative of our existing at all, to honour and love him. Our chief purpose is to accord him, and gain for him, the homage, the esteem and the service that he deserves as King and redeemer.

At the dawn of human history God had but two people to glorify and enjoy him. By the end of time there will be an uncountable number from every language and ethnic group on the globe. Between those two points human history is, before anything else, the story of God's work creating, redeeming and calling to himself this people upon whom his Son's heart is set.[6]

This is what we are for! He destined us in love to be his children 'to the praise of his glorious grace'. God has shown us mercy 'so that we might live for the praise of his glory'. The Holy Spirit is the first instalment of our salvation until we acquire possession of it 'to the praise of his glory'.[7]

We shall never encounter a greater theme than this; there is none. It is the reason why the world exists. Let us frequently remind ourselves, and especially during the times of steady patience or of disappointment, how tremendous a drama it is of which we are a part, and how great a privilege it is to serve it.

Imagine! God from all eternity picturing you and me, with our particular upbringing and background, all our varied experience of life and work, our unique strengths; and, punctual to the second, he has us where he wants to use us.

Who is equal to the task?

Can anyone in Christian work feel sufficient for this? John Chrysostom, explaining why he had avoided ordination, reminds his friend Basil that the Church is Christ's Bride and goes on (I paraphrase):

> The prospect of ordination filled me with fear, tears, dark depression and confusion. How can I explain this to you?
>
> Let us suppose that the daughter of the King of all the Earth is engaged to a certain man; and that she has ravishing, incredible beauty, more than any woman who has ever lived. Not only so; suppose she also has every splendid virtue and that her grace of movement is sheer poetry, alluring and admirable beyond compare. Imagine that her fiancé absolutely adores her: not only for these things, but simply because he loves her, irrespective of them; and that the passion of his ardour has never been equalled or even approached in all human history.
>
> Then suppose that while he is burning with love, he hears that some mean-spirited, abject lout is about to marry this glorious and beloved woman. Do you see why I am so distressed at the prospect of being a pastor?[8]

Here is one of the undeniable pains of Christian work: our sense of unworthiness. But there is also a lesson in this tension between our desire to serve Jesus and our sense of unworthiness: we must learn to take God's decisions more seriously than our own. It is a lesson we see God's servants having to learn time and again. Think of Moses wrestling with God over his vocation: 'Who am I, that I should go to Pharaoh?'

'But I will be with you.'

'But I am not eloquent.'

'Who made man's mouth; is it not I, the Lord?'[9]

Or think of God's word to Gideon: 'Go in *this* your might: have not I sent you?'[10] That was his power for the task: God's sending. When we experience a sense of inadequacy, therefore, God replies as he did to Moses and Gideon: 'But I will be with you.'

Benefits of maintaining our vision

Enjoying the vision and the sense of wonder at being allowed to serve God can, first, *inspire our work* if we will let it. The familiar story of the three men working on the reconstruction of St. Paul's Cathedral under the direction of Sir Christopher Wren still has force. Someone approached them and asked each man what he was doing. 'I'm digging this hole,' said the first, 'to get some money, to buy my food, to give me energy to dig this hole.' 'I'm trying to be the best stonemason I am capable of being,' said the second man. That was better. But the third replied, 'I am helping Sir Christopher Wren build a wonderful cathedral to the glory of God.' Maintaining our vision can inspire our whole approach to our work.

Our vision also *moulds our outlook* amidst the difficulties and pains of Christian work.

> The late Dr. Donald Barnhouse told how once he was conducting a week of services in a large church. The pastor of that church was on the 'hot seat'. His wife was about to have their first child. This was a source of great anxiety for the pastor, but it was a source of real humour for Dr. Barnhouse and he joked about it throughout the week.
>
> On his last night, when he went to the podium, Dr. Barnhouse waited and waited for the pastor to introduce him. But the pastor didn't come. So smiling, and in a knowing fashion, Dr. Barnhouse got up, introduced himself, and conducted the service that night.
>
> Toward the end of that service Dr. Barnhouse noticed the pastor as he slipped in at the back of the sanctuary and made his way silently to the podium. When the pastor took his seat Dr. Barnhouse turned and smiled at him in a knowing fashion. All the congregation joined him in smiling. Then Dr. Barnhouse continued the service and completed it.
>
> It was at this point that Dr. Barnhouse asked the young pastor, 'Everything all right?' No one noticed the pastor's expression.
>
> 'Could I see you in my study, Sir?' the pastor asked Dr. Barnhouse.
>
> 'Certainly,' Dr. Barnhouse said.
>
> So they made their way to the pastor's study. Then the pastor blurted out, 'Dr. Barnhouse, our child has Downs syndrome. I haven't told my wife, and I don't know what I'm going to tell her.'
>
> 'My friend, this is of the Lord,' Dr. Barnhouse said. And he turned to this passage, the most overlooked passage in all the Old Testament, the fourth chapter of Exodus, and he read aloud: 'And the Lord said unto him, who hath made man's mouth or who maketh the dumb or deaf or the

seeing or the blind ... have not I the Lord?'

'Let me see that,' the pastor said. And he studied it very quietly.

As he studied it, Dr. Barnhouse said, 'My friend, you know in the promise in Romans 8 that all things, including this Downs syndrome child, work together for good to those that love the Lord.'

The pastor closed the Bible. He left the study and he went straight to the hospital room of his wife. As he walked in, she was saying, 'Cap, I want to see my baby. I've asked to see my baby and they won't let me. Is anything wrong with my baby?'

' "Who maketh the dumb, dumb and the blind, blind and the deaf, deaf ... is it not I, the Lord?" My precious darling, the Lord has blessed us with a Downs syndrome child.'

The young wife and mother cried long and hard. Then she said, 'Where did you get that?'

'From God's own Word.'

'Let me see it.' And then she read it ....

When that pastor's wife called her mother she said, 'Mother, the Lord has blessed us with a Downs syndrome child. We don't know the nature of the blessing but we do know it's a blessing.'

There were no tears, no hysteria, no breakdown, no coming apart at the seams ....

The following Sunday the pastor was back in his pulpit. In the congregation, unknown to him, were the telephone operator and seventy nurses from that hospital. At the conclusion of that service, as he always did, the pastor stood down front and he said, 'If you've never met Jesus Christ I want to extend to you the invitation to come down to the altar and to receive him as your personal Lord and your personal Saviour.'

The pastor barely glanced up because this was his custom since very few ever came. Thirty nurses from the hospital came to the altar that day! Can you imagine one Downs syndrome child being patently responsible for giving eternal life to thirty nurses? You say, 'How horrible!' No, my friend, not horrible.[11]

Our vision affects our whole outlook.

Thirdly, our vision *gives us confidence*. The American author Zig Ziglar writes of watching a football game between the Minnesota Vikings and the Dallas Cowboys. Ziglar was a Cowboys supporter:

'We headed into the final minute with the Vikings ahead. Many of the Cowboys faithful had lost their faith. As I sat watching the game I am going to tell you there wasn't the slightest doubt in my mind as to the outcome of the game ... (here Ziglar describes yards and kicks which would only be comprehensible to an aficionado; suffice it to say that in the closing seconds a Cowboys kick snatched them the victory). The crowd literally exploded. If there had been a roof on the stadium I think it would have come off. And yet I say to you again in all honesty that I just kept my seat and smiled broadly at what had happened. Not once did my faith ever waver. I knew the Cowboys would come out on top.

'Now in all honesty I must confess to you that one of the reasons for my total confidence was that I was watching a replay. You are probably saying, you knew the final score, why should you worry or get excited? But this is my point. Just so, in the game of life. I know exactly how the game is going to end and I know I have won that game. Knowing what I know about the way the game ends, enables me "not to sweat the small stuff" even if I am unjustly penalised or unfairly treated.'[12]

Vision gives confidence, and that is most telling at the times we are under pressure and most tempted to give up.

Fourthly, vision *nourishes energy and zeal.* David Brainerd, the missionary to the American Indians, said:

> 'My heaven is to please God and glorify him, and give all to him and be wholly devoted to his glory. That is the heaven I long for, that is my religion; that is my happiness and always was, I suppose, ever since I had any true religion. All those that are of that religion shall meet me in heaven. I do not go to heaven to be advanced but to give honour to God.'[13]

Brainerd was not boasting; it was a decision and a commitment that he had made.

The challenge faces each of us, what is our chief motive for being in Christ's service. We might well pause for a few minutes and do business with God, re-affirming what we are for.

References

1. F. Wright, *The Pastoral Nature of the Ministry*, London, SCM Press, 1980, p. 1.

2. Psalm 145:5.

3. H. Heppe, *Reformed Dogmatics*, Michigan, Baker, 1950, p. 58. *The Shorter Catechism*, Edinburgh, Blackwood, 1966, p. 115, qu. 4.

4. Exodus 33:18-34:8; Isaiah 6:1-4.

5. Exodus 40:34-38; 1 Kings 8:10f.

6. John 6:35-40.

7. Ephesians 1:6, 12, 14.

8. J. Chrysostom, *On the Priesthood*, Book 6, §12, NPNF, First Series, vol. 9, Grand Rapids, Eerdmans reprint, 1978, p. 81.

9. Exodus 3:11, 12; 4:10, 11.

10. Judges 6:14.

11. Quoted by T.L. Johnson, sermon entitled 'Outlook', Independent Presbyterian Church, Savannah, GA, 23 Feb 1992. Copyright Ben Haden.

12. Z. Ziglar, *Confessions*, Pelican, USA, 1978. Page not noted.

13. D. Brainerd, quoted by G.I. Williamson, *The Shorter Catechism,* Nutley, NJ, Presbyterian and Reformed Publishing Co. 1972, p. 129.

CHAPTER TWO

OUR PRESENT

Call, character, passion for the work

No-one can even see, let alone enter, the kingdom of God unless he is born again (John 3:3-6).

Check up on yourselves to see whether you are in the faith; test yourselves. Do you not yourselves recognise that Christ is in you? – unless you do not pass that test! (2 Cor. 13:5).

I was walking with a fellow minister in the grounds of a College after an in-service lecture. We had just heard an address on the doctrine of justification that had enlarged my mind and warmed my heart. My colleague said he had not understood a word of it. We explored his statement, and the joy I had found in listening to the lecture, for a few minutes. Finally, I said, 'Would you say you can call Jesus your Saviour?' After a thoughtful pause he replied, 'No.'

Are there prerequisites for being in Christian ministry? If so, what are they? The list deducible from the New Testament is surprising at first sight, containing as it does few specific skills. On reflection, however, the wisdom of this becomes apparent. Christian work has such variety that the gospel lays down few qualifications that have to do with particular tasks, although the ones it does name are significant. As Alec Motyer observes, 'The New Testament does not give a job description but a character reference.'[1]

But if it is not skills, not even pastoral skills, that qualify us for ministry, what does? The New Testament would apply at least the following tests to those who would serve Christ and his cause.

Eternal life

Our Lord uses the most solemn warning about certain Christian workers. They may have spoken God's message and performed amazing miracles but some on judgement day will hear the terrible words, 'Depart from me; I never knew you.'[2] Surely Jesus Christ knows all things? He knows everything about all of us; what does he mean here? He is saying that there was not that knowledge of each other which flows from a union of life and a oneness of mind, heart and spirit between Christ and a person. We may know much about the Christian faith but until, in Jesus' words, we have been 'born from above'[3] we cannot see or enter the kingdom of God;[4] cannot know God, nor his truth and its power, for ourselves. I do not assume that everyone who reads this book is yet a new creation enjoying the benefits which Christ purchased for us. Until Jesus and a person know each other in this biblical sense – as long as Christ remains outside him – he lacks eternal life and all his Christian knowledge is second-hand.

It is the absolute assumption of Scripture that a Christian worker must be a Christian. Saving faith stands before all else and certainly before any authentic service. To that colleague with whom I walked after the lecture on justification, therefore, and to every reader of this book who is in, or who is contemplating, Christian service the apostolic command is, 'Examine yourself to see if you are in the faith.' If we are not, if we cannot call the Saviour our saviour, if we count ourselves amongst the once-born, Scripture urges on us the radical change of heart which brings eternal life.

The term 'born again', of course, has regrettable overtones of a superficial experience, often emotional and devoid of solid moral or even spiritual content. From all cheap, sound-byte new birth, good Lord deliver us. But the abuse of a thing does not take away its proper use. To those, in fact, who call themselves once-born Christians I would simply urge the following three paragraphs.

The Bible establishes beyond argument – as if the daily papers and our own self-understanding did not confirm it – that we are sinners, by nature spiritually dead, guilty before God and in need of a Saviour. It shows us also that our Lord Jesus is the very Saviour we need, crucified for our sins and raised to life with the power to put us in the right with God. How he loves us! He is willing and able to provide the exact redemption we need; there is no other source of it.

So far, so good; but as long as Christ stays outside of us, and we remain separated and estranged from him, it is as though he had never come at all, for all the benefit we get from him.[5] We need to be personally reconciled to him, united with him, in order to enjoy Christ and all he can do for us.

What is our responsibility in this respect? Simply, to repent and believe the gospel.[6] We are to believe that Jesus is the Son, crucified for our sins and actually risen from the dead. Distrusting our own ability and trusting his, we receive him in exchange for our guilt and we surrender our life, all of it, to his reign. Then we tell some trustworthy Christian what we have done.

Vigorous friendship with Jesus

Pastoral work and Christian leadership are not for those who do not greatly care for the Christian cause or about knowing their Saviour better. Just as concerning prayer, the motto of which is 'Pray when you feel like it; pray when you do not feel like it; pray till you feel like it', so it is in respect of seeking to know Jesus Christ better. The enormous privilege of this friendship makes it a subject in its own right and it is addressed in chapter four.

Living discipleship

It is not particular skills but deep and wide-ranging integrity of character which the New Testament requires in the Christian worker. The tasks involved in our work vary, and with them the skills needed; but Scripture calls all of us to become more like Jesus.

What are we to check for? The startling thing about the criteria given us in Scripture is how, largely, 'unspiritual', they are. Extracted from the evidence in the pastoral epistles,[7] they can be summed up as:

Personally moral. Our life is to be above reproach: not perfect but the sort of person against whom no charge would stick.[8] High moral standards pervade the descriptions of people suitable for office: temperate, self-controlled, an orderly life characterised by balance, a sensible person not marked by excess. Alcoholic intake is repeatedly identified as an area in which self mastery is essential. Scripture lays down the additional criterion 'respected by people outside the Church'.[9] Our personal integrity and consistency should be so pervasive as to be evident to all.

Domestically faithful. Absolute faithfulness to the marriage bond in thought and deed is implied by the scriptural language: for example, 'a one-woman man'.[10] Whether we are married or single, that is the sort of person to be. If we are parents we are to be managing our household well and acceptably. The respect we earn should be visible in the obedience which our children give to our lead, and ours will be a hospitable home where others are welcomed.

Relationally peaceful. It is a remarkable list which Paul gives in this matter. Even if we restrict ourselves to 1 Timothy 3 and Titus 1, we have:

· not violent but gentle
· not quarrelsome
· not overbearing
· not quick-tempered

Here is a picture of a peace-making, patient leader whose fair-minded and charitable spirit can be trusted when he speaks of others.[11] I remember, when serving on a committee which decided on staff deployment for our denomination, our having to turn down a request for parish assistance because the minister in question had the reputation of being difficult, an impossible person to work with. To be in oversight of a congregation calls us to be people characterised by respect and constant courtesy towards others; kind to everyone, not resentful nor a person who harbours grudges; gently reasonable with those who oppose us.[12]

Doctrinally able. The pastoral leaders in a church should be capable in teaching so as both to encourage others by sound teaching and also to refute those who oppose it.[13] The reason for this is not hard to discern. The primary task in pastoring is pasturing. The chief action in care for the flock is to feed it on healthy, scriptural Christian teaching. Not only so; we have to expect that there will always be false teachers around wanting to press their wares for a variety of motives. This requires us to be, at least, thoroughly competent in the field of Christian doctrine so as to be able to answer such problems. Even the assistants in ministry, called deacons in the Pastoral epistles, must have a capable grasp of the deep truths of the faith with a clear conscience for the same kind of reason.[14]

Financially modest. Paul puts his finger here on an understandable but besetting sin among Christian workers. I well remember an incident during my ministry when I was helping move furniture for a family after bereavement. As we were carrying an item out of the house my eyes lit upon an old chimney brush set. As it happened it was just the thing we could do with, as a family, at that time. I said nothing. At the end of the removal I was offered it with the explanation, 'The look in your eyes was just like that of a minister years ago when he saw something he wanted.'

I felt ashamed that the Christian ministry, in that parishioner's eyes, included covetousness among its distinguishing features. The authentic Christian worker needs to be clear as to his motives. We are not in the work for honour or financial gain.[15] We can live without kudos and money as well as with them; we sit light to material considerations.

The temptation to let money become too important is understandable. Ministers may be poorly paid and the resultant stringency can come to dominate their families' lives. Nonetheless it is a temptation we must recognise and refuse.

Spiritually vital. As one called to take care of God's Church (not his own!) a pastoral leader should not be a new convert lest he become proud (verse 6). He must so stand as to refuse the devil's wiles (verse 7). Along with his fellow elders he will be wanted at the side of the sick (James 5:14) because he will be a praying person, in substantial communication with the living God: not just in theory, but someone who proves its power and efficacy in practice. If the men appointed to handle finances had to be full of the Holy Spirit, how much more so those whose calling is the prayers and the work of preaching.[16]

What feeds spiritual vitality? A radical mortification of self-centredness and of all that hinders our fellowship with Jesus Christ; behaviour in accordance with the Sermon on the Mount; and the use of the means of grace.

The means of grace are the same for pastoral leaders as for anyone else. Let us take for ourselves the love of God that we make known.[17] Let us preach our sermons to ourselves before we preach them to others. There is a real danger of conveying the benefits of the gospel to other people but never making them our own. What a plight, spiritually to starve while feeding others.[18]

A call from God, including a call to our present work

A few years ago the General Assembly of the Church of Scotland addressed the question of recruitment to the ministry, as though it could be engineered by the kind of procedure used by secular agencies. There is a critical issue here. If we run Christian work along secular lines we get something which looks similar to God's work but is actually quite different. How then shall we recognise *God's* action? Candidate and Church alike will look for at least the following marks of an authentic call.

We really want to do it. Effective Christian work has battles known only to those who engage seriously in it. Some people would rather do anything, as Gregory of Nazianzus pointed out, than let their private beliefs and behaviour be corrected by their pastor.[19] Let us be passionately keen to do this work, difficulty notwithstanding, before considering that we might have a calling from God.

The opinion of others. I cannot emphasise enough the importance of this mark of a call. Every vocational call in the New Testament involved the church in some way as well as the person themselves.

Paul had known since his conversion that he would be a missionary; but he waited years until the praying group of which he was a part was told, 'Set apart Barnabas and Saul for the work,' before he moved.[20] In Timothy's case we do not even know how much he wanted the task; but the believers spoke well of him, Paul took a hand in the matter, and Timothy was in full-time Christian service.[21] Let a person contemplating ministry either wait on God until his church set him aside for the work, or at least submit his thinking to the praying fellowship who know him best.

A pressure on our spirit. In the course of our relation with God there comes the inner awareness of the repeated and irresistible direction of our attention to the pastorate. There is something undeniably 'from outside' about this. It is not a matter of our choosing to contemplate it, so much as something that is being done to us.

A gifting in the area of our calling. Let no-one who is incapable of explaining the gospel, or of forgetting self in the humble service of others, go further. But God-given capacity in the tasks of pastoral ministry, especially in orderly and impactful exposition of Scripture, is a mark of a true call.

God has used us. It is a strange thing this. We engaged in the ordinary activities of healthy friendship; and someone asked to come to church, or found Christ by our side. We gave a talk on some aspect of Christian teaching; and months later one of our hearers told us that they were converted or greatly affected that day. There is something so obviously of God about this that it is to be trusted.

We like people and feel concerned about them. The Christian ministry is not for those whose great interest is themselves.

Even after call and training we still need the call to a particular situation or church. Normally such a call is discerned by the usual combination of objective, subjective and providential criteria by which we make significant decisions in any aspect of life; especially, a call from a congregation combined with the agreement of those whom we trust and an inner drawing within ourselves. Such features are the sweetly reasonable marks of the Father's work.

There is one other thing to note as we deal with the subject of assessing our present situation. A person can be called to minister and called to a particular church – but never notice when it is time to move on. We need courage and wisdom to distinguish such a call from the devil's desire to be rid of us; the latter might come just when the vital need is to stand firm and refuse to submit to the difficulties. As we assess the present, therefore, a proper question to ask is, 'Do I still have, at this time, God's call to this people?'

In this chapter we have proposed ways of assessing ourselves. It is suggested that we now spend some time checking our bearings, before God, in the light of them:

- 'Examine yourselves, to see whether you are in the faith; test yourselves' (2 Corinthians 13:5). Could a fresh surrender to Jesus be anything but good?

- What health rating would I give my 'walking and talking with God'?

- Personally moral; domestically faithful; relationally peaceful; doctrinally able; financially modest: spiritually vital: is there anything I need to adjust in order to align myself with these?

- If considering ministry or a change of ministry, check for the marks of a calling.

- Might there be value in a fresh commitment to choosing, relishing, loving this my life's main work?

References

1. A. Motyer, *Ordination for What?,* Fellowship of Word and Spirit, Disley, Cheshire, n.d., p. 10.

2. Matthew 7:23.

3. John 3:3.

4. John 3:1-6.

5. INST. 3.1.1.

6. Acts 17:30, 31; Mark 1:14, 15.

7. Especially 1 Timothy 3:1-13 and Titus 1:6-9.

8. Thus *anepilemptos*, literally: 1 Timothy 3:2.

9. 1 Timothy 3:7.

10. 1 Timothy 3:2.

11. 1 Timothy 3:11.

12. 11 Timothy 2:23-26.

13. 1 Timothy 3:2; Titus 1:9.

14. 1 Timothy 3:9.

15. 1 Peter 5:2.

16. Acts 6:3, 4.

17. J. Owen, 'On Communion with the Trinity', *Works,* Goold Edition, vol. 2, Edinburgh, Banner of Truth reprint, 1968, p. 24-36.

18. No-one has put this more powerfully than Richard Baxter: RP p. 53.

19. Gregory of Naziansus, *Oration 2: In Defence of his flight to Pontus*, NPNF, 2nd Series, vol. 7, p. 204-227, especially paragraphs 20, 21, 40-46.

20. Acts 13:2.

21. Acts 16:3.

CHAPTER THREE

OUR PAST

The guilt and gospel work cycles

Do not think of yourself more highly than you ought, but rather think of yourself with sober judgement (Romans 12:3).

Nearly all the wisdom we possess, that is to say, true and sound wisdom, consists of two parts: the knowledge of God and of ourselves (John Calvin, *Institutes of the Christian Religion*, 1.1.1).

What sort of person goes into Christian work? In the 1970s Eadie wrote a number of papers on the health of Scottish pastors. He found that people entering pastoral ministry often have a common personality profile. He called it the 'helping personality'[1]: the pitfalls, because it shares features with members of other helping professions.

This type of person tends to be a candidate for a destructive cycle of overwork, fuelled by the very strengths and weaknesses of character which attract us to the work we are in: the very things which make us open to God's call. It is summarised in figure 2.1. The steps in the cycle are as follows.

The 'Helping Personality': The pitfalls

An idealised self image. God has called us into Christian work but there is no way we can live up to the standards we set ourselves. We know we should be thoughtful, patient, considerate, forbearing: so we find it difficult to cope with our sensitivity when criticised or when our plans are frustrated. We know we should not be self-centred, dependent on others, angry; but we are only too aware that these traits keep surfacing.

We perceive a carer within us, nearly always a valid perception, not fully realising that the Christian worker is often a former lonely child who needs to be loved and develops a loving self-image (however subconsciously) in order to be loved. Here is one of the ironies of Christian service. Many Christian workers hate isolation, but their calling often sets them apart and isolates them.

Guilt and self-denigration. The image we set for ourselves produces a powerful inner pressure to meet all demands: a tendency to overwork which has been called 'the hardening of the oughteries'. Failing to meet our unrealistic targets produces a dominating sense of guilt, and, to the irritation of those who love us, we keep running ourselves down.

Compulsive-obsessive characteristics. Guilt feelings exacerbate

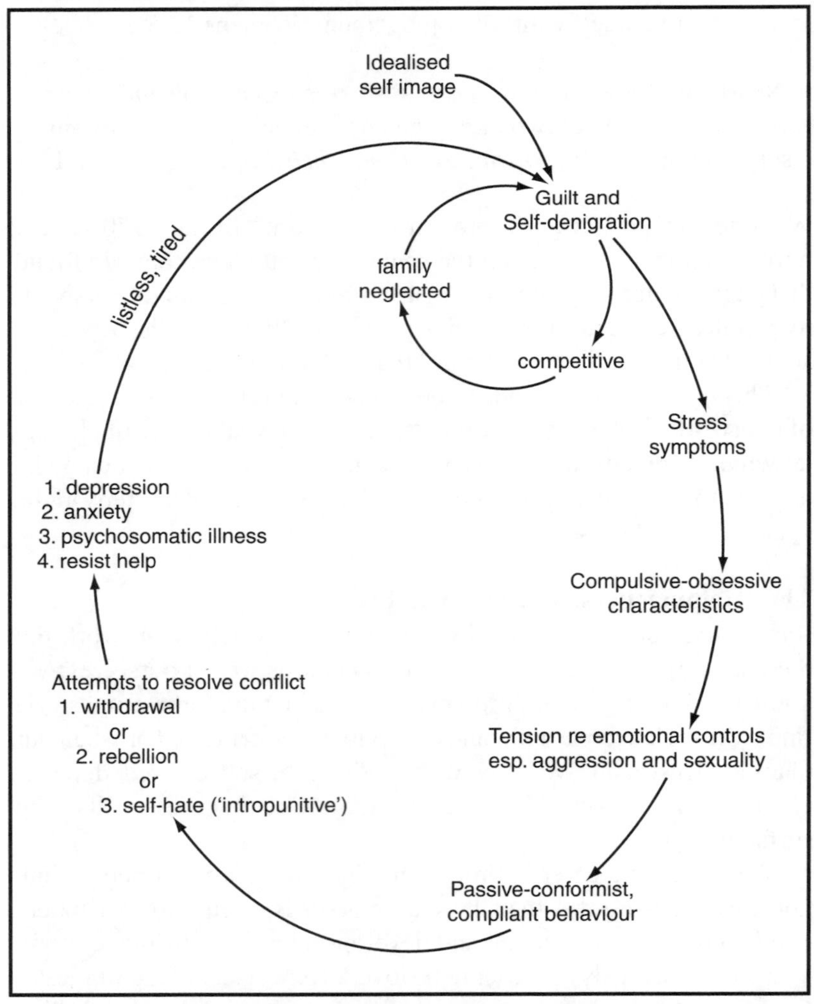

FIGURE 2.1 The Christian Worker's Guilt Cycle

our struggle to perform better and yet, ironically, make that less likely: low morale is debilitating. Hence the inner circle in figure 1. In his perfectionism the Christian servant neglects his family and tries even harder. Here is another irony in Christian work. Surely Christ's service does not involve competition ('how unspiritual!'), but in fact our sense of fulfilment depends on making our presence felt. The result is feedback into the guilt cycle again.

Tension due to these emotional controls. A Christian worker, we say, should be full of drive, yet without aggression. There is obvious tension here. In order to fulfil their calling pastors need to be forceful; the line between this and self-assertion can be virtually invisible.

The same applies in the field of love: let us be warm and loving, but we find it harder to live at peace with our sexuality. Here is yet another irony, for reluctance to accept this facet of ourselves can be a step on the road to downfall. Helpers as a group, and many pastors among them, are sexually more inhibited and less active than their peers. The result is a person outwardly warm and pleasant but inwardly exhausted by the energies needed to repress or deny areas of their emotions.

Compliant behaviour. Since the Christian worker 'shouldn't be aggressive' he often goes to great lengths to meet even unreasonable demands, and to placate uncharitable criticism and opposition. This avoiding of confrontation has a cost in loss of self-respect and in resentment.

Attempts to Resolve the Conflict. Some workers escape into a safe, detached world of study, reading or hobby, only to experience the resentment of their church, fellow-workers and family at such preoccupation. Others rebel into sexual flirtation, alcohol or drug dependency.

Again the costs are high in increased guilt and endangered reputation. Many escape the Scylla of escapism, and the Charybdis of rebellion, only by turning their aggression into self-hate and chronic self-criticism. All three routes, however, have consequences.

Stress symptoms. A high proportion of such conscientious workers experience a degree of depression. Others chronically avoid decision-making in case the decision is followed by failure: an avoidance reaction termed commitment anxiety.

A common alternative is to experience any of a number of psychosomatic illnesses: headaches, vague digestive problems, hypertension.

Yet because he is in the 'helping personality' group the Christian worker is often very resistant to asking for help for himself.

Headache or abdominal pain is in fact the person's unconscious self-protection mechanism, the blessed opportunity for periodic relief from dominating oughtness. Unless the cycle is broken, however, such relief is temporary. The listlessness caused by mild depression is itself seen as failure; the worker feels guilty; and the cycle intensifies.

Understanding the guilt cycle

It is most important to balance this negative picture before exploring its sources and its resolution. An idealised self image does create its problems, but it reflects a remarkable and admirable truth about Christian workers. They are mostly sensitive, kind people, warm and helpful, deeply motivated.

Nonetheless the costs of the guilt cycle are high, which makes the study of their development and resolution vital.

Why are we like this? Why do so very many Christian workers posit a basically romantic and guilt producing self image when their spouse or best friend would gladly tell them – if asked – what impact their personality has on their work?

The uncomfortable truth is that a common factor in the breakdown of Christian workers and their marriages is a reduced ability to love and to receive love. There are two main causes.[2]

Some were significantly unloved when young, perhaps in infancy, resulting in an inner drive to make up for it by doing a good job as a Christian worker. Others were loved conditionally ('I'll love you if you're a good boy', implied, if not necessarily stated), an upbringing that makes for a private, cautious person who is ever asking, albeit unconsciously, 'what is wanted in return here?'

Notice the questions we need to face about our Christian service. To ask them is not to doubt our call but to offer, hopefully, insight into our ministry:

- How much do I need this particular work? What does it give me? Release from the humdrum? Reasonable security without an immediate boss? A sense of being needed? Does it offer me a supply of ready relationships, safely limited yet reassuringly dependent? To what extent is it an escape from reality, even perhaps a fall-back position after feeling unfulfilled, being apprehensive about considering alternatives or failing exams?

- What is my daydream, my secret fantasy? This is something to identify and consider carefully for it is just at this point, the importance to a person of his expectations, that he is vulnerable. So get it out into the open. 'Half the wisdom we possess consists of the knowledge of ourselves.'[3] There is nothing so subtle as the temptation to idolise the work.

- What impact does my personality have on my ministry? This is something to ask our wife or best friend for the sake of those who are our partners in the work.

There is a reason to ask these questions. The more event-dependent and factor-dependent our call, the more vulnerable we are to stress and disappointment later ('what if this work leaves me feeling even more of a failure?'); and the less equable our response to discouraging circumstances and irritating people, and the less able we are to leave a situation and move on.

Conquering the guilt cycle

What can we do about the down side to our helping personalities? What the diagram represents is a theology of works. We might preach free grace, yet live an inner life of justification by works.

What are we to do? Work not suffused by the sense that it is *by grace* that we are saved will, at the end of the day, prove to be bondage. It is the divine wisdom of divine grace that we need to discover: this alone will lead us to be *God's* workmanship engaged in good works.

The primary issue for the Christian worker is always, Do I really understand and experience the grace of God in the gospel? Calvin, as so often, grasps the nettle perfectly: 'There is therefore no other remedy for pacifying our souls than when God forgives us our sins, and deals kindly with us as a father with his children.'[4]

We groan, on the other hand, when we derive our peace from our success. How desolating it is! It fluctuates, dependent on others and on events: this is a whole orientation around works rather than God's free generosity. Make time to reinstall grace in depth and we drive an axe at failure and success, shame and pride alike. David Dickson put it so well:

> I have taken all my good deeds, and all my bad, and cast them in a heap before the Lord, and fled from both, and betaken myself to the Lord Jesus Christ; and in him I have sweet peace.

This can usefully be done on paper when especially needed. We see and grieve over the shortfall in all our behaviour. We recognise Christ crucified for those very sins. We see the Father offering us our Lord Jesus in exchange for them. Then, content with such a way of salvation, we give our consent to it. We give our sins to Christ, and take from him the justification he has bought us. What a swap! Owen said, 'This is every day's work: I know not how any peace can be maintained with God without it.'[5]

There is an illustration of this evangelical freedom in Exodus. The plate on the High Priest's turban signified that he would 'take upon himself any guilt incurred in the holy offering which the people of Israel hallow as their holy gift: it shall always be on his forehead so that they may be accepted before the Lord'.[6]

Our work, likewise, is tinged with shortfall and distortion. Our High Priest, Jesus, accepts those inadequate contributions, takes on himself the guilt involved and presents the Father with a perfect offering. When our consciences, colleagues and congregations accuse us – as they do – happy the servant who can agree. An accuser, human or demonic,[7] has nothing on such a person.

A practical exercise

- Examine the guilt cycle again. *In writing*, work out its evangelical resolution. Pray for such a work of the Holy Spirit that this inner freedom will not be mere wish, but reality.

- Am I 'driven by need', or 'kindled by grace'?

References

1. His three articles are: H. A. Eadie, 'The Health of Scottish Clergymen', *Contact*, 41, Winter 1972, p. 2-22, with comments by Karl S.G. Greenlaw, p. 23, 24; 'Stress and the Clergyman', *Contact*, 42, Spring 1973, p. 22-35; 'The Helping Personality', *Contact*, 49, Summer 1975, p. 2-17. Compare also D. Bridge, *How to Spot a Church Split Before it Happens*, Eastbourne, MARC, 1989, p. 154-161; L.J. Francis and R. Rodger, 'The Personality Profile of Anglican Clergymen', *Contact*, 113, 1994, p. 27-32; E. Sharpe, 'Personality Disorders and Candidate Selection', *Voluntary Agencies Medical Advisors (VAMA) Newsletter*, April 1996, p. 3-12.

2. I am indebted to five addresses given by the Christian psychiatrist Dr. Montague Barker at the Fountain Trust Conference in 1978 for the insights in this and the next few paragraphs. They have also been written up as four articles in *The Rutherford Journal of Church and Ministry*, editions 2.2, 3.1, 3.2 and 4.1: Winter 1995 to Spring 1997.

3. INST. 1.1.1.

4. J. Calvin, Commentary on Romans 8:13-18.

5. J. Owen, 'On Communion with the Trinity', *Works*, Goold Edition, vol. 2, Edinburgh, Banner of Truth reprint, 1968, p. 194.

6. Exodus 28:38, RSV.

7. Zechariah 3:1-7.

CHAPTER FOUR

OUR WALK

You are your ministry

Drinking from the stream as he goes, he can hold his head high in victory (Psalm 110:7).

Power for work like ours is only to be obtained in secret (James Stalker).[1]

Alas! How often have we to reproach ourselves with going on in a round of Christian duty, faithful in a general intention, but not flowing from the fresh realisation of the love of Christ to our souls (J.N. Darby).

It is one thing to describe a day in a pastor's life; it is another to ensure the life in a pastor's day. For it is possible to go through the motions of our work without that walking with Christ which translates the activities into ministry.

But we can turn that thought around. It is possible to have even our poor efforts made mighty by Christ, like the lad with the five loaves and two small fish. All he needed to do was to surrender them to him. The objective of this chapter is to explore what that surrender consists of. It centres on our devotional life: on the way we live out and deepen our fellowship with God.[2]

I do not suppose that anyone could feel they are the right person to write this of all chapters. It has even been suggested that part of Dr. Martyn Lloyd-Jones' greatness lay in refusing to write on the subject at all: that it is essentially private and not something on which we should try to instruct one another.

I disagree. The privilege and potential of the devotional life are revealed in scripture for our instruction. Even the incarnate Son of God made it a priority and connected it with effectiveness in ministry.[3] Paul's letters are replete with assurances of, and requests for, prayer; and they are living examples of, and instruction on, the place of the Word of God in our becoming filled with spiritual wisdom and understanding.

In fact this is probably the most vital subject on which we could be honest with one other. If even Moses needed two friends to help hold up his hands in intercession for the battle as he tired, how much more do we?

The Christian worker's life is a hectic one. Administrative demands, preparation for spoken and written ministry, a plethora of commitments and repeated personal calls on our time daily threaten time alone with God. And yet, we have to know God's Word through and through, not in a textbook way but as true of us, if we are to apply it to unexpected, new and varied situations as they arise. An anxious and guilty world needs people who have *heeded* the invitation, 'Listen to me, and eat what is good, and your soul will delight in the richest of fare;' people who have food to offer from the substantial universe with which to sustain the weary.

Every so often – would that it were more often – we meet someone of whom the burden of this chapter is especially true. The glory shining forth is not loud, nor a matter of their personality; it is seen in quiet and extrovert, male and female alike. But meeting them we are blessed and go away wanting to know Jesus as they do.

The theological basis for conducting a friendship with the true and living God starts with the fact that he wants our friendship. This is why he created a universe, peopled it in his likeness and redeemed it when fallen. He tells us that he takes delight in his people, and that he sent his Son to give us full rights as his children.[4] As James Philip comments, God delights in his people – the thing is fantastic! Think about it: the God who made the rugged grandeur of the mountains and set the stars in their courses wants our friendship. It is flabbergasting.[5]

The doctrinal framework continues with a consideration of our need and his abundance: what remains is for us to ask.[6] For such asking is part of the covenant between us, and God has caused some signal examples of answered prayer to be recorded for our encouragement.[7]

Finally, on what basis do we come to him? Why, as his dear children; we are led by the hand into his throne room, and that by his Son.[8]

What are the benefits accruing from such commitment? Jesus said we can do nothing without him;[9] it is the difference between overwork and overflow.[10] There is a whole protection available, from wicked men and the evil one alike;[11] Owen comments, 'He that would be little in temptation, let him be much in prayer.'[12] We learn intimacy with God there as nowhere else; and it gives reality to our praying in public.

As for our immersion in Scripture, its benefit is directed into our very beings and moulds all that we are becoming.[13] We read the Bible, not to gain knowledge for its own sake so much as to be shaped by God in the process: this is the chief factor in the effectiveness of our preaching.[14] What then are the elements that make up the devotional life?

Main elements in the devotional life

Bible Reading. A pastor should be an expert in scripture – loving it, knowing and believing what it teaches, obeying what it commands, believing what it promises. For this purpose there is no substitute for deliberate, daily, diligent study of the biblical text. This involves setting oneself, it seems to me, a definite aim and system for a given period, and at least sometimes a journalled account of the ground covered and its implications. There is always the danger that we merely read the words of Scripture and go away unchanged: a waste of time which James warns us against:

> Submit to God and accept the Word that he plants in your heart, which is able to save you. Do not deceive yourselves by just listening to his Word; instead, put it into practice.[15]

Whether through Bible reading notes or systematic study of a book or theme, we should work hard to know the truth of the Bible,

> Not only verbally, propositionally, theologically; but religiously, that is devotionally, morally, in worshipping him whom it reveals and in personal obedience to him whose commands it contains. And that is not an experiment, it is a commitment. Knowledge without obedience is useless. You must be doers as well as hearers of the Word in your own lives. This alone will make the image of Jesus Christ appear in your life so that you exemplify your teaching in your own person before you begin to teach. Then your hearers will receive both the teacher and his teaching. [16]

D. S. Whitney recommends six facets to Bible intake: Hearing, Reading, Studying, Memorising, Meditating and Applying. On Bible reading his three suggestions for effectiveness are: find the time, find a Bible reading plan and find at least one word, phrase or verse to meditate on each time you read.[17]

Prayer. There is not a great servant of God recorded in Scripture or in history, I suspect, who was not great in prayer. Abraham, Moses, David, Jesus, Paul, Augustine, Luther, Calvin, Carey, all have significant prayer among their distinguishing characteristics. Mary Queen of Scots is said to have feared the prayers of John Knox more than an army of ten thousand. If Jesus and Paul prayed much for those to whom they were ministering, we do ill if we fail to call on the same resources ourselves. And let us remember *why* it is essential. The only worker in the realm of the spirit, the only bringer of salvation, is the Holy Spirit. Prayer is the tool God has given by which his entry may be appropriated; in John Wesley's words, 'God does nothing but in answer to prayer.'

The Lord's prayer reminds us to put structure into our prayer life.[18] It starts with worship: Our Father in Heaven. The next phase is to proceed to God's concerns: the hallowing of his name, the coming of his kingdom, the doing of his will. There is wisdom in attending first to God and his work.

Only after putting God first do we turn to our own concerns. Jesus instances our provision, our pardon and our protection, inviting us to bring all of our time, present, past and future, into our prayers. It is profoundly encouraging that he includes themes as elementary as our daily bread, as vital as our forgiveness and as necessary as our protection from the evil that might otherwise conquer us. Finally the doxology sees us ending where we began: expressing confidence in God ('for Yours is the kingship and the power') and closing in homage, praise and worship: Yours is the glory, for ever and ever.

Let us pray in a systematic, dependable way for those we serve: not vague generalities, but each person and family by name and in some detail. This is practicable and pleasurable as long as one manages it at a sustainable level. Take your list of members. Select, say, three families a day and talk with God about them in the light of what you know: their current circumstances, what you think Jesus would ask for, their spiritual progress. Pray in a way that takes up your day's Bible reading and directs its implications into their lives.

Maintain some way of asking God into your forthcoming spoken ministry, missionary associates, family and other concerns. For myself, I also need a reminder to be spontaneous! and to close in praise. This helps to avoid a list becoming a legalistic chore and to maintain it as real conversation with God.

Fasting. There seem to be two equal and opposite dangers here. We may either treat fasting as a kind of lever on God as though it had some mysterious potency in its own right, or treat it as a bygone or monastic practice to be avoided altogether. Yet our Lord clearly expects us to fast: 'When you fast' is assumed in exactly the same way as 'when you pray' and 'when you give to a needy person' (Matt. 6:1-18). My proposal is simply this. We live in a pathologically busy age. Since it is better to make good use of fasting than either to suffer from it or abstain from it, start small, perhaps missing one meal a week, or a month. In the time which you would have spent at that meal, speak in detail with God about something which, in your heart of hearts, is more important to you than eating. Whether you and God end up wanting to develop such times will become apparent. In the meantime you have definitely asked God for something that really matters, and probably started to grow a very healthy independence of mealtimes.

Corporate prayer. This chapter centres on the pastor and his walk with God as an individual. It therefore leaves to chapter seven the church dimension of our devotional life.

The practice of the presence of God. I mean by this simply, that we do not go from God's presence when we return from a time of quiet with God back to the details of this restless life. Let us stay in converse, intimately relating each detail, each issue in personal friendship with him.

Spiritual warfare. This vital matter was completely absent from my formal training for Christian service. Yet I know of no subject more important if we are to make sense of our Christian experience and to make ready for what we shall encounter in the course of Christian service.

We live in a day which is bedevilled by two equal and opposite errors. The materialistic scientist will accept as valid only what can be objectively verified. The new age traveller imagines he is able to affect the cosmos by the power of thought. But the Christian, informed by Scripture, knows that while dealing with physical and mental processes, he also deals with personal spiritual beings who influence them. He knows that while he engages in rational argument, the issues are resolved in the realm of spirit, and he depends on God's power to do the work in that realm.[19]

It becomes second nature to all who engage in effective spiritual service, to take account of the practical realities which constitute Satanic opposition. I think of the time when I was within minutes of travelling to speak at a convention. It was scarcely a surprise in the light of past experience when a car started to come out of a side road directly into my path. A friend, about to board ship for the same purpose, was directed by an official to the wrong boat. Another, on returning home on a Saturday to preach the next day, entered his living-room to find the ceiling fallen in and covering the floor. He simply said, 'The devil', closed the door, and deferred dealing with it until the Monday.

It would be easy to scoff and call these things coincidences. There is nothing 'newspaper-ish' about most of the assaults upon Christian life and service. But to become God's friend is to incur the devil's hostility. That hostility can take every form from irrational and almost unbearable spiritual darkness, to sudden and unexpected temptation, to repeated hindrances and difficulties such as those I have described. The wise soldier knows his enemy and experiences these things too frequently to dismiss them as insignificant. We shall never make sense of our Christian experience unless we recognise the devil when he is at work.

Who is this enemy of our souls and what is the nature of his assaults upon us? The word Satan means 'adversary' and his adversarial and hindering work is illustrated in Daniel 9:1-11:1. Daniel had set himself to pray; but the 'prince of Persia', the spiritual source of the resistance to God's will in the Persian empire, prevented the answer to Daniel's prayer from being made known (Dan. 10:12-14).

When we encounter resistance to prayer being answered, therefore, it is true that God is permitting this in order to call forth our courage and promote our perseverance. But the resistance is spiritual, masterminded by the evil one, and effected by his minions.[20]

Doubtless we need to be careful before attributing resistance to our work to Satan. We sometimes cause it by the way we carry it out. Even allowing for that, however, an inability to perceive the gospel as good news is attributable to the devil (2 Cor. 4:3-4), just as the stirring up of antagonism to it is demonic.

Are our prayers hindered? Let us be the more determined to invoke by prayer God's destruction of the demonic resistance to his advance. Do people arouse strong opposition to genuine gospel work? Let us rather be heartened by such evidence that the evil one is stirred up by our work, than discouraged by his hindrances.

If his first name is Satan, the name Devil (*diabolos*) means 'slanderer' or 'deceiver'. We can add the third title 'accuser' (Rev. 12:10)

– in essence, prosecution lawyer – at this point also. Where a Christian is traduced either by his fellow or violently within his spirit by direct accusation from Satan, then this is the devil's slandering work.

This experience is vividly portrayed in Bunyan's *Pilgrim's Progress* where Christian is distressed to find wicked thoughts and words which 'he verily did think proceeded from his own mind'. But they had not come from Christian. The slanderer had implanted them. Has the devil not slandered us similarly, whispering wicked thoughts and then by frontal accusation making you ashamed of them? What liberty, what relief there is in recognising their origin!

Then in Revelation 9:11 Satan is called the destroyer. The tortured suicide of a Judas and the merciless slaughter of the innocents expose his real feelings about us. Whether by slyly hiding his existence or by unleashing its full ferocity, the devil is after the same end, to destroy us.

Let us who are pastors, then, treat the evil one with all care as threatening, genuinely horrifying, cunning. How often Christians say with tears of regret, 'I can't think what came over me!' Are we Christian ministers not sometimes partly responsible for failing to warn them? The question becomes therefore what strategy must we live by and teach in order that Satan should not gain the mastery over us (2 Cor. 2:11).

The passage with which to be familiar is Ephesians 6:10-20: a passage to live for ourselves and press upon our people so practically that they too are strong in the Lord and put on God's armour.

Notice two general features of the introductory verses, 10 to 13. The first is that the devil uses two particular stratagems, his wiles (v. 11) and the evil day (v. 13). As the word 'wiles' reminds us, we are not going to be given a warning in advance that the devil is trying something upon us. Our only protection is a life of Christian integrity which avoids causes of temptation, and alertness to the fact that the devil tempts people just when they are least prepared and least expecting it. It might be when we are very tired, or on holiday out of our normal safer context, or immediately after great blessing. The expression 'the evil day' indicates those times, for which the evil one bides his time (Luke 4:13), when he piles on darkness, loss of health, overwhelming temptation and difficulty. Such a day is evil indeed: too many pastors have fallen at such times for us to contemplate the evil day lightly.

And yet there is encouragement even here. A Puritan theologian commented, 'He that stands near his Captain is a sure target for the archers.' So if all around you is giving way and you are feeling miserably assaulted and uncertain as to the value of your ministry and even as to your sanity or your salvation, recognise what is going on and take heart.

Secondly, note the call to the conscious effort and courage of faith: 'Be strong in the Lord; In the strength of his might; Withstand.' There are times when we simply flee to Jesus and shelter under his protection; others, when we are able to go all out for the advance of the gospel. William Still wrote of three strategies in this war: strategic retreat, unyielding defence and all-out attack.[21] The spiritual armour, set out in verses 14 to 20, resources the second and third phases of that strategy.

'With the belt of truth buckled round your waist.' The broad belt of Paul's day carried money, held the scabbard for a sword and kept clothing in place and out of the way so that one could fight unencumbered. Our lives similarly need to be held by the truth in two ways: a detailed and believing knowledge of Christian truth, and the integrity of lives lived in conformity to it. Are we growing in our knowledge of Christian teaching?

'With the breast-plate of righteousness in place.' How many pastors teach about righteousness freely given to the guilty by the Saviour, yet themselves groan with unresolved burdens of guilt? This strikes at the very heart of gospel living. It is the heart, the vitals which the breast-plate of righteousness is designed to protect. So Christian leader, come back to Jesus. Let the imputed righteousness of Christ guard your heart.

'Your feet fitted with the readiness that comes from the gospel of peace.' So many things steal our gospel readiness. The rush of a week, apprehension about an emotionally unbalancing member, sheer tiredness: these can make us off-balance, unready. But the gospel *has* brought us peace. In spiritual warfare we take it again from Jesus' hands. With it will come a poise, a readiness.

'Take the helmet of salvation.' I assume that since the helmet guards the head, Paul was speaking of the protection for our minds and our thinking which salvation affords as we lay hold of it. I think William Still's illustration is the right model for us here: the young minister who 'had even to preach the Word while the black conviction gripped him that he was himself lost, a Christless soul'.[22] Here was an occasion resolutely to reset his thinking along biblical lines: to have it guarded by the fact of salvation.

'And the sword of the Spirit which is the Word of God.' Here is the first clearly attacking weapon, the very Word of God pored over together with someone seeking faith or with a member needing assurance or wanting principles of guidance and decision making. The Bible itself, explained and discussed, is the sword which the Holy Spirit uses to 'take captive every thought and make it obedient to Christ' (2 Cor. 10:5).

'And pray in the Spirit on all occasions with all kinds of prayer.' Do we not too often forget that God himself is the only one who can make our work effective?

To face the powers of the evil one with merely human resources is like engaging in nuclear warfare equipped with a bow and arrow. That is why the prayerless church and the prayerless Christian present such a tragic and pathetic sight. It takes spiritual weapons to wage spiritual warfare.[23]

God help us to put each piece of armour on with prayer and engage in effective, practical, spiritual warfare.

Journalling. While there are dangers of introversion in keeping a spiritual journal, one only needs to consider that the Psalms and Augustine's *Confessions* are examples of it to realise that the practice has an immense amount to offer.

By journalling we mean keeping a personal account of reading, of events, of decisions, of lessons learnt. The difference between a minister who simply repeats ministry year by year and one who grows and develops is that the latter processes and learns from what he experiences and reads. Journalling is a useful tool in that. It facilitates making decisions, facing crises, making new commitments and learning from our reading. It also has the happy knack of nailing illogical thinking and dispelling panic.

Let the journalling cycle be complete. A journal should record the event, our observation and reflection, the concepts and lessons we have deduced and what happens as these are tested in a new situation. This cycle will include some inner discomfort; that is part of the travail which produces growth.

Other disciplines. A repeated theme in Proverbs, an important element in wisdom is a willingness to take advice, a humble readiness to be corrected and instructed. None of us is 'Gifted with such wisdom and prudence as to be adequate for himself in the guidance of his own spiritual life.' [24] The wise pastor will find a friend straight enough to rebuke his pride as well as comfort his griefs.

The final discipline to mention is *instructional reading*. The minister who confines himself to just whatever reading is essential for the week's sermons will gradually end up boring both himself and his people. If we need stimulation in order to maintain such intellectual growth let us set something up. We might join a study group or simply meet at agreed intervals with a friend, each to deliver a review of a book.

Actually doing it

Method is essentially personal; here is mine. Fix a time for meeting with God daily. As long as we are not legalistic about it (there are days in the week when I do not follow the pattern), I do believe we are better being disciplined about this: stick to it. I find help from the following list in engaging well and definitely, rather than vaguely, in this exercise.

- Greet God aloud and praise him briefly. Ask his help to make this a real time and not to daydream.

- Have a good hymn for the week and sing or say it to him. Find some way of meaning the words rather than saying them with the mind in neutral. For myself this might involve stopping singing and, bearing in mind that God is in the room, placing a seat opposite me and reverently saying the words to God as though he were visible in the seat.

- Briefly confess any definite sins of commission or omission and then leave them resolutely behind, for ever.

- Read a psalm or part psalm out loud: as much sequence of thought as is meaningful for you, then stop.

- Read a few paragraphs of a great spiritual classic. For example, read just enough of *Pilgrim's Progress*, Augustine's *Confessions* or Owen on fellowship with God, to have a unit of truth to savour.

- Read just as much of the Greek New Testament out loud as suits your level of competence, either understanding and translating it or not; not more than one pericope.

- Read a section of scripture using some sort of system: published Bible-reading notes; going through an Old Testament book a chapter or two at a time or the New Testament a paragraph at a time; chasing through scripture for a given theme; or covering the whole Bible in a year: anything to be doing something planned, intentional, purposeful.

- Pray for others, preferably on some sort of rota. You might pray for some people weekly or even daily, others monthly. But also have non-rota time to pray for those you have met recently or those especially on your heart. Use the scripture you have read, as well as your knowledge of their situation, to guide the way in which you pray. In that way, the whole of God's Word to man enters our prayer support of others over a period.

- Pray for your own concerns and day's duties. Using others' prayers, especially at times of dryness, guilt or misery, widens our horizon and vocabulary: the ancient Collects, for example, or Lancelot Andrewes' private prayers.

- Stop for a minute and just be with God. Let him love you.

- Close in doxology: 'for Yours is the kingdom, the power and the glory for ever...'

Time and again we shall find peace, poise and planning flow from such times. They often remind us of someone to visit, phone or write to. The benefits of creating such time and of finding ways to keep it businesslike, and to prevent it becoming daydreaming, are incalculable.

Why do it?

When a person is ordained, says Eugene Peterson, the church is saying something like this: 'We need help in keeping our beliefs sharp and accurate and intact. We don't trust ourselves; our emotions seduce us into infidelities. We know that we are launched on a difficult and dangerous act of faith, and that there are strong influences intent on diluting or destroying it. We want you to help us: be our pastor, a minister of Word and sacrament, in the middle of this world's life. This isn't the only task in the life of faith, but it is your task.'[25]

What kind of person is best suited to give such help? Strachan comments:

> There is a passion for Christ which has set those who have it apart for ever from their fellow men. The trouble with the rest of us is that we are content to dwell in Jerusalem without seeing the face of the King. We are hard at work for him: the freighted hours rush by giving us scarcely time to give a thought to the Lover of our souls who is longing for our friendship. And when we do go into the audience chamber we are burdened with requests: business that must be put through, guidance that we need here, help there, petitions on behalf of this one or that. All important, all urgent, all worthy but – just business after all.
>
> But now and again – at rare intervals – one meets someone who, like Paul, has looked into the matchless face of Jesus and who henceforth sees nothing any more save the face of his Beloved. There is a radiance about such a one, a glory shining forth. What makes the difference? The passion for God.
>
> In our zeal for the better, are we missing the best? The Word of the Lord to us is still, 'he that loveth me shall be loved by my Father and I will love him and manifest myself to him.'
>
> There is reward for the obedient disciple. There are power and authority for the faithful disciple; there is glory of achievement for the zealous disciple; but there is the whisper of his love, there is the joy of his presence and the shining of his face for those who love him for himself alone. And, 'to what profit is it that we dwell in Jerusalem, if we do not see the King's face?'[26]

It would be good to spend a few minutes considering the current health of our walk with God, and to institute any amendments that seem indicated.

References

1. J. Stalker, *The Preacher and his Models*, 1892, quoted by I.H. Murray, *Jonathan Edwards*, Edinburgh, Banner of Truth Press, 1987, p. 147.

2. I do not know any better treatment of the basic grammar of that fellow-

ship than Owen's 'On Communion with the Trinity', *Works*, Goold edition, vol. 2, Edinburgh, Banner of Truth reprint, 1968, especially pp. 24-195. The finest grammar of the prayer life, and one of the warmest, is Calvin's: INST. 3. 20. *passim*.

3. E.g. Matthew 6:1-18; Mark 1:35; 9:28, 29; Luke 11:1-12; 18:1-8.

4. Psalm 149:4 (compare 147:11); Galatians 4:4.

5. Bible Study at Holyrood Abbey Church, Edinburgh, 2 June 1976, privately circulated.

6. INST. 3.20.1.

7. On prayer as part of our covenant with God, see 2 Chronicles 7:14; Jeremiah 29:13 and 33:3; John 14:12-14; 15:7, 16; 16:22-24. On answers to prayer: Exodus 17:8-13; 1 Kings 18:30-39; Acts 12:1-17! On both: James 5:13-20.

8. Owen speaks of this 'manuduction' (leading by the hand) in *op. cit.*, p. 24-36, and volume 9, p.80-82.

9. John 15:5.

10. Colossians 4:3; 2 Thessalonians 3:2.

11. Matthew 6:13; Ephesians 6:17-19.

12. John Owen, *op. cit.*, vol. 6, p. 126.

13. *Ibid.* Owen adduces Romans 6:17 and 2 Corinthians 3:18 at this point in his argument.

14. *Op. cit.*, vol. 4, p. 205.

15. James 1:21-25.

16. W. Still, *The Work of the Pastor*, Aberdeen, Gilcomston South Church, 1964, p. 8.

17. D.S. Whitney, *Spiritual Disciplines for the Christian Life*, Colorado Springs, Navpress, 1991, p. 23-60.

18. Matthew 6:5-15.

19. 2 Corinthians 10:2-5.

20. 1 Thessalonians 2:18.

21. W. Still, *Towards Spiritual Maturity*, Christian Focus Publications, 1992.

22. W. Still, *Ibid.*, p. 38.

23. E. J. Alexander, letter, *St George's Tron Church magazine*, May 1978.

24. J.C. Bona, *A Treatise of Spiritual Life*, trans. D.A. Donovan, New York, Pustet, 1901, p. 5, 66, quoted by E. Peterson, *Working the Angles*, Eerdmans, Grand Rapids, 1987, p. 115.

25. *Op. cit.*, p. 16, 17.

26. H. Strachan, 'The Personal Passion for Christ' in *The Quiet Time*, ed. J.D.C. Anderson, London, IVF Press, 1957, p. 44-48.

2

AMONG THE PEOPLE

CHAPTER FIVE

PREACHING THE WORD

The whole Christ from the whole Bible to make whole people

How welcome is the coming of one who brings good news, who heralds peace, brings happiness, proclaims salvation, and tells Zion, 'Your God is king!' (Isaiah 52:7).

We see that God, who might perfect his people in a moment, chooses not to bring them to manhood in any other way than by the education of the church. We see the mode of doing it expressed: the preaching of celestial doctrine is committed to pastors (John Calvin, *Institutes of the Christian Religion*, 4.1.5).

Christian preaching is an immense tool. No reader of the Bible can fail to be impressed by its place in the forwarding of God's purposes and the coming of his kingdom. It has changed the face of world history. Anyone who has sat under authentic preaching must long for it to be the norm; and it can be.

The fact is that the preached Word is the chief evangelist and pastor in a church. There is no experience quite like that encounter with God when he makes the Scripture, reverently and rigorously unleashed, his life-giving agent. By it he imparts Christian salvation, rips up the conscience, comforts the trembling, enlightens our understanding and empowers our obedience; yet how rare is such a living voice, week by week!

What then is the place of preaching in the scheme of things, and by what process does it do the work of pastoring? Allowing that God is the only Christian worker, what must we do to maximise his working in power through our preaching? It is to these questions that this chapter is addressed.

The place of preaching

Stand back for a moment. God's chief activity through history is that he is 'bringing many sons to glory'[1] by a two-fold partnership. He sent his Son that there might be good news to herald. Now he sends preachers to herald it. Let us unpack that process.

We stated the fundamental assumptions of salvation in chapter two. We are sinners and need a saviour. Jesus Christ is the saviour we need; but as long as he is outside us he might never have come at all, for all the good he is to us.[2] We need through faith and repentance to be reconciled to him.

How does this happy union take place? What is needed is for the Holy Spirit to beget faith in us. God has provided the means: the preaching of the gospel deposited in his church.

We could liken the preaching task to that of the aid worker who is charged with ensuring that vital supplies reach those in need. Similarly, people are perishing for lack of Christ. The preacher's task is to offer him to them, by the plain and loving statement of the truth.

Or preaching is like the experience of Lazarus. He was dead, had been dead for days; but the resurrecting call of God's Son brought that corpse to life again, restored the metabolic processes in his stagnant cells and lo! he came forth, alive from the dead. So it is spiritually with the preached Word. As P.T. Forsyth wrote:

> By the Gospel of this grace I would especially urge that there is meant not a statement, nor a doctrine, nor a scheme, on man's side; nor an offer, a promise or a book on God's side. It is an act and a power: it is God's *act* of redemption before it is man's message of it. Every true sermon therefore is God's Gospel act reasserting itself in detail. The preacher's word, when he preaches the gospel and not only delivers a sermon, is an effective deed, charged with blessing or with judgement.[3]

This deed, this effective act, comes about through personal encounter between Christ and the hearer.

Notice the two interlocking components within that act: the human communication and the divine self-disclosure. Christian conversion and growth are not the result of human persuasion but a manifestation of divine grace. The preacher does not save anybody; God kindles spiritual life in people by his Spirit and then rejoices in their free, uncoerced response to his preached Word.[4]

This meeting with Christ is not confined to the evangelism stage of salvation. It is the active agent in bringing Christians (ourselves first) to maturity. God is in the business of making us fully human by restoring in us all the balance and beauty of his likeness. His method is that we need the whole Christ from the whole Word to make us whole people. For while there is infinite range and depth in Christ, there is a sense in which he has inscripturated himself for this very purpose. Christ is God's Word incarnate, the Bible is God's Word written, and authentic preaching is God's Word preached.

In 2 Corinthians 4, in fact, Paul takes two Old Testament strands to point up just how momentous an activity preaching is. It is, first, new creation work. Gospel preaching is life-giving, creative illumination such as took place in the creation of the universe (Genesis 1:3). The God of Genesis does his new creative work through preaching. It is illuminating to spell out that parallel. God's new creative work is now, as in the beginning:

- *ex nihilo*: out of nothing. God creates life which was simply absent before (Eph. 2:1).

- *per verbum*: through the Word. God makes us new people, and goes on renewing us, by speaking to us through the preaching of scripture (1 Thess. 2:13).

- *et continua*: God continues and upholds what he begins through our preaching (Phil. 1:6; John 10:28).

Secondly, it is new covenant work. The predicted coming of Messiah was described as the manifestation of light out of darkness (Isa. 9:2-7). This long-predicted rescue operation – which consists of the gift of a Son, a Wonderful Counsellor, the Mighty God, the Begetter of Eternal Life, the Prince of Peace – is the New Covenant ministry achieved through preaching.[5]

It is this, no less, in which we are involved in fellowship with God. That is stupendous. As R.A. Finlayson comments, 'No wonder Spurgeon said he would rather have a pulpit than a throne. To be royalty is nothing compared with this.'[6]

Ephesians 4 serves only to magnify further the dignity of this calling as Paul develops its relation to the Christ event. He is exploring the way the ascended Lord Jesus has poured out gifts on his church. He likens him to a conquering hero of the ancient world, who would ride back into his capital city after a campaign and distribute its spoils to those who had come out to greet him and to follow in his train.

In the same way, Paul writes, Jesus engaged in a life and death campaign against sin, sins and Satan; and by his death and resurrection emerged victorious. Having returned to his capital city and his Father's side he now pours out gifts upon the church on earth.

Among these gifts, one is unique in evoking and nourishing all the others. 'He gave pastor-teachers to equip all Christians for their work of Christian service so as to build up the body of Christ ... so that we become united in the faith and in knowing God's Son, mature people, doctrinally stable, people who speak the truth in love, each playing our part so that Christ's Church grows and grows up in a way that is shaped by love.'[7]

It is significant that in all four New Testament lists of the gifts which our risen Lord Jesus sovereignly gives his people, the 'Word gifts' come first. It is so in Romans 12:6ff., 1 Corinthians 12:7ff., 1 Corinthians 12:27ff. and Ephesians 4:7ff. We do not have to look far to see the reason for this. God has given us minds. He addresses and changes us by way of them. This is brought out clearly in the remaining verses of Ephesians 4:

- The heathen live in the futility of their *minds* (verse 17).
- they are darkened in their *understanding* (verse 18).
- you did not so *learn* Christ (verse 20).
- you were *taught* the truth that was in him (verse 21).

and in Romans 12:2:

- let God transform you inwardly by a complete change of your *mind*.

It is a corollary of this that pastor-teachers have a particular place in God's purposes and must be sure to supply, and members of the Church to receive, ministry of the sort that James Philip has described in these words:

> The pattern is as follows: a ministry of the Word at depth, not merely in terms of the recovery of biblical exposition, but particularly in terms of a determination to allow all the vital thrust of that Word to do its costly work in men's lives for the production of Christian character and wholeness; an incisive pastoral work as a necessary corollary to this, helping the Word home in personal application; the establishing of a life of corporate prayer in the fellowship as the power-house for the work and the battleground on which significant advance in the work is made; the self-propagating qualities of such a fellowship by which recruitment for the ministry and for overseas service becomes a spontaneous, unheralded

> and continuing reality; a steady increase over the years in the stewardship of money; and a quiet, steady and unobtrusive building up of the Church of God in the salvation of men.[8]

Paul thus emphasises the given-ness and greatness of preaching. It is not something that humans have thought up as a means of influencing fellow believers. Preaching originates from the exalted Christ. It finds its foundation in his death and humiliation; and nothing less than his ascension is the event which unlocked its release.[9]

Finally, preaching provides for our weakness: by it God addresses us in a way which we are able to receive. We prove our obedience when we are prepared to listen to fellow sinners preaching as if God himself were speaking to us (1 Thessalonians 2:13). 'When a puny man risen from the dust speaks in God's name, we show our obedience to God by being teachable by the preacher even though he is no better than we.' [10]

Such obedience requires humility and so the very method, not just the preached Word itself, furthers our character development. It also unites preacher and hearers and so edifies Christ's church by deepening Christian fellowship: it is the 'chief sinew by which believers are held together in one body'.[11]

The task of preaching: two bridges

The first gap the sermon must bridge is that between the Bible's world and ours. Both types of failure to be a bridge – the failure to start from scripture, and to finish squarely in the world – are seen in sermons. Some are the message of the preacher himself, not of God's Word; others fail in practicality.

Before we preach a sermon, therefore, we should ask ourselves, will my hearers know what will constitute obedience to this message? Authentic Christian sermons exegete, expound and apply: they make clear what the text says, what principles come out and in what way this living message addresses our practical living.

The second gap which the sermon must bridge is the one from where the hearers are in their Christian lives to where they should be. This is illustrated by Titus 2:11-14. In measure all of us are 'active in ungodliness'. The task for the preached Word is to train us to live self-controlled, upright and godly lives. The destination at the other end of the bridge is stated too: the glorious appearing of our great God and saviour.

Here is a test of preaching. Is it merely informing people of Christian theory, or is it dynamically moving Christians along this bridge? This requires pastors to have, and to teach, a biblical understanding of preaching as 'the Word of God which is at work'.[12]

If that is the place of preaching, what criteria must it fulfil in order to be authentically biblical?

Biblical criteria for preaching

It is very instructive to observe just what criteria matter to the biblical writers. To be authentic the message must really be the Word of God.[13] Not a fellow human's opinions, but the truth revealed by God and deposited in scripture, must be its content. Its ethos will not be one of information only, however, but of power from the Holy Spirit. The preacher will long for, and ask God for, the presence of the Holy Spirit testifying powerfully inside the hearers that the message is true, momentous, from God and life-changing.[14] He will proclaim it clearly, boldly and fearlessly.[15]

This last point, fearlessness, is more vital than appears at first sight. Time and again as one preaches, the temptation is to water down the radical nature of the gospel: either for fear of offending the hearers, or out of a sense of discrepancy between it and one's own life.

Preaching defined

We might therefore define preaching as a spoken message, true to scripture and communicated from scripture,[16] communicated boldly and clearly[17] by a Christian given personally to obedience to God,[18] who looks to God to make it a performative and not merely an informative event,[19] with an identified intended impact on the hearers.[20]

On that definition we can check our preaching against certain questions:

- Is this sermon evidently flowing from Scripture: is the Bible doing the talking? If it makes no difference whether the hearers have access to a Bible while we are preaching, our preaching is falling short. The first Christian preachers reasoned from the Scriptures,[21] in such a way that the hearers felt compelled to check the Bible to see if what they said was really true.[22] Preaching is failing if it does not drive the hearers to the biblical text.

- Is the message clear? Do the hearers know exactly what the preacher is getting at? Is the sequence of thought orderly?

- Has the sermon a clear objective? It should be possible to complete the sentence, 'As a result of this sermon the hearers will ...' Will the hearers know what difference I, as preacher, expect in their beliefs or behaviour?

- Is my own life transparently obedient to the message? Is there anything that needs to be amended either now before I preach it, or as soon as possible thereafter?

  For one person can say the right thing with minimal effect; another can use the same words and the effect is lives changed by God and an experience that none of those present will ever forget. This is what makes for what Martyn Lloyd-Jones called the romance of preaching. There is a sovereignty to God's doing such a thing; but power is conditional. There was a petrol advertisement which said, 'A clean engine develops power'; the same is true of a preacher's life. We may speak in the tongues of men and angels; but without love we are as a sounding gong or tinkling cymbal.

  Other things being equal, it is the man whom the Scots call 'far ben' whom God will use: one who has walked close to him for a long time. This is not so much a matter of hours spent with God in themselves, as of basic attitude and theology: of *why* he spends time with him. 'Take delight in the Lord, and he will give you the desires of your heart.'

- Have I asked God to be, and do I rely on and expect him to be, the real author of this sermon, present in power, personally convincing the hearers of his momentous truth, creating a dynamic bond between his own mind and all of ours through my preaching, creating that which he speaks?

- Do boldness, deep conviction and passion mark my preaching? Do the hearers realise it really matters to me? Is my attitude that it is a life or death event?

It is not possible to fake a wish that people know God or a concern that he be honoured as king and redeemer. These are decisions we make; and on them depends our usefulness to God.

Such preaching calls for certain facets of personal and congregational context, of preparation and of presentation.

Anointing: the power in preaching

What makes peculiarly and necessarily for power in preaching is the anointing presence of the Holy Spirit. As Paul says, 'my message and preaching were with a demonstration of the Spirit's power.' [23] 'The baptism of the Holy Spirit remains the matrix of ministry,' says Schillebeeckx.[24] That this will be the defining feature of his preaching, is every preacher's core desire.

If we are to be such preachers we shall work for, and plead with God for, a practical engagement with five anointings.

The inspiration of the scripture. There was a unique anointing on those who wrote the scriptures. To be anointed preachers we must believe that that is so and that God rewards those who respect it, and so treat the Bible not only as a human document to be studied as any other book but also as a divine document to be studied as no other book.

Reverence for plenary inspiration has all sorts of consequences for sermon preparation. It means that we come to the problems of scripture not inductively, led by the difficulty into the assumption that the Bible is making a mistake, but deductively, deducing that the problem is soluble and in no way undermines the Bible's utter reliability for faith and life.

It means coming to Bible passages reverently as the very words of God, alive with truth and life-changing power. It means asking that the Spirit who breathed these words will now breathe on us and be our spectacles to perceive them aright as we study. This decision to treat the Bible deductively breeds a reverence and dependence which are the necessary ground of anointed preparation.

The filling of the preacher. There are two such fillings. Our Lord commands us to 'be being filled',[25] a continuous present imperative directed to all Christians. In order to be transparent to God's truth we shall ask him to fill us day by day; a privilege given only to the obedient and the thirsty.

The second filling for the preacher is that initial, and then continually repeated, anointing which marks out a person as called: a differentness before which one bows in awe, the Holy Spirit bestowed for ministry and maintained by reiterated pourings given in sheer grace. These make a person's preaching like Samuel's: somehow their words do not fall to the ground, they carry weight. It is not a matter of the gift of the gab. Indeed it often accompanies lack of linguistic facility;[26] but there is no gainsaying the association of God with this person's speaking.[27]

There is no magic, no guarantee which ensures the continuance of this filling. We can lose it by disobedience. It is as incontestable when given, as it is inimitable when withheld; yet we need not fear its being removed. Its being maintained is 'to those who walk in his covenant'.[28]

The illumination of the sermon: that is, of the whole process of preparation from choosing a text to having a sermon ready to preach.

The point is, we need the Holy Spirit in the process of unfolding scripture as much as the original writers needed him in order for it to be God-breathed. The Spirit inspired the formation of scripture (inspiration) and the Spirit inspires those who read the Bible with earnest prayer (illumination). These two steps are causally linked. For the original inspiration of scripture had a purpose, the transformation of future readers, which falls to the ground without this second inspiration.

Only the Lord can give us that nice combination of control and liberty that honours both the original meaning and the modern 'fecundity of the text to be opened'[29] for which illumination is essential. We need him lest we either, liberally, cut the Spirit from the Word and preach without scriptural control; or, conservatively, fail its possibilities in modern application and preach ancient text with no contemporary reality.

It is the Spirit's illumination which harnesses both the capacity of the text to communicate a big message, and its actualisation in our space-time horizon.

The enabling of the preaching. We now have a sermon. We have prayed, as Beethoven did over the Missa Solemnis, 'From the heart it comes; to the heart may it go.' We pray again: for that communion between speaker and hearers which achieves a meeting of minds, one common mind in the whole place as we preach; and for utterance, liberty, unction, confidence. We walk up those steps. Just before we preach we pray Robert Murray McCheyne's prayer: 'Lord, forgive my sins, pour your Spirit upon us and take for yourself the glory.'

The dedication of the listeners. It is said of the first Christian community that they devoted themselves to the Apostles' teaching. They gave themselves not only to *attend to* what the apostles taught, but to *do* it: to believe the teaching, trust the promises, heed the rebukes and obey the commands.

Such listening is not achieved casually. It involves praying for the preacher and for ourselves. It involves preparation, getting to bed early enough over the weekend to be alert during the service. It involves coming to worship in the attitude, 'I will hear what God the Lord will say to me.' It involves noting what is said. And since it involves these things, it is up to pastors to teach them so that people know to live by them.

Creating such an attitude in a church is not the work of a moment. It is the fruit, over years, of conviction that where the preached Word is, there is God, 'terrible as an army with banners', savingly communicating himself and his truth, mighty in deeds, creating what his Word declares.

This dynamic presence of God is furthered, moreover, by our asking for it. Why does Paul repeatedly ask prayer for even his astonishing preaching if not because, through prayer, God empowers it? When Spurgeon was asked the secret of his success in preaching he attributed it to his congregation's prayers.

Given these five anointings, 'One has a right to expect the fullness of the Spirit to come upon one. One might not feel liberty, but the fact that the Holy Spirit is getting through can be relied on.'[30] Dr. Martyn Lloyd-Jones said the same: preachers can expect:

> the Holy Spirit falling upon the preacher in a special manner. It is God giving power, and enabling, through the Spirit, to the preacher in order that he may do this work in a manner that lifts it up beyond the efforts and endeavours of man to a position in which the preacher is being used by the Spirit and becomes the channel through whom the Spirit works .... What then are we to do about this? There is only one obvious conclusion. Seek him! Seek him! But go beyond seeking him; expect him. Do you expect anything to happen when you get up to preach in a pulpit? [31]

Preparing the sermon

Everybody prepares differently. David could not fight with Saul's armour and we would not presume to tell others how to prepare. There are, however, stages worth identifying.

Choosing what to preach on. Getting the principles right is vital.

If it requires the whole Christ from the whole Bible to make us whole people, then we shall take care to provide a balanced diet: Old Testament and New; history, poetry, prophecy, gospel, apocalypse and epistle; thematic series such as Christian doctrine and the Christian life as well as expounding through biblical books systematically.

One of the great salvations of such an approach is that we have to cover subjects we would never otherwise have chosen, just because they come up in the course of our systematic method. The short term advantage is not obvious. The appearing of Christ-like character over a period of time, however, in the lives of those who sit truly under such ministry, is worth any cost.

Apprehension! We are bound to come to the most formative activity known to man feeling unworthy of the task and unable to do it adequately. We *are* inadequate for it, and both God's honour and people's destinies hang on it. We are taking a terrible risk in attempting it.[32] So let apprehension stimulate us to prayer and excellence.

Prayer for the Holy Spirit. We have seen why success is totally dependant on him. After the title line – text, theme or whatever – we next write and pray, 'Lord Jesus, pour out your Spirit on me in full measure. Do the hearers great good through this!'

Read the text, pen in hand. Summarise the passage in our own words so we know exactly what is there: content and context. Then comes the more detailed task, without help of books initially, of

■ exegesis: what does it say: identification, divisions, analysis, explanation;

■ exposition: principles at stake, theology involved;

■ application and illustration: what actions constitute obedience to the passage, human stories illustrating the points.

We can set out the page, well spaced out, in three such columns so that it is easy later to add an illustration or another point of principle at the appropriate place. It can be helpful also to consider at this early stage what psalms, hymns and spiritual songs express the principles unfolding, both as possible quotations during the sermon and in preparation of the praise list for that service. The method also forces on us the task of identifying contemporary application as well as biblical understanding, all through the process of preparation.

Read selected literature and develop the content. Sometimes we are full of insight and need less from the commentaries; at other times, blind as spiritual bats and dependant on the insight of our elders and betters. Either way there is now the solid homework stage of developing our understanding of the passage, why it is in scripture, what it contributes to Christian teaching, and how it applies to our specific hearers.

Put the one main thrust of the sermon in a single, glowing sentence. On the broad sweep of Ephesians 3:14-4:16, for example, mentioned below (next paragraph), it was 'Every Christian can know Jesus better, through taking the three steps outlined.' Notice the form of the statement. It is loaded with opportunity rather than with oughtness. To have written 'every Christian *should* ...' would have made it a quite different sermon.

Identify the objective we have for the hearers. For example for the occasion just noted, I chose 'As a result of this sermon the hearers will know what to do in order to know Jesus better; and will want to take those steps.'

Tease out possible outlines. This can require protracted thought, trying out a whole series of alternative headings or stages. There are arguments for and against headings, and especially alliteration. Whether or not these are used, however, a sermon should have logical order.

If headings are used they should be as short as we can make them, as memorable as possible, absolutely true to the thrust of the text and in similar grammatical form. On the sermon just mentioned covering the sweep of Ephesians 3:14-4:16, for example:

not	It is possible to experience Christ's love for us (statement)
	live a consistent Christian life (command)
	Do you take time to study the Faith? (question)
but	Love the Saviour
	Live the life
	Learn the faith

Our favourite: a Scottish preacher, taking the prodigal son story, took as his three divisions:

· sick o' hame …
· hamesick …
· hame.

Its simplicity as an outline, together with its transparency to the scriptural passage as to both story and theology, is perfect.

Write the sermon, the conclusion and the introduction. I distinguish between these so as to make the point that the beginning and ending of a sermon warrant special care. Some people write the introduction last: either capturing the attention by way of a real-life situation which the passage addresses, or introducing the Scripture about to be expounded. Others write it first, after the homework already completed, so as to facilitate and earth the initial writing.

Revise it. We see the discontinuities in thought sequence better by coming back to the sermon after completion and reading it critically. Double check that the language reflects the hearers' lives, and that there is substantial application relevant to different people present: the teenager, the middle-aged, the unmarried mother, the elderly lifelong attender.

Preach it to yourself. It is easier to get the message into others' heads rather than out of our own – an important distinction – if we have 'heard' it beforehand and responded to God from it, perhaps committing ourselves to any obedience for which it calls.

Highlight: underline, circle, put musical notation marks or otherwise remind ourselves of stages, special emphases and anything we want to read word for word.

Pray for the hearers, in terms of the objectives for their lives that we have identified.

Now for that pulpit. It is time to give ourselves in faith-confidence to the last of Griffith Thomas' steps, 'Think yourself empty, read yourself full, write yourself clear, pray yourself keen – and let yourself go!'

Preaching the sermon

We can help or hinder our hearers so much by our presentation. The preacher who preaches once weekly to a hundred members for thirty years will take up 234,000 hours of people's time. What potential for good there is, in using that time as helpfully as we are able!

Our aim while in the pulpit is *involvement* with each other: a living, active communion of mind between God, preacher and people. I shall never forget going to see (yes) and hear Alfred Brendel playing a Mozart piano concerto. After taking his seat at the piano he paused in a fury of concentration. We too were drawn into expectant silence. We could not but feel that this was an event; that something quite different, 'other', would happen that evening; and that it cried out for our attention. Should the same not be true of us, for whom that otherness is so much more momentously true?

Paul asked for prayer for *words to be given* and that he will preach clearly; even 'in opening my mouth'. Content, clarity and the process of preaching all matter to the pastor. We shall be passionate to communicate accurately, clearly and as good communicators. We shall work at the skills of communication: at poise and timing, voice production and the off-putting habits our best friends hopefully tease us for.

If we tend to become tense when speaking, and this can especially be a problem when our ministry is under strain for other reasons, we can quietly practise speaking with relaxed throat immediately before speaking, perhaps by repeating the 23rd Psalm or the Lord's prayer.

As to *stance*, our hearers deserve our attending to nervous-habit fidgeting and swaying. The American communication teacher Ken Davis recommends standing with feet slightly apart, one a little in front of the other, to give both poise and the physical balance for expressing the concepts and emotions of the sermon bodily.

Appropriate *eye contact* can be immensely helpful. Errors to avoid are the sweeper whose gaze endlessly ranges to and fro without ever settling, the shifter who by showing his embarrassment communicates it to the hearers and the bird watcher who gazes at the ceiling (or the back wall just above the highest listener) while avoiding all honest contact.

It is possible for a sermon to be gripping while the preacher keeps his eyes down on the sermon text; Jonathan Edwards did it, and his hearers were transfixed; but we advise working to achieve eye contact. It is good to cover the different sections of the congregation, but not in a rapid sweep: better to stay looking at one person for the duration of a thought before moving on to another.[33]

There can be real benefit in involving the hearers by asking them to consider some practical issue about the sermon for a minute or two, either individually or (sensitively facilitated) with one or two of those near them, in the course of preaching.

We noted earlier that Paul also asks for prayer for *boldness and conviction*.[34] So many preachers say fateful things as though nothing hung upon it! Cicero said, 'He will be eloquent who can speak of small things in a subdued manner, of moderate things in a temperate manner, and of grand things in a grand manner.'[35]

After the preaching

For the preacher. It is not unusual at the end of a service to feel exposed and self-conscious: having had one's soul laid bare before the congregation.[36] One can *feel* both 'God forgive me for making such a mess of your truth' and the need to be affirmed. Recognise this and simply leave all to our Lord. Let us discipline ourselves against introversion and wondering how well we did. There is a place later for objective critique of our content and technique from time to time. Rest in the fact that the essential things have been done already, at Golgotha, and that God is the worker.

For the church. The impact of a sermon is very considerably enhanced by going over its content again, perhaps that lunch time as a family and that bed-time prayerfully on an individual basis.

I do believe there is a place for congregational reflection on and discussion of sermons. We need to be sensitive to people's insecurities. Surely however there is potential in organised discussion of sermons preached; or even, suggests Packer, in pastoral enquiry as to what changes the preaching has effected in people's lives.[37] One method that has proved successful is to distribute questions about the sermon at the beginning of a Sunday service, the questions being then discussed either immediately afterwards by those who choose to, or at a midweek meeting.

■ I suggest there could be value in identifying what steps we actually take in the process of preaching and its preparation, and making some definite opportunity to review them.

References

1. Hebrews 2:10.
2. INST. 3.1.1.
3. P.T. Forsyth, *Positive Preaching and the Modern Mind*, London, Hodder and Stoughton, 1907, p. 6, 83.
4. R. Clements, *The Strength of Weakness*, Fearn, Christian Focus Publications, 1994, p. 83,84
5. 2 Corinthians 3:6 and 4:1-7.
6. R.A. Finlayson, *The Cross in the Experience of Our Lord*, Fearn, Christian Focus Publications, 1993 reprint, pp. 19-25.
7. Ephesians 4:11-16, my paraphrase.
8. J. Philip, Congregational letter, Holyrood Abbey Parish Church, Edinburgh, April 1974. I have retained James Philip's wording.

9. Owen at the ordination sermon recorded in volume 9 of the Goold edition of his *Works*, Edinburgh, Banner of Truth, 1968, pp. 431 ff.

10. INST. 4.3.1.

11. *Ibid.*

12. 1 Thessalonians 2:13,14; compare 1:4-7.

13. 1 Thessalonians 2:13; Galatians 1:6-2:7; Nehemiah 8:1-8, especially 8:8.

14. Acts 16:14; 1 Corinthians 2:1-5; 1 Thessalonians 1:5; 2:13b.

15. Colossians 4:4; Ephesians 6:19f.

16. Nehemiah 8:8; Acts 17:2f; 1 Thessalonians 2:13; 2 Corinthians 4:1.

17. Ephesians 6:19f; Colossians 4:4.

18. Acts 20:18-20; 1 Thessalonians 1:5; 2:10-12; 2 Thessalonians 3:7-9; James 1:5-8.

19. Mark 16:20; Acts 16:4f; Romans 1:16; 1 Corinthians 2:4f; Colossians 4:3; 1 Thessalonians 1:5f; 2 Thessalonians 3:1.

20. Acts 2:37f; 1 Thessalonians 1:6-10; James 5:1.

21. Acts 17:2f.

22. Acts 17:11.

23. 1 Corinthians 2:4.

24. E. Schillebeeckx, *The Church with a Human Face*, London, SCM, 1985, p.121.

25. Ephesians 5:18.

26. Exodus 4:10,11.

27. 1 Samuel 3:19-4:1.

28. Psalm 103:17,18.

29. C. Pinnock, 'The Work of the Holy Spirit in Hermeneutics', *Journal of Pentecostal Theology*, vol. 2, 1993, p. 3-23, to which I am indebted for the argument in this paragraph.

30. W. Still, 'Anointed Preaching', unpublished address to Crieff fellowship of ministers, January 1994.

31. D.M. Lloyd-Jones, *Preaching and Preachers*, London, Hodder, 1971, p. 305, 325.

32. James 3:1; Ezekiel 3:16-18.

33. K. Davis, *Secrets of Dynamic Communication*, Grand Rapids, Zondervan, 1991, chapter 10.

34. Ephesians 6:19,20; 1 Thessalonians 1:5.

35. Quoted by M. Allen, 'Fruitful Marks of Authentic Christian Ministry', in *Captive to the Word*, Burning Bush Publications, no place stated, n.d., p. 53.

36. 1 Thessalonians 2:8. We share not only the gospel but our very life, in this act of 'truth through personality' (Phillips Brooks' definition of preaching).

37. J.I. Packer, 'Introduction: why preach?' in *Preaching*, ed. S.T. Logan, Welwyn, Evangelical Press, 1986, p. 23.

CHAPTER SIX

PUBLIC WORSHIP

Principles, preparation, conduct

Jacob was afraid and said, 'How awesome is this place! This is none other than the house of God; this is the gate of heaven' (Genesis 28:17).

Then the glory of the Lord filled the Tabernacle (Exodus 40:34).

To worship is to quicken the conscience by the holiness of God, to feed the mind with the truth of God, to purge the imagination by the beauty of God, to open the heart to the love of God and to devote the will to the purpose of God (William Temple).

What is worship?

In overwhelming preponderance the words translated 'worship', Old Testament and New, signify prostration. In Hebrew *shachah* means to bow and in the verbal form in which it is used for our purposes it means to bow oneself low, humbling oneself in homage. The concern is to get low before God.[1] In Greek the verb *proskuneo* means literally to kiss (i.e. the dust) before the face of, as when the magi bowed down and 'worshipped' the infant King whose advent had been heralded by the heavens: they kissed the ground before his Majesty, in face of his Presence. The Welsh word for worship, *addoli*, literally means 'on two knees' and expresses precisely the biblical sense.

This is what we aim to achieve in public worship: a people bowed in heart and spirit, in homage, admiration, love and fealty, before God in his glory. When God is being genuinely accorded the weight and worthiness that are his by a people, there is true worship.

If that is our aim in worship, it is also the test of true worship: whether God is being accorded his due as King and redeemer. For a Sunday service can be one of many things. It can be entertainment, it can be the expression of human opinion, it can be a platform for an inflated ego or indeed for an inferiority complex; but it is only a time of worship when God is being exalted as people humble themselves before him.

We need to teach, therefore, that the criterion by which to assess public worship is not our pleasure. There is no greater joy, it is true, than to be glorifying and enjoying God with heart, soul, mind and strength, and to be honouring him by sitting under his Word; but the test of worship is, Are our hearts being bowed, is God being honoured? Not 'Are we being satisfied?' but 'Is God being glorified?'

Would this not do away with much of the self-orientation that accompanies the evaluation of worship? 'I did not get much *out of* the hymns this morning', we say; while the issue that matters is, what God got from them through what we put *into* them. As the Puritan Stephen Charnock wrote: 'When we believe that we should be satisfied rather than God glorified, we put God below ourselves, as though he had been made for us rather than we for him.'[2]

The same defining test sifts the issues of entertainment in worship. Of course humour and pleasure belong here, as does all of life; but Derek Kidner has a characteristically pithy comment on Psalm 22:3, the fact that God inhabits or is enthroned upon the praises of his people. Kidner says, 'The metaphor also puts the question to the church, whether its hymnody is a throne for God or a platform for man.'[3]

A service broadcast from a prominent evangelical congregation concluded with a jazz session, the performers presumably applauded at the end. Surely as soon as it turned from being a throne for God to being performance, at that moment it became entertainment and stopped being worship.

Packer has suggested that there are six components to the activity of worship, each with its characteristic expression:

· Praise: 'Lord, you are wonderful'
· Thanks: 'Thank you, Lord'
· Request: 'Please, Lord'
· Offering: 'Take this,Lord'
· Learning: 'Yes, Lord'
· Telling: 'Listen, everybody'[4]

In each of these *God's worthiness* is being expressed – worth-ship – in different ways.

Note finally that Christian worship is ineluctably Trinitarian. It is addressed to the Father, through the Son, in the Spirit. Our Lord Jesus leads us into God's very presence as we come to worship. This is the only way there: 'No-one comes to the Father but through me' (John 14:6). Jesus is thus the reconciler of man to God and God to man, the foundation without whom acceptable worship is impossible. 'No worship has ever pleased God except that which looked to Christ.'[5] Authentic worship is absolutely full of Jesus.

The issue of inter-faith worship seems solved at a stroke. People are sharing in worship when they worship the Father through the Son in the Spirit. Unless they come through Jesus then whatever else they are doing they are not coming to the Father: our Lord is very clear on that. And if they are not Christians they do not have the Spirit of Christ (Rom. 8:9) and so are not coming in the Spirit. Inter-faith dialogue, respectful and faithful, is a great task; but between Christian and non-Christian worship there is a great gulf fixed: they are simply different activities.

Worship, then, is to ascribe to the Lord the glory due to his name, to worship him as to the splendour of his holiness [6]; this is the activity we aim to achieve.

Why worship?

We know in our heart of hearts that nothing is more important than that God should be accorded the honour that is his due as King and Redeemer, Creator and sustainer – as *God.*

In the end of the day this is why worship is universal among mankind and why Sunday worship is not only a natural priority but the most fulfilling activity in the human repertoire. God is altogether admirable, fairer than beauty, closer than breathing, kinder than compassion, glorious. James Torrance writes:

> God has made all creatures for his glory. The lilies of the field in their beauty glorify God with a glory greater than that of Solomon, but they do not know it. The sparrow on the housetop glorifies God in its dumbness, but it doesn't know it. The universe in its vastness and remoteness glorifies God but it doesn't know it.
>
> But God made man in his own image to be the priesthood of creation, to express for all creatures the praises of God, so that through the lips of man the heavens might declare the glory of God, that we who know we are God's creatures might worship God and in our worship gather up the worship of all creation. [7]

Scripture leaves us in no doubt on this; it calls us 'the people whom I formed for myself *that they might proclaim My praise.*' The psalmist, after a time of mental travail over the unfairness in the world, thinks through to the end of things and concludes,

> Whom have I in heaven but You?
> And earth has nothing I desire besides You.
> My flesh and my heart may fail,
> but God is the strength of my heart and my portion for ever.[8]

The Shorter Catechism spells out our main reason for existing, to glorify and enjoy God. That is what we are for; it is as humbling and as exalted as that. Our Lord explained to the Samaritan woman that God the Father is seeking the kind of worshippers who worship him in spirit and in truth. Peter spells out the reason for the existence of the church in precisely similar terms: to be a holy priesthood offering spiritual sacrifices acceptable to God through Jesus Christ.[9] The term 'sacrifices' is used in the New Testament in a number of ways; in the context here the reference is to the way in which the Church as a priesthood, a people who have access to God in a way others do not, function as the house of God.

The house of God in the Old Testament was the holy place, the tabernacle or the temple. It was the meeting place between two worlds, the heavenly places and this world. Our Lord said it should be a house of prayer, a place of worship not of trade. The New Testament tells us that we are the new Temple. The purpose of public worship is to operate as such a house, the place on this earth where the shekinah glory, the dwelling glory of God, comes down; and God dwells in the midst of congregations, inhabiting their praises, accorded his glory.

Chapter one briefly explored this glory, God's weightiness or worthiness. Worth-ship (old English) or worship (modern English) is our ascription to him of this glory. Since every word of his carries weight, we accord him worth-ship when we esteem every word that comes from his mouth.

This is why to hearken to his words, with obedience following, is not supplemental but fundamental to worship; part, not just of its well-being but its very being. They are greatly mistaken, therefore, who distinguish between the worshipping and the preaching parts of a service. To feed on God's Word is precisely to accord him the glory due to his name, as are to sing his praise in spiritual songs, to admire him in prayers of adoration, to ask him for things in petition, to bring him our offerings and to feast at his table.

The more joyful, the more spiritual: let our final note be joy. 'Come, let us sing for joy to the Lord,' said the Psalmist, 'let us shout aloud to the Rock of our salvation. Let us come before him with thanksgiving and extol him with music and song' (Ps. 95:1-2). 'Rejoice in the Lord always,' said Paul, 'I will say it again: Rejoice!'

The more joyful worship is, the more spiritual: not necessarily happy-clappy, for that is a matter of personal style, but committed to glad boasting about God and his Saviourhood, for that is a Christian commandment. It is as God is glorified and enjoyed that we are fulfilled, outsiders attracted and he honoured as he deserves. Such a people will know God's presence. Such a people will be the church at worship.

Planning worship

The planning of preaching (see chapter 5) provides a theme for a given service, around which public worship is built; but as I have attended churches of every denomination and none, I have often been struck by the lack of order and structure. Sometimes a service has consisted almost exclusively of a number of songs each repeated several times, followed by the preaching and departure. Yet the very thing which holy Scripture emphasises about the conduct of worship, Old and New Testament, is due order.[10]

Look at worship in the Old Testament: structure is clearly built into it. Even the architecture of Tabernacle and Temple speak of several reasonable stages:

- *Preparation*, made careful by the enormous attention to detail (e.g. Exod. 25–30 and 35–40, Lev. 1–9), the removal of one's shoes because one is coming to holy ground, and the sanction visited upon the careless (Lev. 10).

- *Approach*, involving a sacrifice to atone for sins.

- *Prayers*, emphasised by the visual aid of presenting incense.

- The *Word of God* to his people was more basic to their existence even than food: 'Man does not live by bread alone, but by every utterance of the mouth of the LORD' (Deut. 8:3). The ten commandments were contained in the covenant box kept in the holy of holies as a symbol of this. There at the very heart of worship is God's Word: it could not be more central than this. It is clear from passages like Nehemiah 8 and the whole Old Testament corpus, law and prophets alike, that God's speaking to his people is constitutive of their existence and the defining distinctiveness of their life and worship as a nation.

- *Psalm singing*, probably antiphonal, also featured at least in later Old Testament worship,

- ending with the Aaronic *blessing* (Num. 6:22-27) and *departure*.

Similarly when instituting the Lord's Supper Jesus modelled it on the structure of the Passover service and gave it proper planning, preparation, teaching, actions and order, with closing hymn (Matt. 26:17-30).

The church clearly followed him in this continuity and development of the principles of worship found in the Old Testament (Acts 2:46). It was the norm to meet on the first day of the week, clearly the Christians' new living out of the Sabbath principle, and spend time which included the breaking of bread and sustained teaching (Acts 20:7-12).

The Apostles taught thoroughly about worship including its content and significance, the need for orderliness, understanding and order, as well as the connection with concern for the poor (the latter being common to both Testaments).[11]

Worship, in other words, has sequence and contains certain essential ingredients. At the very minimum there should be a sense of three stages:

· approach to God and praise.
· the Word of God read aloud and made clear in preaching.
· response to God and departure under his blessing.

Within that orderly sequence worship is an alternating, two-direction movement between God and man, mediated in both directions by Christ. Consider the dynamic pendulum of movement in a well planned service. Reduced to its essentials it might look something like this:

Since the time of worship has a theme, the whole service will be

ORDER OF SERVICE

God Acts		We re-act
HE CALLS 'Come to Me'	Call to worship	WE COME
	Opening praise/hymn	PRAISE
	Prayer	ADORE AND INVOKE
SPEAKS	Bible Reading	
	SERMON	LISTEN
	Offering	GIVE
	Prayer	INTERCEDE
	Hymn or Song	DEDICATE OURSELVES
	Lord's Supper and hymn?	FEED AND
	Recite Creed? [12]	RESPOND
SENDS WITH BLESSING	Benediction	GO TO SERVE

informed and controlled by it. Each psalm, hymn or song will, if humanly possible, reflect it in some way; it will inform the content of the opening praise, the prayers, each successive item. In preparing for worship the task of the leader(s) is to consider what each part of the service is doing there and how to make it achieve that.

Welcome at door. Having had occasion to visit many congregations as a stranger, I can testify to the power of those who stand at the door. In many buildings it is not possible at first glance to determine where to go. To be resolutely ignored while searching various possible openings for the right one, is daunting. To be swamped ('sit here at the *front*') is unattractive. The doorkeeper who is sensitive to uncertainty without being too forceful can be a power for good. A smiling 'Can I help you?' is a pretty good starting point. Some officebearers are naturals at this; many can be greatly helped by a little training.

The function of the *call to worship* is to decentralise self and centralise God. When a leader says 'Let us worship God!' he isn't saying 'We'll start now', or (as I heard) 'This is the summer so we'll just have a short light service.' He or she is directing our minds and hearts to God and to our reason for existing.

Choosing psalms, hymns and songs and preparing to introduce them.[13] This is not a casual task. Emotions run high over the choice of praise. Well done, it can be a major factor in worshippers' fulfilment in worship and is often part of what God uses to awaken people spiritually.

Does it matter whether we include actual translations of the psalms; and may we include, also, songs and hymns which are not such? We are commanded, 'Sing psalms and hymns and spiritual songs with thankfulness in your hearts to God.'[14] The difference between psalms, hymns and spiritual songs was probably not large in Paul's mind. 'Psalms' possibly means worship songs drawn from the Psalms in the Bible; 'hymns', songs taken from elsewhere in scripture; and 'spiritual songs', made up by the Spirit-filled heart from what one knows and experiences of God.

There are good reasons, therefore, for singing psalms and paraphrases, but all good Christian hymns and songs, old and new, are scriptural in the sense intended by Colossians 3:16: they express Christian truth as revealed in the Bible. We are far better using good material of whatever genre and age, than using items that are bad poetry or poor music because of tradition, or restricting ourselves to direct translations of the biblical psalms.

Every healthy congregation contains a mixture of people, and all reasonable tastes should be able to worship in language they find meaningful. I say reasonable: some new songs are theological nursery rhymes devoid of musicality, cosy words that fit together in almost any order. Others however are very fine and represent many people's natural expression of worship.

The issue is so important because singing psalms and hymns is almost the only way in which people participate out loud in worship. Spiritual songs give people an opportunity to express their faith. Well, they should be chosen so as to be theologically sound and of solid content, but also popular in the best sense: valid for the people present.

This is true not only for the language we use but also for the music to which we sing it. Some old and some new tunes are non-tunes; we should drop them. Some songs, old and new, are probably best sung – for at least a verse or two – without accompaniment. Let us do that. Some definitely go best if accompanied by the organ; others, by other instruments. We should be ready to use whatever best serves our reason for existing: to glorify and enjoy God together.

As far as possible, therefore, psalms and hymns should be chosen so as to fit in with:

- The shape and structure of worship: the approach in homage, the listening in hunger and the commitment in response. The opening praise is not normally the best place for introverted contrition in a minor key. On the other hand bouncy affirmation immediately before the sermon tends to create less of a desire to listen than does a thoughtful, quieter hymn expressing request.

- The theme of the service, which is controlled above all by the preached Word.

- The people present: those particular people in all their variety, with their personal histories, musical preferences and language style, not forgetting those whom you pray will start to come. We need to consider old and young, those with half a century of Christian faithfulness behind them and those who are still thinking about the faith. We want if possible to give all of them opportunity to express to God what is true of him and how they feel about him, in language that is meaningful for them.

Advance preparation on the provenance or recent relevance of a hymn can greatly enhance worship. The circumstances in which Martin Rinkart wrote 'Now thank we all our God' are immensely moving. The Sunday after the over-publicised rape of a London vicar's daughter I changed the opening praise to 'Christ triumphant', written by her father, explaining why I had done so and giving a moment for quiet reading of the hymn before we sang.

When Watchman Nee had his tongue cut out by the Chinese communists because they could not quench his influence even in prison, he asked to sing one last song before they did so; and chose 'O for a thousand tongues to sing my great Redeemer's praise.' Who could not sing it with greater feeling after being reminded of this? There is a wealth of material in the hymnologies, but such introductions should be disciplined to not more than one or at the most two per service lest it become contrived.

Not every verse need be accompanied, nor sung by everyone

present. It can be a constructive part of hymn preparation to consider which verses might be sung unaccompanied, or by only the women or young people, or played on different instruments.

In the *opening prayer* the leader's job is to take us, as it were, by the scruff of our necks to unite and bow our hearts before the majesty and Saviourhood of God; and then, speaking for all of us, to beg him to shine his light upon and touch us in our need; by the end of it the worshipper should be saying, That's what I wanted to say.

The opening prayer is not the time to grovel or mutter. It glorifies and enjoys God and asks his blessing. Its real source is the content and style of our own learning and devotional life during the week: if we have taken time to glorify and enjoy God then (chapter 4), learning more about him even in small stages, we shall usually be able to find something to say to him for the opening prayer.

For the dark nights of the soul he will honour our resolute delivery of words intended but not felt; or we can ask another to take over, or read a prayer written in earlier centuries that says what we should be able to.

Children's Address. It is customary in many churches to include a message to children during the service. My plea is that a serious attempt is made to ensure that it, also, serves the theme of the service; that it is linked to scripture in some way; and that it is really spoken to the children and not to get a laugh from the adults.

It is often possible to find a scripture story that illustrates the theme; or a story from other sources that does the same, preceded and followed by a memory verse from the sermon or a cognate passage.

Scripture Reading. Paul instructed Timothy to give definite attention to the public reading of scripture[15] in a way that implies this is not a part of the service to be taken by just anyone. Preparation for this ministry concerns the suitability of the person reading, study of the passage and advance preparation of its public delivery.

Prayers of intercession. Frustrating are those public prayers that stop short at 'Lord, we pray for (bereaved people, whomever)' and then move on. I want to stand up and call out, '*what* do we pray for them?' When Jesus passed two lepers he asked them to specify what they wanted him to do for them. When Paul urged Timothy to pray during worship for those in authority he specified what kind of thing to ask for.[16]

The scriptures give us a breathtaking vision of what the prayers of believing people can accomplish, even to the fire of God coming upon earth to change the course of history.[17]

An *Offering* is something we do for God; a collection is something others do to us. There is a difference even then between saying 'your offerings will now be received' and 'we continue to worship God in our offerings'. If we include ourselves by using 'we', the reality of that is enhanced by ensuring in advance that we shall be included in the opportunity to give.

Silence. The worship leader is not the only fount of wisdom on what to ask God for and it can be good to propose issues which cry out for prayer and after naming each one to give definite time of quietness for members of the congregation to make their own prayers for them. Times of quiet can be threatening when first introduced; people can be eased through this initial uncertainty by being assured that quiet does not need to be silence.

The Lord's supper (Holy Communion, the breaking of bread, the eucharist). The New Testament does not insist that 'breaking of bread' is weekly. It was initiated at Passover time, after all. The irresistible impression I receive, nonetheless, is that it was so practised in New Testament times. It certainly was in Patristic times, and Calvin urged weekly communion as the most seemly practice.[18]

The Scottish Reformers were not so minded, the *First Book of Discipline* (1560) recommending four times per year.[19] Within the Christian church as a whole, however, this is very much a minority perspective and by 1647 the Westminster Directory urged frequent communion. The contemporary trend to more frequent communion is preferable: in line with practice in the New Testament, in most of Christendom for most of its history, and a help in returning us frequently to remember Christ's passion. As to the outward conduct of the ceremony questions like whether we use common cup or individual glasses, give the elements first or last to those dispensing it and so on, these are quite indifferent and should be decided on the principles of simplicity, spirituality and substance that govern worship,[20] and on that mutual care which must flow when we treat the Lord's supper as the bond of love.[21]

The question of variety. Familiarity with an order of service frees people to think about its content in a way that is simply not possible if they have no idea what is coming next: it is a help to the worshipper if there is a fairly standard order of service.

On the other hand a measure of the unexpected can be stimulating as long as it is well introduced within that safe framework. Interviews, ministry in song by one or more, greetings from a visitor, the opportunity to greet or pray for neighbour in pew or seat, exchanging the peace, exploring the practical implications of the sermon in groups of four or five throughout the sanctuary might all further the upbuilding of the church and the honour of God.

What is appropriate in one context would be threatening in another, but the validity of a standard order of service need not blind us to the enrichment offered by the disciplined inclusion of variety.

What constitutes participation? It is often asserted that to have only one person leading somehow reduces participation ('a monologue to the uncomplaining' is the charge), and that adding to the number at the front increases it. This seems to us a misunderstanding.

Failure to participate is indeed a potential problem. It was the custom before the Reformation to advise those who came to Mass to say their own private prayers while the incomprehensible Latin rite was carried out. A century later the Westminster Directory felt compelled to urge people to attend to the service rather than engage in their own private devotions, reading, 'whispering, conferences, salutations, sleeping and other indecent behaviour'.[22]

That *is* non-participation. But its corrective is not to have everyone leading, but everyone committed together to the one thing that is going on: listening and responding to the lead, given unitedly to the corporate praise, giving themselves to the preached Word. Putting more people at the front can actually make worship less genuinely participative and more of a spectator experience.

Nonetheless, those attending can feel that they are watching the worship experience as outsiders: especially, those sitting near the back in a large building. That is something for both them and the leader(s) to work hard at. We owe it to them to make the whole service as lively and irresistibly involving as possible. This is one reason we have suggested including the creed, at least from time to time. I use it, explicitly as a fresh opportunity to put our faith in the things spoken of, as part of every baptism service, in line with ancient and Reformed practice.

Let us point out members' corresponding commitment. Let us together pray earnestly for the minister and his preparation during the week. Let us come expectant, willing to work at the two movements in worship (God to us, we to him). Let us so give ourselves to responsive praise that we are exhausted by the end of a service. There will be no doubt that such worship is participative.

Leading worship

Let us have passion! I regret to say that there are many evangelicals, self-styled, who need the appeal quite as much as others. Here are some words from William Still:

> It is not the form of worship which is of primary importance, but the presence of the Holy Spirit in the fullness of his power: it is that which makes any service live. The most ordinary style of Presbyterian worship can be fraught with incalculable help and blessing if the Holy Spirit is permitted to release himself and is honoured in it.
>
> What the Spirit does is to infuse into the staidest form of worship such liveliness as will quicken all regenerate souls and make them sit up and take notice – and probably startle others too!
>
> And the way he will do it is by quickening the Lord's servant to such a degree that his voice becomes more lively, more interestingly modulated and his words more clearly articulated – he is on his toes – and he will incline to use the most satisfying language to cloak his thoughts, both in prayer and in the sermon. But the very way he introduces worship will arrest attention, and the praise will tend to inspire and not depress the people, and when he comes to read the Scriptures, it will be clear that he is more than reading them: he is living them![23]

Announcing hymns. The next advice sounds obvious but our experience indicates that it is needed. Since a people like to be taken care of by the person leading in worship, show every confidence and competence. Have a marker in the hymnbook in advance for each hymn: this avoids furious flicking through pages, a nervous experience for those wanting to be led.

Again, the style of announcement needs to take account of human inattention and memory. If we announce the hymn number only at the beginning, many have forgotten it by the time we announce the words. A firm:

> We worship God in Hymn no. x, to the tune y. Ye servants of God, your master proclaim! *Hymn x*.

shows that you know what you are doing (the care factor), indicates that the hymn is an act of worship (the purposefulness factor) and reminds the forgetful of the hymn number just as they were wondering about it: a good, professional quality lead. If you are giving a fuller introduction to the hymn, do so with enthusiasm before that final confirmation of hymn number.

As to repeating units of praise, usually choruses, it can be helpful to sing a short item once by way of praise and a second time by way of reflection but in my view repetition of a chorus beyond, say, twice is an assault upon taste and reason.

Public prayer. There is a nice balance between effective passion, embarrassing emotion and being deadpan which is best solved by thinking through what we want the prayer to express and then being ourselves. Not even God likes being addressed as though he is a public meeting and there is something death-dealing about 'professional' praying, all public address and no personal touch, which treats him like one.

The answer to it is to talk *to him*, not to the listeners, and to do so in a spirit of reverence and not as though we are reading an essay. As to preparation of public prayers there are no rules although those who write nothing need to be aware that they are probably limiting their use of vocabulary and reducing the variety and width of both their intercessory concern and their praying style thereby. Maintaining our theological study in a spirit of devotion is the best source of variety and growth in this vital matter.

One fault to avoid in public prayer is to make it an occasion for preaching at the congregation. This is a gross abuse of power; prayer is to be addressed humbly, as just one of a company of redeemed sinners, to God.

On the act of *preaching* see chapter five; to which I would add that a measure of visual aid does not need to detract from, and can positively enhance, the effectiveness of communication. The vividness and visuality of Jesus' teaching, the research evidence, and our experience, speak with one voice on this.

Such visual help might be as simple as stating in word or picture form the divisions of the sermon. When preaching through Amos I have made part of the sermon a video from a Christian relief organisation. It made quite clear one relevance of that part of scripture. It was unforgettable.

Closure. Some independent church services close without any form of benediction. Apart from being a biblical practice,[24] benediction is profoundly appropriate psychologically and is best given with real emphasis. There is nothing at stake between giving the benediction in the first and second persons ('The grace ... be with *us* all' or 'The Lord bless and keep *you*'). Both are appropriate but in my view the second person form is more so; it is certainly the form in which this ministry is expressed in scripture.

The glory of God is all that this is about: 'honour and adoration expressed in response to his excellence and praiseworthiness.'[25] Every other consideration falls into place when that one is first and last to us. It will make us lead with dignity and reverence, jealous lest anything detract from God's Godhood in the eyes of those present.

The day the Tabernacle was completed, the glory of the Lord filled the place. Let us spend a few minutes recommitting ourselves to this ambition: blessing and honour, kingship and love, glory and power for him.

Concluding exercise

- Do I know of anything, that I am capable of affecting, that tends to reduce the spirit of united worship in my church? If so, what can I do about it?

- Do I so love my congregation, and show it, that they like coming to church and feel able to listen to God's solemn words as well as his affirming ones?

- Do I approve of the steps I am taking to know, and know more about, God?

References

1. D. Kidner, *Psalms 73-150,* London, IVP, 1975, p.345 on Psalm 95:6.
2. Quoted in E.J. Alexander, *St George's Tron Parish Church magazine*, Glasgow, Summer 1981.
3. D. Kidner, *Psalms 1-72,* Leicester, Tyndale OT commentaries, 1973, p. 106, on Psalm 22:3.
4. Unpublished address to Reformed Faith Fellowship, 22 Feb 1975.
5. INST. 2.6.1.
6. Psalm 29:2.
7. J. B. Torrance, 'The Place of Jesus Christ in Worship', in R.S. Anderson, ed., *Theological Foundations for Ministry*, Edinburgh, T&T Clark, 1979, p. 348.
8. Isaiah 43:21; Psalm 73:25f.
9. John 4:19-26; 1 Peter 2:5, 9 in the context of verses 4-12.

10. 1 Corinthians 14:40.

11. E.g. Isaiah 1:11-17; Amos 5:21-24; 1 Corinthians 10:15-22; 11:17-34; 14:1-40.

12. T.L. Johnson, *Leading in worship*: a source book for Presbyterian students and ministers, Oak Ridge TN, Covenant Foundation, 1996, p. 6. Johnson's whole introductory essay is a masterpiece of theological and historical underpinning with respect to worship, combined with a respect for liturgical and Presbyterian history.

13. There is a quite excellent article by Helen Killick: 'Choosing Hymns', in *Rutherford Journal*, vol. 3 No. 2, Winter 1996, p. 11-14. My paragraph is in her debt.

14. Colossians 3:16.

15. 1 Timothy 4:13.

16. 1 Timothy 2:1,2.

17. Revelation 8–10. Compare James 5:16-18.

18. INST. 4.17.43.

19. J.K. Cameron, ed., *The First Book of Discipline*, Edinburgh, St Andrew Press, 1972, p. 183.

20. T.L. Johnson, *op. cit.*, p. 5.

21. Augustine on John 6:51, *Tractate 6*, para. 13 in NPNF, vol. 7, p.172, quotes 1 Corinthians 10:17 (because there is one loaf we, being many, are one body) and exclaims, 'O sign of unity! O bond of charity!' Compare Calvin, INST. 4.17.38.

22. *Westminster Directory for the Public Worship of God*, 1645.

23. W. Still, Pastoral letter, *Gilcomston South Congregational Record*, Aberdeen, February 1989.

24. Numbers 6:24-26; 2 Corinthians 13:14.

25. S.B. Ferguson *et al*, eds., *New Dictionary of Theology*, Leicester, IVP, 1988, p. 271, art. by Packer on the glory of God.

CHAPTER SEVEN

A PRAYING PEOPLE

World Christians; corporate prayer

Pray for us that the message of the Lord may spread rapidly and be honoured. And pray that we may be delivered from wicked and evil men, for not everyone has faith (2 Thessalonians 3.1,2).

Another angel, who had a golden censer, was given much incense to offer, with the prayers of the saints, on the golden altar before the throne. The smoke of the incense, together with the prayers of the saints, went up before God. Then the angel took the censer, filled it with fire from the altar and hurled it on the earth; and there came peals of thunder, rumblings, flashes of lightning and an earthquake (Revelation 8:3-5).

The great orphan

I feel passionate about the theme of this chapter, for I have experienced its benefits in a way that reflects the practice and precept of the New Testament church. Yet it is the great orphan of Christian thought and practice.

That theme is the shared prayers of God's people, world Christians raising their voices together in prayer: prayer for fellow Christians; prayer for secular authorities; prayer for world evangelisation with a view to both the salvation of men and women and the speedier return of Christ; and prayer in response to the world's heartaches and tragedies.

Theologically and biblically it should be a heavy emphasis in Christian work and ministerial training, and therefore also in books on theology and ministry; yet it is astonishingly absent from them. At least a minimal framework of theoretical underpinning, therefore, seems essential.

Relative to the New Testament, this is a minor theme in the Old. This is not surprising: the day had not yet come when ' "they will all know me, from the least of them to the greatest," declares the Lord':[1] which is part of the greater privilege given us through Christ, compared with the Old Testament believer.[2]

The prayers of the people are nonetheless a significant feature of

Old Testament life. When the Israelites were about to enter the holy land at the end of the Exodus period they were commanded, along with presenting their offerings, to speak with God in prayer which included intercession for God's blessing on Israel.[3] After the dedication of the Temple God appeared to Solomon and opened the door to great good being available to the Jewish people through united prayer:

> If my people, who are called by my name, will humble themselves and pray and seek my face and turn from their wicked ways, then will I hear from heaven and forgive their sin and heal their land. Now my eyes will be open and my ears attentive to the prayers offered in this place.[4]

There is also however an emphasis that it was outstanding people, especially those anointed to be prophets, priests and kings, who carried the weight of intercession.[5] The full power of having all the people, a kingdom of priests, praying awaited the new covenant.

In the New Testament we see this greater potential of shared prayer prepared for and taught by our Lord, achieved by his death and resurrection, practised by the early church and commanded by the apostles.

Corporate prayer: the new world power

Jesus prepared the church for it. He said, 'If two of you agree on earth about anything you ask for, it will be done for you by my Father in heaven. For where two or three come together in my name, there am I with them.'[6] When he said that, he was giving a new power tool to humankind.

It was Pascal who said that God gave us prayer to give us the dignity of causality; from our Lord we can add the principle that unity begets strength. Several Christians praying together are handed a power which is greater than the sum of the parts, just as 'a threefold cord is not quickly broken'.[7] Four times in the hours before his death Jesus emphasised the unlimited potential available:

> I will do whatever you (plural, disciples together) ask in my name, so that the Son may bring glory to the Father.

> Then the Father will give you whatever you ask in my name. This is my command: love each other.

> I tell you the truth, my Father will give you whatever you ask in my name.

> Until now you have not asked for anything in my name. Ask and you will receive, and your joy will be complete.
>
> Though I have been speaking figuratively, a time is coming when I will no longer use this kind of language but will tell you plainly about my Father. In that day you will ask in my name.[8]

The astonishing authority Jesus wielded through prayer shines from the four Gospels. His teaching on corporate prayer therefore deserves attention, and all the more so as this area of Christian service is probably the most neglected in the present times. In his teaching on prayer he mentions both individual and corporate praying. The 'you' in Matthew 6:6 is in the singular: 'When you pray as an individual, go into your room and shut the door: this a secret exercise.' Those in verses 7-9 are plural. Our Lord expects us to pray together.

It must be significant, moreover, that the one specific prayer command Jesus gave his disciples was to pray the Lord of the harvest to send out labourers into his harvest field.[9] Hence the concern of this chapter that Christian leaders are an example and catalyst in being world Christians as they lead in the matter of shared prayer.

Jesus purchased it for us by his death and resurrection. At the moment our Lord died the curtain in the Jerusalem Temple, separating the Holy from the Most Holy Place, was torn in two from top to bottom: starting from above, achieved from God's side.[10]

The writer to the Hebrews spells out doctrinally what Matthew records historically. Until Messiah came only the High Priest could enter God's very presence, and he but once a year. The curtain hung as a protection between the Presence and the people lest they be consumed by the glory of God. Christ's atoning death, indicates Hebrews, has removed the barrier between God and man. We may enter the Holy of Holies:

> Therefore, brothers, since we have confidence to enter the Most Holy Place by the blood of Jesus, by a new and living way opened for us through the curtain, that is, his body, and since we have a great priest over the household of God, let us draw near to God with a sincere heart in full assurance of faith ...[11]

This is one of the privileges obtained for Christians through Christ's death: now all believers have direct access into the very presence of God.[12] We are a kingdom of priests, a royal priestood;[13] one calling of a priesthood is to pray, especially for God's people.[14]

What activities constitute obedience to this calling? It is true that a church does this during Sunday worship, with the pastor leading. Not only pastors are priests, however. We all are. An implicate of the priesthood of all believers is that it must be natural to hold meetings where anyone may lead in prayer; but we can put it more strongly than that. The priesthood of all believers is being best expressed when all may pray: such a meeting as to copy the New Testament church in raising up their voices together in prayer. The priesthood of all believers was not, for them, theory so much as a simple fact of experience. Naturally, spontaneously, they engaged in joint prayer.

The early church noticeably availed themselves of it. Of the four key exercises of Christian living started on the birthday of the Christian church and chosen for mention in scripture, one is that they devoted themselves rigorously to 'the prayers', the appointed seasons for united prayer in the new community. These were distinguished from their attendance at worship, the apostles' teaching and the breaking of bread. They were clearly a factor in the difference about this new community which filled with awe those who observed it.[15]

After the first arrest for Christian witness, the first thing the church did when Peter and John were released was: 'they raised their voices together in prayer to God' to enable them to speak with boldness. As a result the place where they were meeting was shaken, they were all filled with the Holy Spirit and they spoke the Word of God boldly.[16]

A little later when Peter was imprisoned 'the church was earnestly praying to God for him'. The story of his resultant release, together with the church's total surprise at such an answer, is one of the delightful gems of scriptural history.[17] It was at a time of corporate worship and fasting that the Holy Spirit got through to them to initiate the first missionary journey, which was then commissioned by united prayer.[18] Given our Lord's teaching on this practice, the early church's implementation of it must surely be a model for us, especially considering what it achieved.

The final picture of the New Testament church at prayer is momentous. Amidst the persecution of Christians for their witness and the varied quality of Church life, John was shown that there is a throne in heaven and that from it the one who unfolds history is Jesus Christ, once crucified but now reigning.[19] That which calls fire from God down on to the earth, changing world history, is the prayers of the saints.[20]

The apostles commanded it. Paul urges the church in Rome to join him in his struggle by praying to God for him.[21] The word, *sunagonisasthai* (yes, there are connections with our word 'agony'), bespeaks sharing together in a contest and is suggestive of the persistent wrestling which is required; and don't we know it! And although the close combat dimension is obviously a matter of spirit and not of geography, there is a suggestive thought even there: separated as Paul and the Roman Christians are, they actually meet in the throne room of the universe when they are wrestling together in prayer.

I find very moving the conversation between the young Hudson Taylor and his mother just after his conversion. While she was on holiday he read a tract:

> Little did I know at the time what was going on in the heart of my mother, seventy or eighty miles away. She rose from the dinner table that afternoon with an intense yearning for the conversion of her boy; and feeling that, absent from home and having more leisure than she could otherwise secure, a special opportunity was afforded her of pleading with God on my behalf. She went to her room and turned the key in the door, resolved not to leave the spot until her prayers were answered. Hour after hour that dear mother pleaded, until at length she could pray no longer, but was constrained to praise God for that which his Spirit taught her had already been accomplished, the conversion of her only son.
>
> I in the meantime had been led in the way I have mentioned to take up this little tract, and while reading it was struck with the phrase, 'the finished work of Christ.'
>
> 'Why does the author use this expression?' I questioned. 'Why not say the atoning or propitiatory work of Christ?'
>
> Immediately the words 'It is finished' suggested themselves to my mind.
>
> 'What was finished?'
>
> And I at once replied, 'A full and perfect atonement and satisfaction for sin. The debt was paid for our sins, and not for ours only, but also for the sins of the whole world.'
>
> Then came the further thought, 'If the whole work was finished and the whole debt paid, what is there left for me to do?'
>
> And with this dawned the joyful conviction, as light was flashed into my soul by the Holy Spirit, that there was nothing in the world to be done but to fall down on one's knees and, accepting this Saviour and his salvation, praise him for evermore.
>
> Thus while my mother was praising God on her knees in her chamber, I was praising him in the old warehouse to which I had gone alone to read

> at my leisure this little book.
>
> Several days elapsed before I ventured to make even my sister the confidante of my joy, and then only after she had promised not to tell anyone. When mother returned a fortnight later I was the first to meet her at the door and to tell her I had such glad news to give. I can almost feel that dear mother's arms around my neck as she said,
>
> 'I know, my boy.'
>
> 'Why,' I asked in surprise, 'has Amelia broken her promise? She said she would tell no one.'
>
> My mother assured me that it was not from any she had learned the tidings, and went on to tell the incident mentioned above. You will agree with me that it would be strange indeed if I were not a believer in the power of prayer.[22]

On that occasion just two people were meeting in prayer though far apart. It is exciting to think that when a congregation labour in prayer with missionary partners the other side of the globe, they are actually meeting.

How specific may we be in our prayers? What topics are proper objects of intercession? The New Testament includes deliverance from deadly peril (so much for the idea that prayer doesn't affect the material realm), from wicked and evil men and from prison; that circumstances will bring them together again; that they will live honourable lives; for fearlessness and clarity in declaring the gospel; to be given the words when preaching; that God would open a door of opportunity for the message; and that the message will spread rapidly and be honoured.[23]

The New Testament writers not only ask for congregational prayer and model it; they also give instruction in it. It is to be prayer in the Spirit, all kinds of prayer on all sorts of occasions, alert, awake and persevering; for everyone but being sure to include governing authorities so that it will be possible for populations to live quiet, peaceable and godly lives. Let it be so done that we receive mercy and find grace to help in time of need; for example, in the confession of sin and the assurance of forgiveness, for healing in special sickness and for the riches, clothing and insight that matter.[24]

What scripture teaches, history confirms. The historian J. Edwin Orr claims that there has not been a major turning to Christ throughout the Christian era that has not been characterised by (I think he would also say, preceded by) special attention to committed, expectant, corporate intercession. In fact, he records that in the 1859 revival a quarter of the members of the Church of Scotland were found at the prayer meeting. If this were to be replicated today, what a transformation might be seen.

The rule of the kingdom

We conclude that asking is the rule of God's kingdom. C.H. Spurgeon comments:

> It is a rule that will never be altered in anyone's case. If the royal and divine Son of God cannot be exempted from the rule of asking that he may have, you and I cannot be expected to have the rule relaxed in our favour. God will bless Elijah and send rain on Israel, but Elijah must pray for it. God will bless Paul, and the nations will be converted through him, but Paul must pray. Pray he did without ceasing; his letters show that he expected nothing except by asking for it. The Gospel ministry is so dependant upon the power of prayer that it should be a pastor's main object to educate the praying faculty among his people.[25]

It follows that a pastor who wants to avail his people of the life-giving touch of God, will give a lead in encouraging and developing prayer, including times of shared prayer where anyone may pray, among the church.

This might be easily achieved in some parts of the world and at times of widespread fervour; but in the Britain of our day it takes mighty gifts of indefatigable leadership. It is not natural in our society for people to contemplate praying together and much thought needs to be given to sensitive ways of encouraging it. In the passage just quoted Spurgeon recommends 'numerous prayer meetings, and that of a varied order, that women, youths, children and illiterate persons may unite in the holy exercise.... There may be more real prayer in a little gathering of obscure desirers than in the great assembly where everything is done with ability rather than with agony of desire'.[26]

Church leaders are often reluctant, rightly, to abandon the one main congregational prayer meeting in favour of several smaller ones. While scripture leads us irresistibly to gather to pray, it lays down no order for doing so. One solution is to stick with a main prayer meeting but also, following Spurgeon's lead, to be alert to other possibilities.

When there was widespread turning to Christ in Dundee in Robert Murray McCheyne's time there were twenty-eight prayer meetings in the parish. People often feel unable to pray out loud in a large meeting; any way of reducing the barrier to making their own more stumbling attempts must be helpful. It is possible, for example, to split up a larger meeting for some of the time into groups.

The best size for the group is greatly affected by the character of the church. Groups of about five people might suit a gathered church who know each other well. For most churches a group size of ten, where possible, gives opportunity to all to pray aloud without being threatening or oppressive for those who react against intimacy.

Developing a congregation's shared prayer

How can we encourage ourselves and our people fully to avail ourselves of the good things our Lord holds out to those who will pray? I am indebted to Stanley Davies of the Evangelical Missionary Alliance for the following sevenfold strategy. It centres on world mission but can be applied to other prayer objectives:

Instruction. From Genesis to Revelation scripture reveals God's dealings with the nations. Therefore the teaching programme of the church in all of its departments must deal with this aspect of divine revelation, reflecting God's plan for the nations and the way in which he commands his church to be involved in sharing the good news to the ends of the earth.

Information. There is a vast amount of information available about world mission. One pastor passes on to members magazines he has read. The expectation is that each member will come with at least one prayer item to share with the church's prayer group. The same can be done from prayer information books like *You Can Change the World* and *Operation World*, and (best of all) from the letters of missionary partners.

Inspiration. The key here is spiritual leadership. Of the prayer meetings I have known, the most remarkable have been led enthusiastically and with competence by people who have put energy into collecting items for prayer, from missionaries and others. They have stirred the people to pray, week by week, year on year. Inspiration can also very helpfully be imported in the way of visiting speakers, with or without visual material, to bring news and a new insight.

Intercession. People learn to pray by praying. I so well remember the first Saturday evening prayer meeting I attended. After 50 minutes of scriptural exposition came prayer news and then a full hour of intercession; I was exhausted. It is hard work.

And pray for the prayer meeting. Those who give themselves to reliable labour in prayer often find that the day of their prayer meeting is strangely assaulted: sometimes by a dark cloud of depression or of anxiety, fears, temptations or vague guilt; sometimes by the way every accident seems to make attendance difficult. The one consistent suggestion for relief is that we miss the prayer meeting.

We need to encourage people to expect this and come to terms with it for what it is: opposition from Satan and his dark forces of wickedness. This is not mere imagination or coincidence, and too much is at stake for us to give in.

Investigation. Stanley Davies suggests that the leaders of children's and youth activities give opportunity to learn about different areas of the world and about Christian projects. Youth groups can put on an excellent mission exhibition when given some guidance and a small budget. I don't see that it need be restricted to young people...

Illustration. That is, include visual material. Many churches have prayer boards reminding the praying group(s) of those for whom the group has a commitment. Many societies now produce videos and other multimedia (see, hear and do) materials to further the partnership in Christian work.

Involvement. Plan to encourage every member of every age group to be involved in some meaningful way. A time such as now in the west, when the number of elderly in the population is rising so dramatically, is a strategic time to mobilise this potential for prayer.

We arranged that for three months of her first furlough our missionary member would be part of the ministry team. She lived in her own home and re-established friendship links with the church. Her work was Theological Education by Extension, so she read up in the discipline and gave a critical review at the weekly staff meeting.

For her the furlough was more stabilising than traditional furlough and developed her competence in her area of service. For the congregation the friendship with her deepened. Prayer-and-letter links were strengthened not just among those who attended the prayer meeting but across the whole life of the church. We on the ministry team had helped and been helped by her. No compulsion was needed to pray for her on her return to the field; the whole congregation felt personally involved with her.[27]

Involvement is furthered if we are selective about prayer support. We cannot pray for the whole world. Let us be selective and pray, and give, responsibly to a few. Give guidance on praying so that, for example, the shy are encouraged to participate and the long-winded to keep to the point. Education in being supportive can include aspects of:

- sharing: joys and sorrows, both ways, in confidence.
- caring: sending post-cards from holiday, tapes of music, a book you have enjoyed, a magazine subscription. Telephone them or send a fax or email. If you send personal money, make clear that it is for the person himself and not for the work.
- bearing: their burdens, especially by prayer but quite possibly also by looking after their UK home and by practical arrangements, e.g. handling finances, distributing their prayer letters, sending out things they need but could not take with them.

This work, of developing the shared prayer life of a church, is not supplemental but fundamental to all that it does. It could be only good for our church if we stopped at this point to plan some way of cultivating it.

References

1. Jeremiah 31:31-34.
2. Hebrews 8:7-13; Romans 3:19-25.
3. Deuteronomy 26:(1-)13-15.
4. 2 Chronicles 7:14.
5. There are fine examples of its power scattered throughout the psalms but also in, for example, 1 Kings 8:1-61; 1 Chronicles 29:10-19; the ninth chapters of Ezra, Nehemiah and Daniel; Exodus 17:8-16. J.G.S.S. Thompson attributes this 'anointed one' emphasis to the pre-exilic period in particular: J. D. Douglas, ed., *New Bible Dictionary*, London, IVP, 1962, p. 1020, art. on prayer.
6. Matthew 18:19, 20.
7. Ecclesiastes 4:12.
8. John 14:13; 15:16; 16:23; 16:26.
9. Matthew 9:38 // Luke 10:2.
10. Matthew 27:50,51.
11. Hebrews 10:19-22.
12. Hebrews 9:1-13; 10:11-22.
13. 1 Peter 2:9; Revelation 1:6.
14. Hebrews 7:24f.
15. Acts 2:42 (and note how fruitful: 2:43-47).

16. Acts 4:23-31.

17. Acts 12:1-19.

18. Acts 13:1-3.

19. Revelation 1:9; 2; 3; 5:1-6.

20. Revelation 8.

21. Romans 15:30.

22. Dr and Mrs H. Taylor, *Biography of James Hudson Taylor*, London, Hodder and Stoughton, 1973, p.16f.

23. Romans 15:30-33; 2 Corinthians 1:11; Ephesians 6:19, 20; Colossians 4:2-4; 1 Thessalonians 5:25; 2 Thessalonians 3:1, 2; Philemon 22; Hebrews 13:18, 19; James 1:13-20.

24. Ephesians 6:18; 1 Timothy 2:1, 2; Hebrews 4:16; James 5:13-20; 1 John 5:16,17; Revelation 3:18.

25. Quoted by T. Torrance, *Expository Studies in St John's Miracles*, Edinburgh, James Clarke, 1938, p. 131.

26. *Ibid.*

27. M. Griffiths, *Get Your Church Involved in Missions*, Sevenoaks, OMF, 1974, pp. 20-23. Compare his recent and more broadly developed *A Task Unfinished*, Crowborough, MARC/OMF, 1996, p. 98-101.

WITH INDIVIDUALS

Chapter 8. Caring

Chapter 9. Listening

Chapter 10. Discipling

CHAPTER EIGHT

CARING

Could mere loving be a life's work?[1]

When he saw the crowds, he had compassion on them, because they were harassed and helpless, like sheep without a shepherd (Matthew 9:36).

Jesus looked at him and loved him (Mark 10:21).

Keep watch over yourselves and all the flock of which the Holy Spirit has made you overseers (Acts 20:28).

The eager young pastor starts visiting his people, full of expectation that many a conversation will concern eternal matters; full of hope that he will be used day by day as a catalyst in his members' meeting the Saviour. He knows that true love is mostly hard work and he is willing for that; but he did not anticipate the sheer reluctance to speak of spiritual things which he encounters week by week, visit by visit. What, he asks himself, is pastoral care?

There is great salvation in putting our faith in the distinctive assumptions, values, tasks and methods of Christian pastoral care. Lived out for their own sake and not for the sake of ministerial success they nourish persevering expectation and spiritual ambition during the endless, sometimes discouraging round. Pastoral care, in other words, comes alive and stays alive when exercised theologically: when we remember what it is that we are doing.

What distinctives does the pastor bring to his caring that make it genuinely pastoral during the long faithful spells?

Pastoral care: its Christian assumptions

To recollect the ultimate, building block truths which brought us to the pastorate is one handle on the 'dead routine' problem. There is, first, the reference point of our *world view*.

- God exists. He is the God with whom we and our members have to do day by day. We engage in our routine not alone but in company with the Godhead and as the incarnate expression of his compassion and purpose.

- The Word became flesh; the normality of Jesus' infancy and manhood are resources available to the situations we encounter.
- Men and women are made in the image of God; man is a spiritual as well as a physical and psychological being. Although they may deny it, every cell in their bodies knows they were created for him and are sustained by him. In pastoral care we retain the confidence that this knowledge is there for us to appeal to.
- We are sinners. We can expect spiritual blindness to our assertions and moral resistance to our questions and our exploration of issues with people. We must reckon also on our own sinfulness intruding into our exercise of care.
- There is a difference between right and wrong and we have the Bible as a trustworthy directory to values.
- The church is God's family on earth; the fellowship and prayers of a caring church are vital resources unavailable anywhere else.
- Above all the pastor is distinguished by the resources of spirit available to him. The carer walking close to Christ has in the Holy Spirit a unique wisdom and kindness. If we have prayed for a person and do not yet see evidence that our care is useful, we remember that the Holy Spirit loves the person more than we do. This does not let us off the respons-ibility to go on trying, but we should allow these facts to give us peace and hope when we see no visible benefit from our caring. While the secular carer looks either outside the person to therapeutic activities or inside them to self-acceptance, the pastor can look up to God for his Spirit's wisdom and working and for Christ's pardon and partnership.

Michael Taylor has suggested that the distinctives which Christianity brings to pastoral care can be summarised in the words formation, information, transformation and support. Faith is formative of our care in that Christ is steadily shaping us. It is informative in providing information to the caring process: the nature of man, the possibility of a new heart. It is transformative because a Christian is a distinctive person and because the Holy Spirit has unique power to change a person. It is supportive because of our world view; Taylor instances hope, sin and the Holy Spirit.

The results, as Taylor points out, will not necessarily be distinctive. Our caring is Christian not because it always reaches different conclusions but because it has distinctive points of reference.[2]

The fact is, only the Christian carer is engaging with the whole of a person: a body-soul-in-community, with an eternal destiny. This is our confidence: he may expect to reach areas which no other carer can touch.

The pastor also has, in the end of the day, distinct *aims*. Our singleminded desire is to be able to say, to our congregation, what Paul wrote to Corinth: 'I betrothed you to Christ to present you as a pure bride to her one husband.' A true pastor aims for this one outcome as what he most wants to achieve in this life. The beauty of the Church, her family unity, her ethical purity, her enjoyment of God, her desire for his glory: these most interest him.

Such singleness of purpose will keep us going when others have dropped by the way for lack of encouragement, for it is independent of success and circumstance. Pastoral care of this order deals with the whole of a person and cannot be ineffective or insignificant.

Pastoral care: its Christian values

The work of caring springs out of three underlying values: our knowledge of our people, our love for them and the kingdom of God.

The first value is to *know our people*. A good shepherd really works at this. Having had a seriously ill son for some years and observed attention good and not so good from the medical profession, I can testify with authority that the doctors who have been any significant use have had a great interest and pleasure in people, enthusiasm for their work and have shown above-normal thoroughness in the performance of their tasks.

How important for a pastor, the significance and difficulty of whose work is so much greater, to do at least as well. He will take an interest in each person. He will particularly watch out for change in people. He will keep notes so as to remember the important things about them. He will build the kind of information system that enables him to show care at special occasions such as the anniversary, especially the first anniversary, of serious bereavement.

The second value, *our love for our people*, lay behind my choice of the quotation from Elizabeth Goudge at the head of the chapter. Mary Montague, lame and in constant pain, would never marry; and no other career was open to her. What should she do? *Could mere loving be a life's work?* So she took a vow to love. Millions before her had done the same, but she was different: for she kept her vow, even after she had discovered its cost.

Until now she had only read her Bible as a pious exercise; now she read it as an engineer reads a blueprint and a traveller a map: with profound concentration, because her life depended on it. Slowly she discovered that Christ's love held and illumined every human being for whom she was concerned; and, slowly, she discovered that pain deepens love.[3] Mary Montague would never have dreamt it, but hers was precisely pastoral care.

The meaning of the Old Testament word translated 'to care'[4] is very significant. Its basic thought is to search, seek or enquire. Thus in Deuteronomy 11:12 the holy land is a land God cares for in the sense that he keeps a close eye on it with its welfare at heart. In Psalm 142:4 the Psalmist longs to have someone looking out for his soul or his life: the same idea of energetic interest based on the importance of the object of care for the carer. The issue in Jeremiah 23:4 is whether Jeremiah is seeking the 'shalom' – the overall health, harmony and wellbeing, spiritual and physical – of the people. Are we diligently seeking others' shalom?[5]

The New Testament words add a dimension for us. Paul and Timothy feel a concern amounting to anxiety for the church, and especially for its future: so much so that if someone sins Paul burns in distress, and if they are weak, he feels weak.[6]

The question for us to ask ourselves is how greatly people weigh with us, whether we have them so much on our hearts as to lead to care in action. Our Lord made the point in the story of the good Samaritan. He who would care must do so in a thousand particulars; if we are not *taking care* of people, we do not *care* for them.

The third foundational value is the *kingdom of God*, the saviourhood and reign of our Lord Jesus. It is remarkable that Ezekiel 34 writes so clearly of the centrality of Christ. Having berated the then leaders in Israel for caring only about themselves, God states his alternative:

> I will place over them one shepherd, my servant David, and he will tend (literally, feed) them; he will tend them and be their shepherd. I the Lord will be their God, and my servant David will be prince among them.[7]

God makes clear what a good pastor is working for: that Christ shall be people's king and shepherd.

Pastoral care: its Christian task

Ezekiel 34 is a very remarkable chapter. Quite apart from its curse on leaders who only take care of themselves it is an absolute window on the responsibilities from our side which open the door to 'showers of blessing' (verse 26) from God's.

1. The first such responsibility is *spiritual nourishment*. 'I will raise up shepherds to look after them and feed them.'[8] It cannot be emphasised too strongly that bringing the Scriptures to bear on living human situations is the primary task of pastoral care in biblical Christianity. I mean first of all authentic pulpit preaching, but also every situation where the Word of God is introduced, explored and relevantly applied.

For I define preaching, not institutionally but functionally. In any situation where it is possible to explain the Word of God and apply it, there is preaching. It may be formal preaching in a church service, or informal preaching as we gossip the gospel in a casual conversation: the kind of thing that, as ministers and spokesmen for the Lord, we seek to do in the study as we sit down with someone who has a problem and begin to explore with them how the message of scripture bears on their situation.[9]

In both Old and New Testaments, the chief action of pastoring is such pasturing. A shepherd's first task is to provide food; both the literal and metaphorical usages of the key terms put this beyond dispute.[10] The word for shepherding in the Old Testament means, primarily, ensuring that domestic animals receive food.[11] When used of God or his servants pastoring his people it is also used for feeding, spiritual nourishment;[12] the chief way in which the Lord is a good shepherd is that he feeds and provides for his people.[13]

It is the same spiritually. A good pastor ensures that the people are fed;[14] and spiritual nourishment is the input of God's truth, for man does not live by bread alone but on every word that comes from the mouth of the Lord.[15]

The New Testament emphasis in this regard is, if anything, even stronger. The person who enters by way of Jesus the good shepherd will find pasture.[16] The content of feeding the 'sheep' is explicit: it is as they listen to Jesus' voice.[17] Similarly Peter's task after the resurrection would be to ensure that the lambs and sheep were fed.[18]

Paul's model of pastoring, likewise, is primarily nourishment of the spiritual life by the process of conveying the gospel and its implications;

Paul uses words like preach, teach, declare, testify, proclaim and warn.[19] The description of good pastoring as consisting above all of sound, healthy teaching is thus underlined. That which builds up God's flock is the 'message of his grace'.[20] By contrast, enemies of the gospel provide bad food when they distort the truth.[21]

William Still is but reflecting the genius and emphasis of holy scripture, therefore, when he writes:

> Look at it like this. The Christian life is Christ in us. Christ is revealed 'in all the scriptures' (Luke 24:27). We can only learn him there, and become transformed into his image through feeding on His Word. All that many sick people need is a good and balanced diet and a disciplined routine. My principal surgery, clinic, visiting hour, committee room, call it what you will, is the pulpit and teaching desk.
>
> It is through the ministry of the whole Word, every part of it – e.g. I think of the inestimable value of some studies in the book of Proverbs which proved to be an eye-opener as far as the practical details of daily living are concerned – it is through that ministry that men and women are made and, when they resist it, are marred.
>
> It is that ministry which makes Christian character so that healthy feeders need the pastor less and less.[22]

The 'how' of this – the factors which ensure that preaching is divine food and not mere human words – is explored in chapter 5. The first task in pastoral care is to gain an entrance for the Word of God into people's lives just as the shepherd's first task is to lead the sheep to pasture. Most of us are not as good at this, I suspect, as we should be. Faced with a practical problem in someone's life we are (for the most part) excellent listeners; but the wit and courage to bring scriptural teaching to bear on it is our distinctive calling. The first act in pastoral care is spiritual nourishment.

2. If the first pastoral task is to feed the flock, the second is to *collect and keep it together*: to 'herd' it. God complained to the leaders of his people in Ezekiel's day, 'You have not brought back the strays or searched for the lost.'[23] Jesus is especially committed to be present where his people gather together[24] and some of God's most terrible condemnations are for pastors who scatter his flock, allow it to be scattered or fail to major on its gathering together.[25]

The second task of pastoral care, therefore, is to nourish a sense of the church, especially the church at worship, as the heartfelt desire and priority of every Christian; and to encourage responsible, accountable and sacrificial commitment to the life of the congregation as the life and gifts of each member allow. We shall encourage members to notice who is not there and to enquire after them if the absence is repeated. We shall take every opportunity to foster a spirit of family under God's fatherhood as the most important truth in our members' lives – for such it is.

3. The third part of a shepherd's job in a land of wild animals is to *protect* his sheep. What is the spiritual equivalent of this? It is not just that in time of persecution or plague the Christian leader should be active in protecting his people physically; in addition, peace with God loses us peace with the world, the flesh and the devil. These dangers to our salvation call the minister to protective skill of a special order.

Alastair Campbell is surely right in drawing attention to the courage called for in this kind of care.[26] To speak about the dangers that the world and the flesh introduce into people's lives, calls for resolution as well as love. How often does the pastor 'rebuke with all authority' (Titus 2:15)? The pastor who would take action to protect his member from the pull of the world, the flesh and the devil risks the relationship.

Such a choice faced me some time ago, and it was my secretary who made me take action. Someone had written of bad relationships with in-laws. I dictated a bland reply; my secretary inserted an exhortation to be reconciled.

Some examples of such protection can be suggested. In respect of the world, the temptation to 'get on and better oneself' is good but it can be self-centred, drawing one away from God and from true quality of life. Job security can subtly take over from Jesus as one's first love and lead a person, sadly, to miss all that matters most.[27]

What of the 'flesh'? Self-will and overreaction when it is crossed, self-indulgence, lust, covetousness, any habit or hobby which ends up taking a person over – all can prove bitter enemies to our faith. Dangers from the devil include hindrances and sudden unreasonable accusations on one's conscience; how much a pastor can do for people if he trains them to recognise and resist these devices.

Another vital area for protection is in the realm of truth. As Gregory of Naziansus observed, people 'would sacrifice anything rather than their private convictions'.[28] Paul spoke of false teachers as 'savage wolves not sparing the flock'. Clearly their influence was a danger to the church. Truth really does matter and the dangers of error are real. In fact, Paul's command 'be on your guard' means literally to stay awake and he set the pattern to follow: 'I never stopped warning each of you night and day with tears.'[29]

We may not abdicate our responsibility to protect folk from spiritual danger. When to speak and when to pray and wait: this is a judgement that calls for wisdom. Well might we covet Isaiah's gift: 'The Lord has given me an instructed tongue to know the word that sustains the weary.' [30]

4. Feeding, gathering and protecting are accompanied, fourthly, by *healing*. God complains to the leaders in Ezekiel's day, 'You have not strengthened the weak or healed the sick or bound up the injured' (Ezek. 34:4). The good leader will defend the afflicted and save the children of the needy.[31] A distinctive of pastoral care is that it follows up distress with practical mercy and kindness. [32]

Just as a diligent shepherd examines every sheep after dipping and shearing, the Christian pastor approaches conversation sensitive to griefs and guilts. By hospitable greeting and warm enquiry we must make it clear how very interested we are.

None of us is whole. We must learn how to deal with the different types of disease: more firmly with men than women, arguably, and with the rich than the poor; unembarrassed to put down the cocky, but gently showing the crushed and faint-hearted the good in themselves.[33] Guilt and guilt feelings are very painful; happy the congregation whose pastor heals and builds faith. 'The aim is to help people see what the Lord is saying to them,' says Still.[34]

5. The fifth service which caring renders is to *lead*. A spiritual shepherd 'leads them out. When he has brought out all his own he goes on ahead of them, and his sheep follow him.'[35] The responsibility to include leading as part of pastoral care is present whenever scripture covers the subject.[36]

The pastor gives a lead whether he likes it or not. The mind-set and progress of a congregation is more influenced by the leadership team than by any other single factor. If the pastoral leader trusts the awesome potential of the preached Word; if only the best will do in everything; if his conversations have the character of faithful witness and his relationships breathe esteem of and interest in others; if he has made a wise audit of the congregation's state and is developing a strategy for its progress; if he treads down unbelief and looks to God for the reaping from such sowing, these things cannot but breed a spirit within the congregation.

Even not to give a lead, gives a lead, for a church's life is dynamically affected by the approach of the leaders. Let us seek advice and support, therefore, so that each person is playing to his strengths.

Pastoral care: its Christian methods

Pastoral situations are so varied, we often wonder how best to respond to different problems. In a fascinating study Derek Tidball has identified pastoral methods implicit in the different sections of Scripture and proposes that we select from them as appropriate in our own work.[37]

Matthew's special distinctive, says Tidball, is the direct way in which he takes the teaching of Jesus and uses it to address the problems of the church of his day; well, let us boldly do the same. His special concerns are discipleship – notably obedience to God's law and open profession of Christ – and the Christian community, especially its brotherly care and the discipline needed to maintain it.

Mark, written during a time of persecution, points to Jesus' compassion and to his example in experiencing and enduring suffering. He shows a very human Jesus who nonetheless had identified his calling and refused to be deflected from it; who, through trusting the authority of God, continued faithful amidst assault and suffering. As we are called, time and again, into the mystery of suffering there are times for following Mark's example in turning people's attention to a Jesus who knows their experience from within.

Luke's pastoral method, suggests Tidball, is story-telling. Rather than preach at his readers he tells in Acts an orderly account of (for example) how, every time the church came to a crisis and things seemed hopeless, the result was a new advance. He lets the history speak for itself, including the place of prayer in being filled with God's Spirit and as a factor in the church's forward progress.

To a church torn by different understandings of Christ during a time of persecution, John's pastoral method is to fix their gaze on Christ: fully human, genuinely God, all-sufficient, self-giving, highly exalted and now the very centre of heavenly worship.

Paul's pastoral method is in essence two-fold. There is first, as the Christian experience of thousands would testify, immense pastoral power in the way he links his teaching of the gospel with the explication of its behavioural implications. Secondly, he is himself an example, whenever possible providing a positive and appreciative climate for his teaching, very open about his own experience and needs and always concerned to enable Christians to work things through for themselves.

And so a study of the New Testament writers' pastoral methods provides tools for us to choose from in different contexts. One time, to tell a story; another, to show the bearing of Jesus' teaching on an ethical problem. It aims to present people mature in Christ, to Christ, as a pure bride to her husband. Its primary task is unambiguously to bring the Word of God to bear on the lives of people in Christian community.

Integral to such caring is a diligent, living knowledge of our people flowing from a burdened concern for their *shalom*, their rounded wellbeing. Who is sufficient for these things? The conscientious pastor (there is no other sort) will cast himself helpless, yet hopeful, on God: whose love and care he longs adequately to express.

An exercise. Take ten minutes today to consider, and diarise your response to, the following questions:

- Are there any steps I could be taking to know and love my people better?
- Can I do anything differently to enhance this church's experience of the gracious reign of Christ?
- Is the effect of my influence to nourish, gather, protect, heal and lead in a genuinely Christian way?
- Am I honestly, expectantly depending on the Holy Spirit to be the effective pastor for Christ here?

References

1. E. Goudge, *The Dean's Watch*, London, Hodder and Stoughton, 1960, p. 113.
2. M. Taylor, *Learning to Care*, London, SPCK, 1983, p. 19-37.
3. E. Goudge, *op. cit.*, p. 113-116.
4. Hebrew *darash.*
5. C.P. White, 'The Church: A Caring Community', in *Scottish Tyndale Bulletin*, 1977, p. 48-63, spells out the Old and New Testament words and their implications.
6. 2 Corinthians 11:28f.; Philippians 2:20.
7. Ezekiel 34:23,24.
8. Jeremiah 23:4; and the theme is repeated throughout Ezekiel ch. 34.

9. J.I. Packer, *Aspects of Authority*, Orthos Papers, no. 9, Disley, Cheshire, n.d., p. 13.

10. E.g. R. Harris et al, eds., *Theological Wordbook of the Old Testament*, Chicago, Moody Press, 1980, on *ra'ah* (vol. 2, p. 852f.).

11. E.g. Genesis 29:7.

12. Proverbs 15:14.

13. Genesis 48:15; Psalm 23; Isaiah 40:11.

14. Ezekiel 34 esp. verses 14 and 26-31; Jeremiah 23:1-4.

15. Deuteronomy 8:3.

16. John 10:9.

17. John 10:16.

18. John 21:15,17.

19. Acts 20:20, 21, 24, 25, 26, 27-31.

20. Acts 20:32.

21. Acts 20:30.

22. W. Still, *The Work of the Pastor*, Aberdeen, Gilcomston South Church, 1976, p. 18,19.

23. Ezekiel 34:4.

24. Matthew 18:19, 20.

25. See, for example, Jeremiah 23:1-4; Acts 20:29-31; Hebrews 10:25; 12:22-29.

26. A.V. Campbell, *Rediscovering Pastoral Care*, London, SCM, 1986, p. 33-36.

27. As with Demas: 2 Timothy 4:10.

28. Gregory of Naziansus, *Oration 2,* Section 40; NPNF, second series, volume 7, p. 213.

29. Acts 20:31.

30. Isaiah 50:4.

31. Psalm 72:4. Compare Isaiah 42:2f.

32. B.B. Warfield, 'The Emotional Life of our Lord', *The Person and work of Christ*, PRPC, 1950, p. 93-145.

33. Gregory the Great, *Pastoral Rule*, Book II, in NPNF, 2nd series, vol. 12, spells out such considerations in great detail. They are also explored in Gregory of Naziansus: *Oration 2*, NPNF, 2nd series, vol. 7, pp. 204ff.

34. W. Still, *Dying to Live*, Fearn, Christian Focus Publications, 1991, p. 111.

35. John 10:3,4.

36. E.g. Ezekiel 34; John 10; Acts 20:17-38; 1 Peter 5:1-5.

37. D. J. Tidball, *Skilful Shepherds*, Leicester, IVP, 1986, pp. 31-143.

CHAPTER 9

LISTENING

Spiritual direction: objective and process in pastoral care

I long to see you so that I may impart to you some spiritual
gifts to make you strong – that is, that you and I may be
encouraged by each other's faith (Romans 1:11,12).

That we may present everyone perfect in Christ:
to this end I labour, struggling with all his energy,
which so powerfully works in me (Colossians 1:28b, 29).

At a certain time there were four of us in the pastoral team. We were united, keen Christian servants and there wasn't one of us who didn't like people. But we vied in avoiding the next visit to – well, let's call her Mary. Mary's commitment to resentment and vilification had the touch of genius about it. Malice had become her friend, her relief, her food. Visiting her was an effort, the farewell a relief; then you needed a shower. We reckoned we had tried everything, got nowhere and run out of options.

Looking back I should say we had chickened out of the real remaining ones, rebuke and avoidance. Mary exemplified a recurring pastoral problem: the frustration of getting nowhere and not knowing what, other than prayer, to do about it.

And yet, observe our Lord in his encounter with the woman at the well of Samaria. He starts where she is, with naturalness and esteeming friendship. There is nothing contrived about his request for water, no spiritual scalp-hunting. He was thirsty and, disdaining contemporary chauvinism, asked the woman for a drink.

This was a woman with a major problem, however, to be drawing water at midday; and Jesus takes the conversation steadily deeper. 'If only you knew what God gives and who it is that is asking you for a drink, you would ask him, and he would give you living water!' And then when she takes up that signpost reply, Jesus unpacks the next possibility: 'Water welling up to eternal life ... never thirst.' As she continues to respond the kind surgeon identifies the abscess: 'Go, call your husband': and the conversation becomes an occasion for saving faith.

J.I. Packer identifies five principles in Jesus' method: approach whoever is there, appeal to whatever is there, arouse a sense of sin, allow spiritual interest to grow and affirm his own authority and claim.[1] While this was a particular kind of encounter we learn from Jesus the desire, in every pastoral conversation, to see the person move 'from here to there': from their current spiritual maturity, to make progress. Is it possible to propose a structured approach to effective listening that will serve for different kinds of interview?

This chapter offers a way of keeping our bearings in the process of spiritual direction. It outlines a three stage management model for listening and spells out key listening skills and some other criteria for good practice.

We are not offering 'pastoral care by numbers'. Every person is unique. Flexibility is of the essence when we listen. We do say, however, that it is possible to be purposeful in our approach. If our listening is helpful, our members will be in a better position to live lives worthy of God and pleasing to him.[2] Whether they then do so is their choice; but they will be in a better position to, if they wish.

The aim of the model is to stimulate the identifying of objectives so as to guide and maintain the momentum of the listening process. It also helps us to orientate ourselves: to perceive where in the process we are.[3] It is suggested that fruitful listening identifies three stages: where the person is now ('present scenario'), where it seems he should be heading ('preferred scenario') and how to get there.

In ordinary talking with folk we are not 'acting as counsellor' as though the only relevant conversations are those in which people are seeking help. Our interest is genuine and the conversation goes, as life does, from the mundane to the momentous, moving quite naturally between 'basic human issues and theological and spiritual exploration'.[4] We can expect nonetheless that because of the preached Word there will be opportunities to talk of serious things.

When there are, and especially when we meet people by arrangement, two factors to consider are the direction to take and the skills which facilitate effectiveness. Our task is not to impose our external advice but to facilitate people's own insight, their perception as to what God is saying to them: and to help them make a response which is authentically theirs.

Helping: a three stage management model

Stage 1. How things are now: the 'present scenario'. As the first stage in medical treatment is accurate diagnosis, so the first stage in spiritual direction is self-understanding.[5] Three factors in this are the story itself, the blind spots and the possible leverage on the problem.

As we elucidate *the facts*, the first help we provide is clarification. Merely to ask the facts helps; and a person will often come with a presenting question far removed from what is really troubling them. Be gentle; lack of sensitivity can lose a whole opportunity for a person's healing. As we ask, members gain insight and learn things about themselves. At the same time the relationship deepens; and the most crucial factor in progress is the quality of relationship between pastor and member. It builds a climate in which members can openly discuss and work on their problems.[6] Good listening is both empathetic and action- or strategy-orientated: the goal, whether or not reached, is always to identify progress of some sort.

Common to so many problems is our own blindness to features of them; especially, to the contribution we ourselves make. This is the phenomenon of so-called *blind spots*. Sometimes a person denies the problem altogether; they might be misinterpreting parts of it; they might avoid the effort to change as too costly.

Faulty perception needs to be challenged. I suspect that ministers are good at supporting people but not nearly so good at challenging them over their blind spots. We might be afraid to hurt them, or wish to be liked; sometimes we are scared of letting our own negative feelings out. Perhaps we would do it more if we realised it is in the member's interest that we attempt it, even if tentatively.

> Jean asked to share something. After her 'woman's operation' she had found sex a dirty experience and her husband John had moved to a separate bedroom. Now, however, she longed for the support of physical intimacy. It had not occurred to her that John's self-esteem had been hurt by her rejection. Once her blind spot was identified it was possible to devise ways of bridging the gulf between herself and John, and in prayer to seek the Lord's hand on the process.

The task is to highlight significant considerations which might be only lightly alluded to or hinted at, and to clarify what is stated confusedly. Of special value is to challenge defeatist thinking: 'I'm so hopeless at making relationships; I always do everything wrong.' Challenge such; foster faith and courage.

The term *leverage* is used of that helping process which identifies, out of the many components to a story, which ones are most worth working on so as to make a difference. Begin with what the member sees as important and encourage as the first response something manageable which the member is willing to work on.

Stage 2. How they would like things to be: the preferred scenario. Our goal is to help the person to perceive Jesus' ambition for him and to motivate him to achieve it.[7] If it is difficult to see what improvement is really desirable, develop a *range of possibilities*.

> Jennifer is experiencing stress because she simply has too much to do. A part-time job, individual tutoring after school hours, church committees, a house to keep clean, a husband who does not share the housework and children with different gifts and needs all compete for her attention. What she would really like to do is help with the congregation's work among young prostitutes.
>
> Over tea after church the minister asks how she is managing to keep all these pots boiling and they arrange to meet for 50 minutes. By asking future-orientated questions the minister helps Jennifer brainstorm a range of more livable scenarios. After listing the things she likes to do and feels committed to, and measuring each against her identified values and goals, Jennifer realises she will also have to negotiate her final choice with others' expectations of her.[8]

The next step is to turn the intent ('I must trim down my activities') into *a goal* ('I'm not going to be out at meetings more than two evenings a week'). The goal should be clear and measurable: not 'I must spend more time with my children' but 'by October I will be reading at bed time not less than two evenings a week with each child'. This is the time to consider the consequences of such a decision: in the case above, a willingness to withdraw from other activities.

Now is the time for definite *commitment*. This can be quite frightening. At the point of taking the first step we are 'dealing not just with possible selves that we want to become, but possible selves we are afraid of becoming'.[9] It is important that this is their own choice, not externally imposed. We can help the dynamics of commitment by drawing attention to the attraction and challenge of the new goal, by talking through the fears, seeing ways of overcoming the obstacles ('management of disincentives') and agreeing the practical steps needed to move towards their goals.

Stage 3. Getting There. All of us have pains and propensities which we can learn to manage better, but many people feel helpless about the whole process of getting there.

We can ease that process by supporting a brainstorming session to dream up as many concrete *strategies* as possible, suspending all assessment or criticism of the ideas in the first instance. The one that is the best fit will be detailed and realistic but should hold out the promise of making a real difference; and the person should own it himself; it should not be imposed on him by some other person.

A strategy is demanding and may have costs for the person's family or associates. *Best fit* includes weighing the benefits and costs of alternative strategies. Sometimes one can try a strategy for a time, for example taking a trial year off a commitment for the sake of testing one's giftedness at a new form of ministry.

Now is the time to tie down a specific *plan*: actual dates for the activities required to reach a person's 'preferred scenario'.

> Brian, a Christian worker, is a typical 'type A' driving personality, overweight, hypertensive, whose father died of a heart attack in his mid-40s. Recent dizzy spells make him perceive a physical fitness regime as more than just vaguely desirable. A handbook from his local sports centre indicates the objectives for his sex, height and age and the timescale within which to reach them. Each day Brian knows what to do and he is now lighter, fitter, has more energy and feels better about himself.

Brian had an easily soluble problem; too many useful plans end up in drawers. The final skill is ensuring delivery. The pastor needs to enable his people to overcome inertia ('I know I should do that but I keep putting it off') and entropy ('I'm always starting exercise regimes and then giving up').

In a way this is just a matter of saying, 'Get on with it – I'll check up next week whether you've started.' It can help nonetheless to be aware of strategies for overcoming procrastination and fear: take the first easy step, delay giving yourself a particular reward until you have taken it, set up a support arrangement to monitor progress and the like.[10] It is important for the member to take responsibility for changes they identify, and for us to keep our own bearings in the process.

Effective listening

Why do some pastors shine in the usefulness of their pastoral conversations and listening? It is interesting that the effectiveness of professional counsellors is most affected not by the particular school they follow but by two factors: by their personal qualities[11] and by what they actually do when they listen.[12]

One friend asks how I am, but his lack of attention shows that he is taking no interest in the answer. Another gives people his eyes, smile and whole attention. How much we give just by the (very tiring) art of utter and well managed listening.

Extensive research has clearly identified three qualities for effectiveness in listening. They are genuineness, non-possessive warmth and accurate empathy; Roger Hurding draws a parallel between these and the fruit of the Spirit.[13] In addition it has been shown that the effectiveness of pastoral work is enhanced where pastor and speaker share the same values.

The pastor who is *genuine* consistently matches his words to his feelings. He does not lie, nor pretend to a care he does not feel. He is open, honest, sincere. There is no real alternative to genuineness if a relationship is to be healing. Hurding comments:

> Even if he were a skilled, polished actor it is doubtful that a therapist could hide his real feelings from the client. When the therapist pretends to care, pretends to respect or pretends to understand, he is only fooling himself. The patient may not know why the therapist is 'phony' but he can easily detect true warmth from phony and insincere 'professional warmth'.[14]

Warmth includes two factors. The first is attitudinal: to like people, and in particular the person we are meeting, whatever they have done and whatever they are like. Secondly, warmth is most healing when it is *non-possessive*. In his powerful study Carl Rogers found that patients and clients value having independence in making choices and decisions.[15] They grow, and like it, not when told what to do but when helped to come to their own internally made decisions by a helper who is interested in them. Rogers writes of 'unconditional positive regard': liking and accepting people without emotional over-involvement. This does not mean detachment. A merely clinical relationship, withholding oneself as a person and dealing with the other as an object or a case, is unhelpful.

The third quality is *empathy*: skill in understanding and matching the person's emotional state. Can I so attune myself to this person that I enter the world of his facts and feelings? Can I make myself at home in it so that we can explore them together without my trampling on his values or the meaning for him of his experiences?

I identify three imperatives that flow from the qualities we bring. They might seem repetitive but I find they act as a profitable reminder when available as an instant *aide-memoire*, especially if meeting with several people in succession when one is tired.

Take a deep interest in the person and their situation. Profound attentiveness is a ministry in itself and can only flow from a genuine interest in, and the choice to be curious about, a person. None of us is spontaneously like that about all people, the awkward and unattractive as well as the more normal and those to whom we are spontaneously drawn. It takes a decision, a commitment for Jesus' sake and sustained energy: *interest* in people!

Take pleasure in, admire them. Imagine meeting Jesus walking down the street. Would you not be aware of how fond he was of you, even though he knows all about you? All that lies behind 'You shall be Peter ... neither do I condemn you ... I have appointed you' would be there in his respect for us, his appreciation of (and ambition for) what we will become, his pleasure in our friendship. What of ourselves: do *we* like people, see them as Jesus sees them, approve of them? If we are like that, wholeheartedly and warmly, with those whom on a natural level we would avoid, it will be easy to be like that with all.

Feel their concerns and potential with them. This is simply to live out accurate empathy: energetically to put oneself into the person's shoes. At the simple level this is hearing the story accurately; more deeply, it is 'identifying with the (client) enough to feel something of his or her anguish or despair' so that 'we begin to perceive the events and experience of his life as if they were parts of our own life':[16] together with the ability to *communicate* this 'I am with you', to the other.

To be really interested in, to take pleasure in, to feel people's feelings with them: the listening imperatives require energy. These are the essential underlying attitudes; but have we the skill to show them? To that we turn.

Body language

Communication research indicates that the words we use count for 7%, their tone 38% and non-verbal communication 55% of our impact on folk, the impression that they go away with. It is vital to understand the main components, therefore, of this communication. The main microskills can be summarised in the acronym SOLER.[17]

Square on. This varies with culture but in British society to face a person more or less squarely, or with the body at a slight angle, indicates involvement and attention; to turn the body away from them implies turning from them in attitude also.

Open Body Position. To have arms and legs crossed can indicate a defensiveness against what the other person is saying. The main issue is whether one is bodily indicating that one is open and available to the other person.

Lean forwards. This shows interest in the other. It can be overdone, especially if your chairs are at different heights. If the chair is higher, leaning can be dominating and daunting. The key is to be sensitive to body position that shows real and responsive attention to what they are saying.

Eye Contact. Maintaining only minimal eye contact with frequent looking down or simply looking away leaves a person feeling we are not taking interest in them. Clearly, staring can be as off-putting; a shy person can be as helped by our relaxing and not forcing eye contact. We can learn things about ourselves from difficulty in showing interest by eye contact: perhaps an inner reluctance or a problem with the matter under discussion. Work to sustain warm, interested eye contact.

Relaxed. The listener who is tense or fidgety introduces these distractions into the listening process. Aim, therefore, to relax and to use body language in a natural and flexible way.

Overall, there is much to offer people in learning to understand the signs the body sends us ('why am I tensing up at this point?') and to convey involvement.

The place

Again there is an acronym – CLOWN – to summarise desirable features of the surroundings where we meet.

Comfortable and private. A person feels safer, and valued, if we make the opportunity for conversation physically comfortable and design ways of preventing people barging in or telephone interruptions.

Light, not dim. We facilitate openness, lighten mood and build confidence if the surroundings are not dark and gloomy.

Open, not obstructed. Hiding behind a desk covered high with clutter is less confidence-enabling than arranging chairs in such a way that nothing more than perhaps a low table comes between you. When tears might be involved, let the table carry a box of paper hankies.

Warm. A room that is either too cold or too hot can increase a person's nervousness; a comfortable temperature helps us relax.

Near, but safe. Having the chairs too far apart is not conducive to sharing of confidences. It is threatening, however, to have someone too close. The need for personal space varies between cultures and the wise listener will arrange it so as to be close enough to give ease, and distant enough to reassure the person of their security.

The safeguards

Good listening can be sexy. It creates very significant bonds between listener and speaker, whether they are the same or different sexes. It is important to know this both to be prepared for it when it happens and in order to guard against its obvious dangers. Particularly when engaging in meaningful talk with someone of the opposite sex, the wise pastor will avoid excessive privacy and ensure that some form of very available chaperoning is to hand in case of need, perhaps discreetly knocking and offering refreshment half way through an arranged fifty minute session.

Stewardship of time is another safeguard and in the normal run of things it is wiser to confine serious listening sessions to about fifty minutes, arranging for a number of sessions one or two weeks apart, than to have a very long single session.

The third safeguard is that of control. The listener who lets the 'client' dictate the length and frequency of sessions is hindering the helping process. It is up to the helping person definitely to give a lead in the way the agreement between the two parties is managed.

The final and crucial safeguard is confidentiality. This does not always mean secrecy and we might have to tell a person who insists on secrecy that we are unable to promise to give it in every instance. An example might be in some situations when a serious crime has been committed. It is essential, however, that a Christian worker be absolutely trustworthy in not gossiping or passing on news about someone to a third party.

The perspective we take

Pastoral work can sometimes seem a deadening routine. That is not surprising: all of us resist being improved by others. There is no work as difficult. Our task as pastors is to take the long view. The Holy Spirit loves our people even more than we do: let us look to God for the results. Eugene Peterson makes three suggestions:

> First, I can cultivate an attitude of awe. This face before me, its loveliness scored with stress, is in the image of God. Every meeting with another person is a privilege. Second, I can cultivate an awareness of my ignorance. There is so much about this person that I don't know. God's grace is in operation and will persist. Third, I can cultivate a disposition to prayer. It is God with whom I have to do.[18]

We are not the Christian workers: God is. We go on listening, loving for its own sake yet also longing to be God's servants in the development and healing of his children.

David Atkinson has suggested essential components to the way in which theology informs pastoring.[19] Using covenant as its unifying concept he draws implications from four features of it: the covenant relationship, the covenant mediator, the covenant resource and the covenant fulfilment.

The covenant relationship. God's covenant with us is one of grace. To those in need God says, 'I am and will be your God, who brought you out of slavery' – even though they deserved anything but. The style of this is to be reflected in our pastoral care: the importance of each person, our positive regard for them unconditioned by their attractiveness or behaviour. It will be personal. Its Torah background will give it, in contrast to some so-called client-centred therapy, a moral framework before which each individual is responsible. The wider covenant literature provides additional guidance. Wisdom literature reminds us to tease out the practical ways of living; the Psalms, to give space for the expression of every emotion, rage and despair as well as sweetness and light.

The covenant mediator. In uniting Godhead and manhood in one person our Lord took our whole situation on himself and assumed our frame of reference ('Who touched me?', 'He was amazed', 'Jesus wept'), while remaining himself. Because he suffered when tempted, he is able to help those being tempted. He prayed with loud cries and tears (Heb. 2:14-18; 5:7-10) and learned from what he suffered. In our pastoral care we also learn to assume other people's frames of reference while remaining ourselves. We are vulnerable, we take no superior position and we give space for expression of the whole range of emotions, with the 'wonderful counsellor' within us.

The covenant resource. In the Holy Spirit, the Christlike provider of insight, love and healing, we have a perfect and personal resource. One of the keys to sticking to our ambition for folk without being discouraged is that he 'so breathes divine life into us that we are no longer actuated by ourselves, but are ruled by his action and prompting'.[20]

One of his awesome gifts is discernment. It should be used with care, for there is a constant interplay between the Spirit's illumination and our own psyche. We must be kind and tentative about such insights in case we have misread the Lord.

To use this gift supportively is relatively easy; the need for courage comes when we should use it to confront or to draw attention to an aspect of a person's life which needs review ('Thou art the man!'). The pastor who does that *when appropriate* will not have an easy life but will be worth his weight in diamonds.

Packer encourages us: 'The more we deal with people, the more skill we shall develop in seeing our way into people's hearts and putting our finger on the things they are covering up.'[21] The wise pastor will, when possible, consider carefully in advance, not only how to raise this issue but also what reaction he might receive, so as to be prepared.

> I often say to people consulting me, 'I never give advice.' The most I can do is, having listened sympathetically, to advise believers to find their counsel where I find mine, from God by his Holy Word and by his Holy Spirit. Our aim is to help people see for themselves what the Lord is saying to them: not to tell them what we think, which is utterly inappropriate. At least this assures people seeking help that their personalities and individuality are being respected. Only God himself can enable the faithful discharge of such an onerous responsibility. God help us! [22]

The covenant fulfilment. An advantage the Christian worker has over the secular therapist is the divine promise. God's Kingdom has entered history in Jesus Christ. We have eternal life and taste its benefits in first instalment. So we have expectation about Christ's ministry in people's lives.

We recognise however the not-yet-ness, the incompleteness of this. We see it exemplified in the 'eschatological reserve'[23] or pause between the two words of Christ, 'Your sins are forgiven' and 'Rise, take up your bed and walk.' We experience this pause painfully. But the very groaning and yearning, the completeness of which our 'already' is the first instalment and down payment, gives us hope.

In the new heaven and earth all will be well. Our work is part of our response to the covenanted truth that all shall be well, and all shall be well, and all manner of things shall be well.

Concluding exercise

- How well do I combine sincere, relaxed friendship with well planned pastoral practice, so that members and I are mutually encouraged by each other's faith when we spend time together?
- What steps can I take to grow in genuineness, non-possessive warmth and accurate empathy?
- Evaluate the microskills of your listening practice.
- Do I trust the Holy Spirit to be the real lover and spiritual doctor in this congregation?

References

1. J.I. Packer, 'The Practice of Evangelism', in *St Andrews 73 Report on Conference in Evangelism*, ed. S. Anderson, 1973, circulated privately, pp. 13-22.

2. Colossians 1:10-14; Ephesians 3:14-21.

3. The model is heavily built on G. Egan, *The Skilled Helper*, Pacific Grove, Brooks-Cole, 1990.

4. M. Jacobs, *Still Small Voice*, London, SPCK, 1982, p. 19.

5. INST. 1.1.1.

6. J.L. Deffenbacher, 'A Cognitive-behavioural Response and a Modest Proposal', in *Counselling Psychologist*, vol. 13, p. 261-269, quoted in Egan, p. 58.

7. Egan's term is the 'dynamics of commitment', p. 269.

8. altered from Egan, pp. 276f.

9. Egan, p. 311.

10. See chapter 15, especially p.219f.

11. C.B. Truax and R.R. Carkhuff, *Towards Effective Counselling and*

Psychotherapy, New York, Aldine, 1967, p. 34-46.

12. D.G. Bennett, *Therapeutic Love – an Incarnational Interpretation of Counselling*, Lingdale papers, No. 1, Clinical Theology Association, Oxford, 1985, p. 3.

13. R. Hurding, *Roots and Shoots*, London, Hodder, 1985, p. 29-37.

14. Truax and Carkhuff, *op. cit.*, p. 4, quoted in Hurding p. 30.

15. C.R. Rogers, *On Becoming a Person*, Houghton Mifflin, Boston, 1961. Rogers's remarkable findings were based on measuring four parameters: genuineness, liking, empathy and mirroring the client's emotional intensity.

16. Hurding, *op. cit.*, p. 33.

17. Egan, pp. 108f, with some transatlantic modification.

18. E. Peterson, *Working the Angles*, Grand Rapids, Eerdmans, 1991, p. 128-131.

19. D. Atkinson, *Counselling as Covenant*, Lingdale Papers no. 11, Clinical Theology Association, Oxford, 1989.

20. INST., 3.1.3.

21. J.I. Packer, *op. cit.*, p. 19.

22. W. Still, *Dying to Live*, Fearn, Christian Focus, 1991, p. 111.

23. T.F. Torrance, quoted in R. Anderson, *On Being Human*, Eerdmans, Grand Rapids, 1982, p. 129; itself quoted in Atkinson, op.cit., p.15.

CHAPTER TEN

DISCIPLING

Building a church. Members and their gifts.

In being united to Christ you are being built together to become a dwelling in which God lives by his Spirit (Ephesians 2:22).

Using whatever gifts they have received to serve others, as winsome stewards of God's many-coloured grace (1 Peter 4:10).

The ways in which energy is invested in pursuing and then harnessing congregational development vary widely. In a pattern of church life devoted to simplicity these goals will be pursued in one way; in a city fellowship of house groups with a developed discipleship course, in another; and in a large church with much community involvement, differently again.

But are some goals and methods frankly more valid than others? It is vital to be clear what progress we are most aiming at in people's lives, and what it is that most fundamentally constitutes advance in a congregation.

It follows from Ephesians 2:22, quoted above, that we have a primary vision that is definitive. We aim to see people united to Christ and being so built together as to become, as a people, a spiritual dwelling place for God. Without this defining goal we are not building a Christian church, whatever else we are doing. With that in mind this chapter considers three terms: edification (upbuilding), discipling and spiritual gifts.

1. Edification

The building process is that the preaching and teaching of the message of God's grace strengthens both individual believers and congregations, settling and confirming them in the faith.[1] Christians should likewise act to exhort one another and further one another's spiritual growth;[2] 'the individual helps to edify the community by receiving for himself the exhortation of the gospel and then passing it on to others.'[3]

It is not just a matter of 'passing on the exhortation of the gospel'.

Christians differ in their strength of conscience over secondary areas of conduct. They are commanded not to please themselves but to choose that which strengthens and assures the faith of others. We are warned in the strongest terms against making the faith of others less stable or more faltering.[4] We make it our aim to bond Christians together, to contribute to their faith rather than pull it down; and we do so by laying a good foundation of teaching the faith and Christian living, correcting what is amiss.[5] Unwholesome conduct and conversation undermine faith; ours should do people good.[6]

It is as our union with Christ grows that there is in the church a growing unity, and it increasingly becomes a dwelling place for God. As the pastor-teacher prepares people for works of service, more and more people end up believing and cooperating. Christians become more and more united in knowing Christ, and in a Christlikeness of character. Love grows. This is edification and this is to be the main thrust of a pastor's energy.[7] Note that the patient teaching of a body of doctrine, to be used as a yardstick for sound belief and practice, is all part of the building work to which we are called.[8]

We have seen that sound teaching is edifying but also, in order to edify, we must disciple.

2. Discipling

To 'disciple' is to make someone a Christian learner or apprentice; to train in the Christian life. For all that it only occurs four times in the New Testament it is a good word for a vital ministerial priority. Our Lord Jesus commanded us to disciple all the nations,[9] involving the twofold:

- Requiring of public Christian allegiance: 'baptising them in the Name...'
- Teaching of obedient Christian living: 'teaching them to obey everything I have commanded....'

This needs spelling out. A disciple is an apprentice to a master craftsman, learning his particular trade, following his teaching; an adherent of his method, imitating his approach. The New Testament includes all these overtones in the term disciple but its defining feature is personal attachment to Jesus as one's Master. This personal relationship shapes the whole of a person: the inner life as well as the behaviour.

The attachment of the disciple to Christ is personal, but not in a mystical so much as a moral way. Features of discipleship in the Gospels include obedience to Jesus, suffering with him and being co-workers with him.[10] It is worth spelling out the constituent elements of discipling from the rest of the New Testament because it has a bearing on the debate between different modern schools of discipling. We are clearly responsible to inculcate the following aspects.

- *Sanctification*, in principle and practice. The basic principle is 'let not sin reign in your mortal bodies: rather offer yourselves bodily to him as instruments of righteousness'.[11] In the 'let not' and the 'rather', are the two aspects called mortification and aspiration.

  Mortification is to put to death what belongs to our lower nature. The New Testament contains several lists to illustrate what is meant. A typical one would include sexual immorality, greed, anger, malice, slander, filthy talk and lying.

  Aspiration speaks of clothing ourselves with behaviour that accords with our new natures: kindness and patience, bearing with each other, forgiveness, truthful speech, honest work, self-control, keeping our public behaviour above criticism.[12]

- *Setting our minds on the things of the Spirit.* This includes valuing salvation, learning about it, assessing ourselves maturely, putting our talents at the disposal of the church, working to be at one with other Christians without jealousy or strife, putting on the whole spiritual armour, knowing God's will with spiritual wisdom, praying for fellow believers especially in their Christian service and not forsaking meeting together with them.[13]

- *Good relationships* in the family, at work and as citizens, obeying the governing authorities for conscience' sake and being good employees because we are living every department of life in such a way as to please Jesus.[14]

- *Living lives of practical love for others.* The general 'do good to all people, especially those who belong to the family of believers'[15] is spelt out in no narrow way: prison visiting, feeding

> the hungry, welcoming the stranger, clothing the naked, taking care of the sick, visiting orphans and widows in their affliction, washing feet, giving of our goods when we see our brother in need.[16] Love is not a feeling, it is a practical commitment to others' highest wellbeing.

If these are some of the lineaments of discipleship, by what process are we to pursue it? This important question is given a spectrum of very different answers in our day. I propose to describe five alternatives and draw some guiding conclusions.

(a) The early Church's pattern of activity was built on the social structures of the day. The church in a given city consisted of a number of house churches, the houses in question belong to converted citizens with large households including various slaves.[17] On the Lord's Day they met for worship, teaching and the breaking of bread as a church; and informally in each other's homes during the week, including further teaching as appropriate.[18]

Discipling consisted of teaching at the Sunday meeting, commitment to the times set for prayer in the Christian community[19] and informal care for each other's Christian lives during the week at a domestic level as circumstances allowed. There is some evidence that there were courses of instruction from early days,[20] at least for those preparing to make public allegiance to the Faith. The bubbling up of gifts was furthered by the Spirit-full openness of their gatherings for worship.[21]

(b) Richard Baxter in the seventeenth century describes in his classic, *The Reformed Pastor*, a fourfold pattern of activity. The *public ministry* consisted of the preaching, the sacraments, and worship. There was a vigorous, orderly *catechising* of every family in the parish, described in detail later in this chapter. There was a *discipline* of those who lived 'in known sin through wilfulness or negligence'[22] which started gentle and private but could in the case of serious sin, bringing public scandal on the church, call for public rebuke. Lastly there was *pastoral care*.

The result was thus a congregation drawn from the parish (for Baxter, the two were virtually coterminous)[23] who by Sunday and Thursday preaching and the work of individual catechising were becoming more united, orderly, Christ-like and strong in knowing God, understanding the faith and valuing heaven. This was Baxter's discipling. It is difficult to imagine him involved in gift identification except as needed for the orderly arranging of the church's business affairs and in keeping an eye open for possible future ministers.

(c) In a typical very active evangelical Church of Scotland congregation, Sunday service(s) are complemented by a system of house groups, possibly a monthly congregational Bible Study and prayer meeting in place of them, and by a profusion of other midweek activities. These may be classified as:

- totally church: choir, women's guild, youth fellowship, men's club;
- mixed: lunch club, badminton, uniformed organisations, youth club;
- secular: playgroup, youth employment service, snooker for the unemployed in an abundance of bridge relationships with and service to the world, alongside the religious life of the congregation.

Discipleship is inculcated by a combination of Sunday teaching, house or discipleship group and the pressure to support almost any number of the activities. From the point of view of being a good spouse, parent or neighbour there is a real danger of being 'the out and out Christian who is never in'.

In fact 'discipleship' can consist largely of helping keep the show going: six or seven days a week if one is not in gainful employment, and the same number of evenings if one is. I heard one unconverted husband say, 'You should take your bed to the church: it would save you coming home.' In real terms discipleship is keeping things going and gift identification is the leadership group considering who might take over an activity when necessary.

(d) The shepherding and house church movements, and writers such as Juan Carlos Ortiz and David Watson,[24] represent a reaction against such churchianity (however evangelical) and an attempt to return to Jesus' method with his own disciples. The discipling process is a deeply pervasive sharing of one's whole life including, sometimes, one's home with a small committed group, on a detailed 'Watch me, I'll teach you, we'll do it together' basis.

Each church member is accountable to his house group leader for his spiritual growth and for the identification and deployment of his gifts from the Spirit. In some cases ('heavy shepherding') the disciple must ask his leader's permission on whom to marry, what employment to be in and his use of time. The apprentice serves the leader, who may require him to cut his grass or do his shopping. Christ is seen theoretically as the discipler, through the leader. House group leaders are in turn accountable to elders, and the elders to the pastors; sometimes the pastors to an 'Apostle'.

The activities on this model are (note the order) weekly house group, meetings with one's leader and the Sunday meeting. The church is a city- or area-wide congregation of house groups. A feature of times together, whether in cell (house group) or congregation, is the exercise of the gifts identified in 1 Corinthians 12 and 14. A fairly prolonged time of singing is followed by some of the following: a word of knowledge, a word of prophecy (a fairly informal word 'from the Lord', usually encouraging, in quasi-scriptural language or with promise for a better future), a description of a vision, speaking in an unknown 'language' sometimes with an interpretation from someone else, and Bible reading. There is a lengthy inspirational message, sometimes expository.

Discipling is thus the major industry on this model. The process of discerning one's spiritual gifts is a major, mostly message-and-healing orientated, component of life. Corporate life is deeply coherent. The result is a very alternative society with enclave features.

(e) A fifth model lays its emphasis on simplicity of congregational structures. Preaching takes place twice on Sunday and once midweek. The congregation meets as a church family for prayer weekly, the children sometimes leaving with their parents after perhaps forty-five minutes. Backed up with vital personal work, that's it. Organisations are excluded and formal arrangements discouraged; even a day out together is arranged between friends rather than announced as a church activity.

Discipling on this model is achieved by the prayer-powered preached Word dealing in depth with people's personalities. Those people are thus free to be themselves in society, untrammelled by churchy activism; it is almost the exact opposite of the 'Keep them busy and you'll keep them happy' philosophy. Gift identification is virtually unnecessary except as it becomes clear, in the process of people's spiritual growth, that some have expository gifts or could share in the minimised administrative burden.

What principles can we take from studying these five models in the light of the New Testament?

- Church leaders are responsible to inculcate, model and monitor a personal bonding to Jesus Christ as Master; including a growing Christian understanding, moral behaviour, the spiritual exercises (attendance at worship, shared prayer, the Lord's Supper, the preaching), Christian relationships at home and work, and lives of loving service.

- The means by which these priorities are achieved are not laid down and we need not feel bound to any one model however compelling or successful.

- Not many pastors, or members, can afford the time needed to achieve Ortiz/Watson discipling in depth, including a sharing of home and hearth with disciples as well as family.

- The level of accountability between one Christian and another, church leader or not, may legitimately be exercised only as far as is plainly according to Scripture.

The last point is not a small one in these days of the shepherding movement. Calvin had to protest against the Roman Catholic church using Matthew 18, the 'power of the keys', to justify a whole range of control from confession to the sale of indulgences. No, he said, the Church's authority is to be judged 'solely according to God's law'.[25]

The shepherding movement is sometimes guilty of the same illegitimate argument. From the command to 'obey your leaders and submit to their authority'[26] they arrogate the right to forbid a change of employment and a hundred other uses of time and behaviour. It will not do. 'Necessity ought not to be imposed on consciences in those matters from which they have been freed by Christ.' The Church may only insist on what is demonstrable from Scripture; beyond that a Christian's conscience is free.

I cannot believe, however, that attendance for an hour on a Sunday adequately fulfils the biblical criteria for discipling. Some more detailed approach is surely essential, whether a large weekly meeting that breaks into groups for questions and discussion, or a system of house groups that still ensures solid corporate prayer; or an orderly system such as Baxter's for ensuring that pastors or the leadership team 'catechise and teach personally (he does not say frequently!) all who are committed to their care'. To Baxter we turn for more detail.

Since our first concern is for the whole Church, our first duties are the public duties: the preaching, sacraments and worship. Our second concern is for individuals: somehow, every one of them.

That which Baxter regarded as his most important contribution has been, as it seems to me, so little carried through with any thoroughness, and yet its impact was so momentous and amazing, that it cries out to be given an airing. Those who try it, find God blessing it.[27]

Baxter's greatest contribution was his system of discipling on a detailed individual basis, family by family, member by member. For Baxter the pastor's duty (yes) was personally to catechise everyone in his parish who would submit to it.

By catechesis he meant to teach the essentials of the faith contained in a published catechism, by the method of question, answer and discussion, in private conference. Privacy gives 'the best opportunity to impress the truth upon their hearts, when we can speak to each individual's particular necessity, and say to the sinner, "Thou art the man," and plainly mention his particular case.'[28]

I've a suspicion that being catechised by Baxter must have been a formidable experience. We'll come to his sensitivity and generosity in a minute; meantime notice the benefits he claims. Our sermons are better understood. A good foundation is a hopeful means of conversion. We become familiar with our people, and may thereby win their affections. And so Baxter continues, in Puritan thoroughness, expounding some twenty benefits.[29]

How did he run these private interviews? Baxter gives advice so practical as to warrant summary:

- Justify the meeting.
- Speak with people individually: in a separate room or a little distance from the rest of the family (but do not be alone in a room with a member of the opposite sex, for the avoidance of scandal).
- Find out what they have learned of the catechism.
- Choose one or two important matters and see how far they understand them. Start with what is obviously about their lives, e.g. 'What do you think happens to people when they die. What

should our heart be most set upon?' Avoid difficult or doubtful questions; make them such that they can see what you mean. Do not ask 'What is God,' for example, but 'What is God – is he made of flesh and blood as we are?' If they do not understand, frame the answer in a follow-up 'easing' question so they need only answer yes or no. If they really cannot answer, do not push them: give the answer yourself.

- Go on with a little more teaching appropriate to their capacity.
- If you think they are not converted, gently explore the issue with them. For example: 'You know how the Holy Spirit makes the faith clear and softens our hearts; have you ever known this?'
- If they seem unconverted, bring to their heart a sense of their condition.
- Conclude by pointing out our duty to believe in Christ and use the means of grace.
- Before you leave, again justify the time spent and express appreciation of their giving it.
- Keep a good record of visits in a book.
- In your manner be sensitive to people's ages and stages, and be easy to understand. Give scriptural evidence for what you teach. Prepare and pray in advance, do it lovingly; and if they are not well off, give money to relieve their poverty.

Baxter concludes: now get on with it!

Baxter spent Monday and Tuesday each week interviewing from morning to nightfall. Astonishingly, he actually asked the men to stay home from work and recompensed them for their lost wages. He took some fifteen or sixteen families per week between himself and two assistants in order to cover his eight hundred families each year. That divides up at about three families per day each: say, two to three hours per family. For years he held back from it because of the difficulties. Out of fear that few would want it and the sheer added burden of work, he ended up asking them to visit him; and was never refused by a single family.

He says, 'I find more outward signs of success with those who come than in all my public preaching. I found the benefits and comfort of the work to be such that I would not now forgo doing it for all the riches in the world.'[30]

I can confirm this from personal experience, having engaged in Baxter style visiting with the congregation coming one by one (couples together) to the manse after careful explanation. Some initially felt daunted but it proved one of the most happy and fruitful pastoral exercises I have ever undertaken.[31]

A complement to personal catechising was that Baxter held a weekly meeting for discussion and prayer. He preached once each Sunday and Thursday; 'every Thursday evening my neighbours met at my house, and there one of them repeated the sermon, and afterwards they proposed what doubts any of them had about the sermon, or any other case of conscience, and I resolved their doubts: and last of all I caused sometimes one, and sometimes another of them to pray.'[32]

Before we dismiss Baxter we do well to notice that the churches that have been characterised by the most spectacular growth in numbers, and in the major features of true discipleship, in our day have also featured, like Baxter, a systematic approach to the detailed discipling of individuals.[33]

The vital thing however is not which method is used but that we keep before us Christ's command to make disciples. Obedience must involve identifying by what means we shall achieve that in our context, and implementing them.

3. Gift identification and exercise

Convictions on the question of the spiritual gifts vary so widely that I had better make my assumptions clear. I assume that every conversion to Christ is a miracle, a work of God's Holy Spirit in which he persuades and enables a person to turn to Christ in faith. I assume that the Holy Spirit is engaged in continuing his 'radical and complete transformation'[34] in us. I assume that in Christ we who are many form one body, each of us belonging to all the others, each with different gifts by God's grace.[35]

The New Testament word for these gifts, *charismata*, indicates that they are given by God's mere kindness. They are to be used for the good of the body. The New Testament has no complete list of gifts; the lists we have are illustrative. A person's gift might be prophesying or administering, teaching or serving, for example; or more than one. Whether or not the 1 Corinthians 12 gifts have died out, there are significant lessons for pastors.

In 1 Corinthians Paul indicates a number of directives on which one should be clear. *Pneumatikoi* (v. 1) indicates that such gifts are breathed into us by God's Spirit, while warning that He is not the only source of them (v. 2f). *Charismata* (v. 4) indicates that they are bestowed graciously: that he is very kind in his free generosity to give them to us. The word *diakoniai* (v. 5) tells us to use them in the service of others, and probably also bespeaks the dignity of having such a commission from the Lord himself.[36]

Energematoi (v. 6) calls us to think highly of our gifting because it is the fruit of God's mighty work in us. Billy Graham's approach to the results of his preaching illustrates this. When he has preached he always makes it clear, without a hint of pride but simply as a matter of fact which he observes with great respect and expectancy, that many people will leave their seats and come forward. It is like watching a dentist with a drill or a JCB operator with his digger – here is an excellent tool, in the right hands, doing a good job. It does its work. That is how to exercise in God's service the particular ability he has wrought in us.

Phanerosis (v. 7) indicates that these gifts are not for our own private unseen enjoyment but are given in order to make the Spirit's work apparent: making its useful appearance to contribute to the common good.

The 'gift' passages[37] teach us:

- The gifts and their expressions will reflect and further the Lordship of Jesus Christ. Any that do not make this testimony and pass this test are spurious (1 Cor. 12:1-3). The key expression is in v. 3: 'Jesus is Lord.'

- They are to be used for the good of the Christian church, a profitable contribution (*sumpheron*, v. 7) to the body life (v. 4-10). The key expression is in v. 7: 'for the common good.'[38]

- The distribution of gifts to people is the Holy Spirit's absolute prerogative (v. 11-13). The key expression is in verse 11: 'he gives them to each one just as he determines.'

- No gift is better or less useful than another. All are equally valuable and equally essential, whether they are up front or behind the scenes, impressive or less so (v. 14-26). The key expression is verse 25: 'so that the members have equal concern for each other.'

- There is no gift that is given to every believer. The Greek is worded in verses 29, 30 to give the force, 'Not all are apostles, are they; not all speak in tongues, do they?'

Whatever view one takes of the cessation of the 1 Corinthians 12 gifts (all of them? some of them? only the ones not also listed elsewhere?), these five principles tell Christians 'using whatever gifts they have received, to serve others, as winsome stewards of God's many-coloured grace'.[39]

We do not need to be adherents of the 'fill this questionnaire to discover your charismatic gift' school, for this Christ-centred, church-serving teaching to guide our pastoral practice. Every congregation of believers is a charismatic church. As people get stuck in to humble Christian service, the way in which they have been made gifted to serve others should become apparent to a minister with an eye for what people are becoming, and are capable of becoming, in Christ.

I think of the student minister who saw in a new convert a gift for making the gospel come alive to young children and encouraged her to become a Sunday School teacher. That is the identification, affirmation, encouragement, development and exercise of a charisma. It takes an eye for God's footprints and a functioning delight in other people. Ask God for it! Start exercising it. Discern who else has it, and enlist their help. It is the *living* God we are serving; expect the living experience of him in the everyday life of a congregation.

A word on the variety evident in the Bible's treatment of charismata. We are expecting the development, not of mini-ministers but of maxi-Christians. Our aim is not the delegation of pre-identified tasks, but the discernment of God-provided gifts, resulting in a gloriously varied ministry of all God's people. Every pastor longs for a multiplication of pastors; but it should be only one of boundless possibilities for which we shall be watching.

For that very reason I want to question the view that what constitutes progress is to have a larger number at the front on a Sunday taking parts of the service. It might be so, if God is evidently pouring out such gifts: perhaps with a view to new church planting. If pursued dogmatically, however, such an approach can turn worship by the whole people into performance by the few, and a coherent service into confusion. There is even something to be said for the view that the public reading of scripture should be reserved for those with a call, such as is explored in chapter 2, to minister the Word.[40]

To fail to give opportunity to gifts that would profit the church's work, however, is an even more unattractive imbalance. 'Quench not the Spirit:'[41] the person who denies expression to a spiritual gift is surely grieving a generous Lord and impoverishing the church. The church generally has, in Cyril Ashton's phrase, an 'unemployed problem'.[42] Its leaders should be 'constantly reviewing the church scene, alert to the existence of embryonic ministries and willing to spend time nurturing them'.[43]

Individuals will find growing in them a desire to be involved in a particular activity, either within the church or as salt and light in society. There must be steady teaching so that, for example, members visiting each other pastorally regard this as the genuine ministry it is: and not at all as second best to a visit from 'the minister'.

The results may not be tidy; but as Ashton observes, better a schoolyard than a graveyard.[44] May our congregations be steady eruptions of every member service, in every field of life.

For further reflection

- Make a check-list of the goals of edification and evaluate one week's activities. To what extent are your energies serving your priorities?

- Compare the five models of discipling. Is there any practice you can introduce, or any current practice you could usefully drop?

- List those who attend your church at least three times per month. Pray for the appearance of spiritual giftedness in them on a rota basis, three each day, and note down when you see prayer answered.

References

1. Acts 9:31; 20:32; 1 Thessalonians 5:11, 14; 1 Corinthians 14:3ff.
2. 1 Thessalonians 5:11.
3. O. Michel in TDNT 5.141 s.v. *oikodomein* (edify, upbuild).
4. Romans 14:13-21; 15:1ff.
5. 1 Corinthians 14:26; 2 Corinthians 10:8; 13:10.

6. Ephesians 4:28-30.

7. Ephesians 4:1-16.

8. Galatians 2:18.

9. Matthew 28:19.

10. TDNT s.v. *mathetes* (disciple).

11. Romans 6:1-14.

12. Colossians 3:12-17; Romans 12:16-21, esp. v. 17, J.B. Philips version.

13. Romans 8:1-39; Colossians 3:1-4; Hebrews 2:1-4; Romans 1:18-8:39; Ephesians 1:3-3:21; Romans 12:3-9; 1 Corinthians 12–14; 1 Corinthians 1:10-13; Ephesians 6:10-20; Colossians 1:9,10; Hebrews 10:21-25.

14. Ephesians 5:21-33; 6:1-4; Colossians 3:22-4:1; Ephesians 6:5-9; 1 Peter 2:13-17; see note 5; compare 1 Peter 2:18.

15. Romans 13:8-10; 1 Corinthians 13:1-7; Galatians 6:10; Ephesians 5:1, 2; 1 John 3:11-18; etc.

16. Matthew 25:35, 36; James 1:27; John 13:14; 1 John 3:17.

17. Acts 18:7,8; Romans 16:3-5; 1 Corinthians 16:15, 19; Colossians 4:15.

18. E.g. Acts 18:26.

19. Acts 2:42.

20. E.g. Ephesians 5:14 is a citation from a baptism hymn; 1 Timothy 3:16 is a quotation from an early Christian confession.

21. 1 Corinthians 12:7-11; 14:26-38.

22. RPH p. 143.

23. Baxter saw his own special contribution to Christendom as threefold: individual instruction, church discipline and the fostering of fellowship meetings for pastors for the sake of unity.

24. J.C. Ortiz, *Disciple*, London, Lakeland (MMS), 1971. D. Watson, *Discipleship*, London, Hodder & Stoughton, 1981. Article 'Shepherding Movement' in *New Dictionary of Theology*, ed. S.B. Ferguson *et al*, Leicester, IVP, 1988, p. 639f.

25. INST. 4.11.2.

26. Hebrews 13:17.

27. See, for example, W. Benn, *The Baxter Model: Guidelines for Pastoring Today*, Orthos booklets, no.13, Fellowship of Word and Spirit, Northwich, 1993.

28. RP p. 175.

29. RPH p. 106-111; RP p. 173-192, numbers 1-17.

30. RPH p.6.

31. C.Peter White, *Sandyford Henderson Memorial Church Congregational Record,* Glasgow, Pastoral letters of Sep and Nov 1998 and Nov 1999. See also n.27 for Benn's guidelines which I followed.

32. *Reliquiae Baxterianae*, part 1, p. 83, quoted by J.I. Packer, RP, Introduction, p. 13 n. 11.

33. It is the second of five features which E. Gibbs identifies as common to

such churches. The five are: relevant, eventful worship; a fellowship network designed to integrate every believer; a concept of ministry which enables the body to grow; a steady rather than occasional approach to evangelism; and a certain approach to church structure. E. Gibbs, *Urban Church Growth*, Nottingham, Grove Books, 1977.

34. B.B. Warfield, 'On the Biblical Notion of Renewal', in *Biblical and Theological Studies*, Philadelphia, Presbyterian and Reformed Publishing Co., 1952, p. 351.

35. Romans 12:4-6.

36. Thus the context: 'a wide choice of types of service, and the same Lord (who commissioned them)' (12:5); compare John N. Collins, *Diakonia: Reinterpreting the Ancient Sources,* Oxford, OUP, 1990.

37. Romans 12:3-13; 1 Corinthians 12:14; Ephesians 4:7-16; 1 Peter 4:7-11.

38. 1 Corinthians 12:7.

39. 1 Peter 4:10, my translation.

40. 1 Timothy 4:13 in context.

41. 1 Thessalonians 5:19.

42. C. Ashton, *Church on the Threshold*, London, Daybreak, 1991, p. 92.

43. Ashton, p. 97.

44. Ashton, p. 98.

DEVELOPMENT AND OUTREACH

CHAPTER ELEVEN

STRATEGISING

Taking a Christian work forward

I know the plans I have for you: plans to prosper and not to harm you, plans to give you a hope and a future (Jeremiah 29:11).

Each one should be careful how he builds. For no-one can lay any foundation other than Jesus Christ. If any man builds on this foundation using gold, silver, costly stones, wood, hay or straw, his work will be shown for what it is, because the Day will bring it to light (1 Corinthians 3:10-13).

Ministry is just not as simple as giving oneself to preaching, praying and caring. Decisions still have to be made about the use of time and human resources at both the strategy level (are we a gathered or a parish-orientated congregation? What *is* the church for? Shall I copy Richard Baxter and engage in systematic catechesis?) and the immediate activity level (now there is new housing in our area, shall we visit?). We cannot evade strategic management, whatever name we give it. Even not to plan is, paradoxically, a plan.

By strategic management we mean the process by which we identify our distinctive vision as a congregation and by which we then seek to realise our aspirations.[1] Its purpose is to match our activities to God's call in concrete obedience, in a particular context: this congregation with its own unique history, gifts, catchment area, network of relationships and ministry.[2]

The particularity of our obedience is not identified by prayerful study of scripture alone. Consider Paul's adaptability, shown so clearly in his preaching as recorded in Acts. He had just one evangel, the Lord Jesus Christ, crucified and reigning; but with Jews he packaged that good news quite differently from the 'begin at creation' approach he adopted in an untaught pagan context.[3] We do not know whether his use of urban centres for evangelism was chosen in conscious preference to less strategic alternatives; but strategic it was.[4]

Quality: the people we need to be

There is something very frustrating for spiritually ambitious members when those appointed to lead the congregation are sleepy, content with second best or fail to think ahead. I would identify six key desirable qualities in a pastor or Christian in leadership who wants to be part of the forward move of his work.

Of the directly spiritual qualities the first is faith. Expect God to work. Seek a view of his gracious purpose for the work. The next is prayer. Ask God to work, lay hold of his gracious purpose, refuse to let go of him. The third is holiness. There is no greatness without a radical break with sin and a radical passion for God.

The remaining three qualities are less obviously 'spiritual' but reflect the spirit of a true leader nonetheless.[5] The first is a sense of strategy that keeps looking ahead and always seeks to gain shared ownership of the large vision. The second is congeniality: to be a person who likes people, people of all types, the unattractive as much as the attractive and compatible, and whose demeanour is winsome. For my sixth key quality I would nominate energy. Leaders should be wholehearted, hard working, the sort of people who will turn out and help you in your need, passionate rather than hireling [6] in their approach to work.

We are responsible to God for our particular work whether it be the whole world, as in the case of a missionary alliance, or a tiny rural community. Let us then approach our task strategically. When we do, other advantages accrue. To agree the ethos and ministry of a work strengthens the team, helps decide between priorities, clarifies vision, sets direction and grows commitment; although it can lose some people who do not share the vision.

Planning: the components we need to include

Tensions in a church often arise either because those with a significant stake in its work have not been consulted or because they have different assumptions about the work. When planning change, therefore, the following considerations form a useful checklist. One of the skills in taking a work forward is to cover these areas.

- Our church's particular vocation: what our church or Christian group exists for, broken down into concrete goals and purposes which constitute our practical obedience at this time, having regard to the congregation's maturity and situation.

- Our external constituency: whom are we trying to reach and serve?
- Our resources: how many members and officebearers, with what gifts, the building and facilities, the current local and worldwide relationships: all that we can draw upon to fulfil our calling.
- Our organisation: the individuals and boards or committees who get the different things done, and the relationships of responsibility, accountability and communication between them.
- Our processes. It is sadly possible to be active and hold the statutory meetings but to be getting nowhere and not even to know it. The 'processes' component is that which lists and evaluates the church's activities. For example, does the leadership group know whether the youth work is growing or declining, and if declining whether the reason is social change locally or boring leaders? Does it ensure that the work has enough money for materials? The 'processes' component also ascertains by what instrument or procedure we find out these things.

The management spiral: linking the components

The textbooks, if they call it anything, call this the management circle or cycle. I call it a spiral with the aim of indicating its commitment to progress. It is often said that to manage is to plan, organise, direct and control.[7] My own proposal is of three stages (I find three easier to remember than four): planning, implementation and review, linked by prayer:

Plan. The first step is to be seeking God's face together to gain a sense of his heart for the work. It is true that the large priorities are

FIGURE 11.1 The management spiral [8]

clear: the church's calling to glorify and enjoy God, and her desire for people to be saved and sanctified. The priority of worship, however, does not exhaust what the church is for. We also exist for each other in fellowship and for the world in evangelism and service. The question to be asked by each congregation is, 'What are we for, *here* – here in all its ethnic, economic, social and environmental dimensions?' The shapes of church life in a tiny Papua New Guinea church plant, the heart of an English university city and a deprived Scottish housing scheme contain real differences. The here-ness of our calling needs prayerfully to be sought.

Audit involves taking stock of the situation both internally and externally. To know how many we are, whether our numbers are increasing or declining, to make also some assessment of the quality of our congregational life: these are wise activities that the New Testament church engaged in[9] and are part of good stewardship. The accurate understanding of our situation can mould our mission and earth our work in the realities of people's lives.

Being specific about our objectives, the targets they imply and the steps to reach them is a great way of avoiding just beating the air. If we have specified our purpose as being to further the honour of God through building a church, it is still right to ask how we do that. This might spell out as:

OBJECTIVE 1 Develop the ministry of the eldership.
    TARGET 1 Keep this vision in their mind
    TARGET 2 Train the elders
        STEP 1 Elders' meetings to include time for systematic training at four meetings (or one retreat) per year.

We ensure thereby that our vision for this congregation is identifiably worked for and not just vaguely hoped for. Good plans are usually specific, realistic, challenging and have a time limit.[10]

Organising is the process of 'dividing up all the activities and material and assigning them to people'[11] to be carried out so as to fulfil the underlying target and purpose, in line with what the congregation stands for (our values).

A feature of good organisation is first to identify the necessary action steps accurately enough for people to perceive what needs to be done, to select appropriate people for each ('best fit') and then to delegate appropriately, supportively and clearly so that everyone knows who is responsible for what and to whom. Chapter 10 proposes characteristics of good delegation.

Implement. The difference between a congregation that is abounding and one that is just getting the work done is almost invariably traceable to good communication and to the affection for people that underlies it. A good strategist is voracious to share and to hear how people are doing. He keeps himself in touch with each operation and keeps people informed and feeling part of the work. It starts inside us. If we like and trust people the different components of communication are likely to be delivered.

We who are in Christian leadership are communicators by vocation and might not always be aware how poorly we communicate at the personal and delegation levels. We do well to be aware of the results of a huge survey: of over 8,000 people in many types of organisations, 'virtually everyone felt that he or she was communicating at least as well as, and in many cases better than, almost everyone else in the organisation. Most people readily admit that their organisation is fraught with faulty communication, but it is almost always 'those other people' who are responsible.'[12]

There is nothing more discouraging for a follower or a task leader than to feel that the minister or leadership group has abdicated the task or is uninterested. It is essential that we set the example, and accept the responsibility in our part in the work, as well as encourage and appreciate others in theirs.

A particular instance of this is training: to ensure a person is helped to become proficient in their work of service. This might involve the sequence:

- Watch and I'll do it and explain.
- Let's do it together.
- I'll watch while you do it, and I'll give feedback on your performance.
- You do it.

I add 'Perform and Monitor', to emphasise that in the end of the day getting something done for Jesus involves actually delivering on our planning rather than vaguely intending to initiate something some time.

As D.L. Moody said to a critic of his evangelistic practice, 'I prefer my way of doing it to your way of not doing it.'

As to the monitoring, we are wise to have a tremendous interest in how people's Christian service is getting on and to keep our finger on the pulse of a project, especially in the early stages.

Review. William Still wrote, 'Have the courage to turn to Christ – never mind anyone else – and ask him to tell you honestly what he thinks of you and your life.'[13] That was advice to individuals but it can be applied to congregations. The healthy strategist takes stock of how the strategy is going. The two stages in review are fact-gathering and evaluating: not backward-looking (let alone apportioning fault) in motive but with a view to further forward planning and progressive improvement of practice.

The way to evaluate effectively is to decide what criteria we shall apply. This saves us from vague impressions and gives instead a clarity and an objectivity to the evaluation process.

There is great difficulty however, and some danger, in applying measurable standards to Christian work. We cannot specify numbers of conversions or count the impact of a sermon. Nonetheless the scriptural command to assess ourselves, and the examples in Revelation chapters 2 and 3 of congregational review by our Lord Jesus, imply that there are standards against which to judge ourselves.[14] Here are possible starting points.

Congregationally, if we set ourselves an agenda it should be possible to give examples of effective and ineffective performance in attaining it. For example if we have a number of missionaries for whom we have promised to pray, it is possible to know whether we have corresponded with and prayed for them over a period; and even, if we mean business by them and are prepared to make ourselves accountable, how long it takes to reply when they write.

Individually, the main leaders in the congregation have written or implied job descriptions. The same procedure can be followed: specify effective and ineffective behaviours, group them by categories which fit the job description, and (to be thorough) use a scale to rate each description. An example: reply to each personal letter within ten days. A rating might be from 5 (always manages to) to 1 (never bothers).

This process has the acronym BARS: behaviourally anchored rating scales.[15] Evaluate only what is worth evaluating, and devise ways of doing so without taking too much time. If the test is not cost effective (cost in terms of time, effort, importance to our ministry) it should be eschewed. Leaders, however, should know whether numbers are growing or declining, whether the building is in good repair and the church's financial state represents honourable stewardship. They should also be able to evaluate their 'team-ness'. Such an exercise can be most useful; two examples of team work review are given as appendices to this chapter.

How to start: using the components to develop a congregation
It is very important indeed to consider our people's sensitivities at this stage. We might have a vision for progress but the very suggestion causes surprise and fear in many hearts. A change of leader or a new ministry by the church involves loss for some members – loss of stability, of power, of identity, of role. Such bereavement can be profound and its power needs to be understood by those who would institute change.

One personality facet has the mnemonic DISC: dominance, influence, steadiness and compliance:

Members high on Dominance fear losing control. A person who scores high on Influence fears rejection. The high S person – Steadiness – fears change. Members high on Compliance fear having work criticised.[16]

The ethos of our approach, therefore, is to consider how members perceive the changes; to treat their feelings as important.[17]

Start as you mean to go on. This is most easily done at the start of a ministry: it is easier to set a desirable pattern, than to change a static one. If the new minister is able quite early on to introduce a certain amount of change that everyone knows has been needed, people's first experience of change will be a positive one. But it is never too late to change; start with a really good change, even if small. In fact 'small wins' is good strategy. My advice would be not to introduce more than three changes at a time, to gain the consent of the main stakeholders in advance and always to visit and talk with those most nervous about the proposed changes.

This first point – start as you mean to go on – is questioned by some. There are those who recommend making no change for the first year or so in a new situation. Certainly it is a mistake to institute too much change at first. Change is disturbing and people need time to learn to trust a new leader. The fact is, however, that we start setting a pattern as soon as we arrive. Better to start a consistent pattern of sensitive progress than to institute an ethos of no change which we then break in a year's time.

Let development be corporately led. Far better a decision genuinely owned by the whole leadership team than something which comes over as critical of the people, their leaders and their history.

Explain and prepare people for any proposed change and show its advantages. To have something foisted on to us without explanation or preparation is upsetting for any of us.

Do not give up. Awkwardness about change is natural. If people are not feeling awkward doing something new, they are not doing something new. Therefore do not stop because of inertia or resistance; these are inevitable.

We have written of the ethos of sensitivity. It is no help however to a congregation's development if we allow sensitivity to degenerate into diffidence, apology or doublemindedness.[18] Bunyan's insight is so accurate: Diffidence was the wife of Giant Despair, and she made sure that he gave Christian and Hopeful some terrible beatings.[19]

Meetings

Committee work can produce lowest common denominator planning and action. Nothing is more irritating than a chairman not in command of the facts or the meeting, who starts late, fails to moderate chaos and from whom no decisions are made. In the right hands, however, meetings can be immensely powerful. It can help to identify, from their armoury of functions, which ones are to be achieved on a given occasion.

- Meetings can add to our knowledge. As different members contribute they learn from each other in a way that is greater than the sum of the parts: the 'social mind' has a special creative power.

- Meetings help us understand our particular task and provide cumulative insight: elders discussing approaches to visiting, for example.

- Meetings strengthen commitment. Since all share responsibility for the final decision, the ownership of it is constituency wide: as in Acts 15, where in a remarkable way the Jewish and Gentile churches agreed on gospel freedom from legalism.

- Meetings cohere a group and strengthen both the relationship between leader and group, and mutual support between group members quite beyond the meeting itself.

- Meetings are a powerful way of exploring complex problems, especially when the progressive stages of the argument are laid out visually to discourage repetition and encourage orderly resolution. This is particularly the case when modern methods like Nominal Group Technique[20] are employed to maximise corporate brainpower and minimise dominance by individuals.

- Meetings are an effective tool in training.

Planning a meeting

Good planning can make a tremendous contribution to the value of a meeting. The four tasks to be alert to are advance consideration of the agenda, the objectives, the people and the time.

Draw up the Agenda. It should be clear and include enough explanation for members to know what is at stake and what to read up in advance. Agendas should reach members sufficiently in advance to make this possible.

Briefing papers setting out the background to an item and what the speaker proposes to recommend, are immensely useful on significant items. They should be kept as short as possible. It can be helpful also to be clear whether items are for decision, discussion or information.

Define the objectives. Each item is likely to be one of the following:

- Informative, for example leaders receiving the annual report of the youth work and discussing its implications.

- Constructive, as when a body formulates a policy – the procedure by which a person is considered for and received into membership, for example. Constructive business answers the question, what shall we do?

- Executive items answer the question, how shall we do it? In assigning responsibilities a meeting ensures that people see their place in the overall task and tends to facilitate consent.

- Legislative: the 'organisation and rules' business of a committee.

If people are aware beforehand which of these types of business each agenda item is, they will be more ready to treat them appropriately: exploring an informative item, ready to decide policy on a policy-constructing one, and assigning responsibilities when acting as an executive.

A wise chairman will also consider in advance which business is significant enough and controversial enough to warrant being put on the business on more than one occasion: 'counsels to which time has not been called, time will not ratify' (Francis Bacon). I remember a chairman admirably saying, as an item dear to him was in jeopardy, 'Ladies and gentlemen, I can see that we are not ready to decide at this time; we shall defer and return to it on another occasion.' A year later it went through with almost complete unanimity and in a good spirit.

I said 'controversial *and* significant', above. Plenty of matters should never reach a meeting agenda. Many are best resolved by one person deciding and taking action.

Discuss it with the people responsible. God forbid that we fix decisions in advance, but we can at least ensure that those responsible for presenting an item will be there and prepared to do so. It is a help to know also what to expect in the way of response: forewarned is forearmed. A few words with a member the day before can alert us to the considerations likely to be raised, or might spare the meeting unnecessary resistance or irrelevant objections.

Divide out the time. The chairman can help a meeting by proposing the amount of time to be spent on different items. He will put items that call for lively and creative brainpower early in the agenda. He will also consider which items will unify members and which will divide them: it is good to end a meeting in unity. He will consider ways of avoiding spending too much time on trivialities. This can be achieved by delegating such details to an individual or small group.

Plan for a total meeting time of something under two hours. Better to have two two-hour meetings than a single four-hour one. The corporate brain, in meetings of 5-20 people, starts to deteriorate after about two hours; and, worse than that, introduces the phenomenon of 'group shift'. While individuals tend to entrench their original approach, with both conservative and risk-taking members becoming more so, groups shift towards the risky.[21] There is solid evidence that decisions made more than two hours after the start of a meeting are unreliable.

Tasks during a meeting

Structure the discussion. Trusted practice involves an initial proposer or presenter, opportunity for questions, time for discussion and closes with the motion summarily proposed and seconded. This may be followed by opportunity for amendment with supporting speeches and the decision, reached by vote if there is division.

Many a time procedure can be more relaxed; but the danger once we depart from formal practice is always that we give more scope for fudge and make it less easy to explore alternatives. At worst, people do not know if there has been a decision at all.

There are those who believe that decisions should not be made by Christian groups until there is unanimity. This is not realistic in every situation. Christians are allowed to disagree (!) and we help when we make that easy, acceptable and savouring more of light than heat.

In introducing business, Anthony Jay's medical model can be useful:

- 'What seems to be the trouble?' – explain the issue which brings this item on to the committee's agenda.
- 'How long has it been going on?' – analyse the past, explain the background.
- 'Let me examine you' – this is how things stand now.
- 'You've slipped a disc' – we assess the situation.
- 'Take this prescription to the chemist' – the group considers different options as to the most helpful way forward, chooses the best fit, states plainly what conclusion or decision has been reached and waits while it is written down for the minute.[22]

Achieve the objective. It is most important to achieve the aim set for each item on the agenda and to identify closure: 'We have agreed in principle to set aside a budget for training and the treasurer will report to the next meeting with recommendations.' A very satisfying outcome for every member present; morale and commitment are enhanced when the group has both achieved something and knows it.

Enable the people. The chairman is the servant of the group, not its master. The most effective discussions have in fact two leaders:

the social leader (chairman) who furthers the process of discussion, and the project or agenda item leader who leads off the content of discussion. A good chairman contributes not so much content as process; his calling is to keep the discussion going, not to determine its direction.

Choice of seating arrangement is significant. For the chairman to sit in the centre of the long side of the room or table makes him more part of the team but makes those beside him less so. Start on time. If you don't, you reward the latecomers and punish the diligent.

The most significant contributions often come from the quiet thinkers who might not speak unless we are alert to a raised eyebrow. Alertness needs to be backed up by impartial treatment of different people appropriately: the norm is not equality but fairness. The repeated participant needs, 'Bill, you've done well making your point; I should like to give others an opportunity to contribute on this matter, please.'

When chairing a large multi-church committee, I used to set aside time for contributions from those who were not ministers(!), from the women present and from any who had not yet spoken. The shy person needs gentle invitation. The thoughtless need firm control: including, at the next meeting, perhaps, the request to sit next to you. That gives them minimal chance to catch your eye.

Two kinds of silence worth unfreezing are those of diffidence and of hostility. Protect the weak. In one situation we had a sniper who repeatedly made clever remarks about a paper drawn up by a vulnerable member. I indicated that it had been tabled at my request and in face of its author's diffidence. The sniper never criticised it again and the author expressed thanks.

Detailed discussions are kept on course if someone summarises each distinct contribution visibly, e.g. on flip chart. Have the chart where everyone can see it without turning round. The ideal person to do this is someone other than the chairman, a person who is good at summarising the point and is willing to sacrifice some participating role for that purpose.

The ideal is not always possible, however, and in fact the chairman can sometimes be the best person to do it. If so, his own position is dictated by the optimum position for the flip chart. If right handed and the chart is just to his left, he will not have to move across the chart in order to write on it.

Encourage suggestions and the interplay and even clash of ideas, but not of people. The member who seeks dominance by knowing what is wrong with others' tentative ideas breeds defensiveness, is an adventure-spoiler and should be controlled. 'Generate before you evaluate.'[23]

The capacity to facilitate and moderate a discussion is a considerable skill and the most crucial component in excellent chairmanship. The hindrances to effective process come in standard forms and management textbooks offer guidelines on how to deal with them: the hostile, the know-all, the dominant.[24] There are general pitfalls worth identifying.

- Groupthink. When a group gets together, new dangers arise which do not apply on a one-to-one basis. Members become reluctant to express views contrary to the sentiment currently prevailing, especially where these have been propounded by dominant or awkward personalities. This pertains even when better options are subsequently offered. The result can be worse than if the committee had never been consulted in the first place.

- Social loafing. This is to hold back from participation, whether out of a sense of insignificance or because 'no one else is trying'. It increases, the larger the committee. The chairman has a responsibility and his force of personality is the most significant factor: expecting people to contribute and showing so; inviting individual contributions; reminding them of the importance of the topic.

- Personal Agendas. People can come to a meeting with their own gripe about how things are going, their frustration from being manipulated at work, reaction from a conscience stirred by a recent sermon. Keeping control of the meeting constructively is not always easy. Being prepared in advance for the different types of disruptive behaviour is one skill; overall the way we handle 'problem people' (aware that we are a component in both the problem and its solution) can set the tone for a committee's life. Open-ness, problem- rather than person-orientation and supportive forbearance are key factors in success; you can always punch a pillow, or unload to a friend, when you get home.

After a meeting

The Minutes. The chairman is not usually the person who writes the minutes. They are however his minutes and he should ensure a clear brief minute which records who was present, where and when held, who was in the chair; all items discussed: briefly set the scene, where necessary summarise the main considerations adduced, state clearly what was agreed and who is responsible for any action arising; the time the meeting ended and the date of the next meeting.

A wise chairman will make brief notes on the meeting, immediately afterwards if possible. It is my opinion that minutes should be cleared with the chairman before distribution to the members.

The Follow Up. Arising from our notes of the meeting we should diarise both immediate follow up to the meeting's key players especially if there was controversy or emotion at the meeting; and dates at which to ask after the progress of action agreed.

Meetings, in fact, call for:

> Patience to sit through endless tedious discussions, good humour to counter the tensions of disagreement, fair-mindedness to enable you to see both sides of the question, tenacity of purpose to press persistently for the needed policy, absolute integrity to avoid the underhand trick, humility to admit that you may be mistaken, and perceptiveness to get to the heart of a problem quickly.[25]

Apart from that, they're effortless.

For consideration

- Have I confused the organisational busyness of my congregation with the discipleship of Jesus and the obedience of faith?
- Have I avoided decision where God's Word and the welfare of the congregation demanded decision?
- Are there skills in the preparation for, or chairing of, meetings which I could note for future use?

APPENDIX TO CHAPTER 11

EXAMPLES OF REVIEW INSTRUMENTS

1. EXAMPLE OF PERSONAL WORK REVIEW

AREA OF WORK

RATING: 1-4:
1= poor
2 = not so good
3 = good
4 = excellent

Comprehension of job
Quality of work
Quantity of work

Self Discipline
Initiative
Enthusiasm

Ability to communicate
Lead in public worship

Ability to delegate
Ability to define others' activities
Ability to direct others' activities
Ability to inspire others

PLEASE MAKE BRIEF NOTES FOR DISCUSSION. Continue on separate sheet if necessary.

1. What have been your best achievements?

2. What do you believe yourself least good at overall?

3. Were there obstacles hindering you accomplishing what you wished? If they are likely to recur, how could they be eliminated?

4. What do you think should be the key aims in your workplan at this stage?

5. To improve your performance, what additional things might be done by:
   Others in the team?
   Yourself?
   Anyone else?

2. EXAMPLE OF TEAMWORK REVIEW INSTRUMENT

A. PREPARATION: done individually in advance

Each to prepare answers to the following questions.

SECTION 1: CONCERNING MYSELF

1. What am I doing well .... and what badly?
2. Where do I need help?
3. How do I feel about how things are going?
4. What's my biggest headache in the work?
5. What's my biggest blessing?
6. What potential do I see for the future?
7. What should I start doing?
8. What should I stop doing?
9. What should I do differently?

SECTION 2: CONCERNING MY PARTNER(S) IN THE TEAM

10. What am I dissatisfied with in my team partner(s)?
11. What am I most grateful for in my team partner(s)?
12. What are the contributions for which the Church, and my partner(s), should hold me accountable; and what should they expect of me?
13. What is the best utilisation of *my* knowledge and ability?
14. What is the best utilisation of *your* knowledge and ability (re each team member)?
15. What points need raising from our original job description/contract of employment?
16. Write a personal set of objectives, and steps by which to attain them, over the next six months.

B. PROCEDURE ON DAY OF REVIEW: whole team, plenty of time

1. **Review the team's work:**
   a. Who has done what and why; what were the results?
   b. How well did I/you/we do the work? Sharing of answers to preparation questions.
   c. How good were the results of the work?
2. **Construct the team's plan:**
   From the resources available and identifying the work confronting us, construct the *team's* objectives.
3. **Execute the team's plan:**
   Who is to do what. Check each person is clear about what has been delegated to whom and how we help each other get our jobs done.
4. **Arrange the next review:**
   Put next assessment date into diaries now: 6 months?

Main source: J.W. Alexander, *Managing our Work*, Downers Grove, IVP, 2nd edition, 1975.

References

1 A secular analysis of the stages involved is given in G. Johnson & K. Scholes, *Exploring Corporate Strategy*, New York, Prentice Hall, 1989. The three key tasks are strategic analysis in which we understand our strategic position under God; strategic choice in which we formulate possible courses of action, first generating, then evaluating and finally selecting between the options; and strategic implementation, which decides how to put into effect those choices and acts accordingly. Johnson and Scholes identify resource planning, organisational structure and management systems as the components involved in implementation.

2. E.P. Clowney, *Resource of Divine Guidance*, unpublished paper given at Westminster Theological Seminary, n.d., offers a theological overview starting from God's planning.

3. Contrast, for example, Acts 13:16-41 with 17:22-31, and see F.F. Bruce, *The Speeches in Acts*, London, Tyndale Press monograph, date not noted.

4. E.g. Acts 19:8-10 in context.

5. C.J. Cox and C.L. Cooper, *High Flyers*, Oxford, Blackwell, 1988, pp. 85(yes)-105,170-176, offer a powerful secular analysis.

6. John 10:1-28.

7. E.g. Patricia King, *Performance Planning and Appraisal*, New York, McGraw-Hill, 1989, p. 22.

8. Adapted from J.W. Alexander, *Managing our Work*, Downers Grove, IVP, 2nd edition, 1975, p. 16.

9. E.g. Acts 2:41-47; 1 Corinthians 5:1; 11:17-22; 2 Corinthians 13:5; Revelation 2; 3.

10. King, *op. cit.*, p. 25. Compare S. Chalke, *Making a Team Work*, Eastbourne, Kingsway, 1995, pp. 67-71, 122-123.

11. Alexander, *op. cit.*, p. 39.

12. W.V. Haney, *Communication and Interpersonal Relations*, Homewood, Illinois, Irwin, 1979, p. 219, quoted in D.A. Whetten and K.S. Cameron, *Developing Management Skills*, New York, Harper Collins, 2nd ed., 1991, p. 231.

13. S.B. Ferguson (ed), *Letters of William Still*, Edinburgh, Banner of Truth, 1984, p. 160: congregational letter of August, 1976.

14. Compare, uncomfortably, 2 Corinthians 3:2-3.

15. King, *op. cit.*, p. 132-144.

16. 'Turning Vision into Reality: an interview with Ken Blanchard', *Leadership*, Spring 1996, p. 114-118.

17. Quoted by P. Goh, 'Mission Agencies and the Management of Change': EMA Personnel Secretaries Group presentation on 30.11.95, p. 3, from R. Harrison, *Organisation Culture and Quality of Service*, AMED, 1987.

18. James 1:8.

19 J. Bunyan, *Grace Abounding* and *The Pilgrim's Progress*, London, OUP, 1966, p. 231-234.

20. C. M. Moore, *Group Techniques for Idea Building*, Newbury Park, California, Sage, 1987.

21. Whetten and Cameron (p. 470) quote research by McGrath and Kravitz, 'Group Research', *Annual Review of Psychology*, vol. 33, p. 195-230.

22. A. Jay, 'How to run a Meeting', *Harvard Business Review*, Mar-Apr 1976, p. 53.

23. R. Kraybill, 'Ten commandments of meeting facilitation', in *Mediation and Facilitation Training Manual*, Akron Pennsylvania, Mennonite Conciliation Service, 3rd ed., 1995, p. 191f.

24. Whetten and Cameron, p. 472f, suggest responses to eleven categories of disruptive and inappropriate behaviours.

25. Stanley G. Browne, *Medical Missions: Regaining the Initiative*, London, CMF, 1978, p. 8.

CHAPTER TWELVE

EVANGELISING

Reaching out in our area

I will make you a light for the nations, that you may bring my salvation to the ends of the earth (Isaiah 49:6).

All authority in heaven and on earth has been given to me.
Therefore go and make disciples of all nations, baptising
them in the name of the Father and of the Son and of the Holy Spirit, and
teaching them to obey everything I have
commanded you. And surely I am with you always,
to the very end of the age (Matthew 28:18-20).

In Scotland the decline in church going in the period 1984-1994 averaged 225 people weekly. Taking into account all the denominations this is the size of an average congregation lost each week in Scotland over a ten year period. It is a land where half – 48%, in fact – of those aged 10-19 in 1984 had left the church ten years later: a huge haemorrhage of young people.[1]

Equally serious, missionary support is preponderantly given by the over 60s. Two complete generations of Christians have for the most part not been caught up in the vision of sacrificial giving, supporting by correspondence and praying for worldwide evangelisation. Missionary meetings are largely attended by the late middle aged and older.

Across Britain the only growing churches, with individual exceptions, are the charismatic churches; and their growth is more by transfer from other groups than by conversion. A relatively recent factor is competition from other religions, especially Islam; one new mosque will have been added each month to the British scene over the years 1985-2000.

If these are the cold statistics, the facts of underlying attitude are equally challenging. The normal British, even the average Scottish family (England's decline was a generation earlier) is totally secularised. A generation ago the majority of Scottish families had church connection at least to the extent of baptism and Sunday school attendance by the children.

In the 1950s most Scots understood the basic tenets of the Christian faith. This gave a shared basis of knowledge and understanding for evangelistic enterprises such as the 'Tell Scotland' movement and the visit of the evangelist Billy Graham to the Kelvin Hall, Glasgow in 1955. Very large numbers turned to Christ and a stream of candidates converted at that time continued to enter Christian work right to the end of the 1960s.

In the late 1990s, however, the whole thinking of the vast majority of the nation is humanistic. There is a growing trend to New Age thinking, monistic and largely mystical in its world view and increasingly influencing education, political thought and morals. Nine out of ten couples who marry are already living together. Schools are permitting Christmas services on condition that they are not Christian. Popular attitudes to honesty, covetousness and sexuality have undergone a revolution.

The missionary statesman Lesslie Newbigin said that, next to Islam, western Europe is the most resistant culture in the world to Christianity today. Some of the trigger words identified by the London Institute for Contemporary Christianity as marking our society are pluralism, materialism, individualism, sex and the new paganisms already mentioned. In addition in these early years of the 21st century, there is an almost universal recognition of the need for every individual to have a spirituality, however defined.

This is a very different Britain from the one in which all but younger Christian leaders grew up and it calls for fresh understanding of the communication task. The old bridging language is inadequate for the new gulf in thought between Christianity and the population.

The evangelistic task is the same as ever, but even more urgent: to face men and women effectively with the fact that our Lord Jesus is good news, the Saviour they need, crucified for their self-centredness and their guilt and risen as Lord. How are we to meet this challenge?

Church leaders should be concerned not just for maintenance but to identify those means by which a given church, with its current membership and minister, in its geographical and denominational context, will most effectively further God's kingdom.

But what *will* most effectively further God's kingdom? There has been much debate about what to value in the matter of progress. It has centred around the qualitative-quantitative axis: should numbers and quality be equally important ambitions?

The Church Growth school has sometimes valued numerical growth in preference to other gospel values: for example, in espousing monocultural congregations because these produce a larger response. I would claim that such a strategy jeopardises a higher gospel value, the barrier-destroying work of Christ reflected in Ephesians 2:14-18.

Others have valued quality to the exclusion of any programme for evangelism. R.C. Halverson comments:

> When I was called to the Fourth Presbyterian Church in 1958, I had an agreement with the officers that there would be no pressure to increase the membership. It was understood that our responsibility was to care for the people, nurture them in the Word of God, strengthen their fellowship with Christ and one another, and help them grow in love. The conviction was that numerical growth, as it occurred in the New Testament, was the spontaneous and normal result of a healthy community of faith (Acts 2:47; 6:7; 9:31; 16:5).
>
> The New Testament does not define evangelism as a department of church life. Nor is it one of many programs initiated by the church. Rather, it is the normal outcome of a spiritually strong community.[2]

The New Testament reflects rather a 'both-and' than an 'either-or' on this debate. Orlando Costas writes of 'holistic expansion'.[3] It may be said to include:

- Growing up to maturity: conceptual growth. Hebrews 5:11-13.
- Growing together in community: organic growth. Acts 2:42-46; 6:1-7.
- Growing out in service and influence: incarnational growth. Matthew 5:14-16.
- Growing more in numbers: numerical growth. Mark 4:1-20.

Whatever view one takes of 'progress', however, it will not do for a church's leadership merely to administer the present congregational life. Scripture makes them responsible to God to plan, pray and labour for congregational and Kingdom progress.

The chief agent in lasting evangelism is the life of the local church; the pastor's priorities, to build Christ-centred, Christ-like communities where people will say 'God is among you' and will meet him.[4] There is no easy route to this. It involves creating not only a prayerful but also a learning environment so that members and interested non-members can ponder the truth and move forward with support.

The temptation is always to avoid the labour of such work and to short-circuit it with lighter and easier alternatives, less mortifying and more attractive to the flesh for all involved.

The most effective ongoing evangelism is not contrived but has a naturalness and an inevitability about it. It is the natural outcome of the impact of Christian lives well taught and well loved by their church leadership. We do indeed need to plan strategy but it is this spontaneous impact of the life of God, in all its distinctiveness and greatness, that is core evangelism.

The sermon recorded in Acts 2, for example, was not preached as a result of a decision on evangelistic strategy. After much joint prayer a people came alive with the promised fire of the Holy Spirit and their distinctiveness was so marked that people asked, 'What does this mean?'

The same is true of the sermon recorded in Acts 3. Peter simply responded to the question provoked by the evidence of God's power. In other words the Christian community was so remarkable as to raise questions in people's minds.[5]

There is ample evidence of God's use of this phenomenon throughout history. In AD 112 the local governor Pliny wrote to the Roman Emperor Trajan about a problem. He had started to put the wretched Christians to death for not worshipping the emperor as a deity but his conscience troubled him: their only fault was that they prayed to Christ as God and were bound by an oath not to steal, commit adultery or break their word! Pretty wretched reasons for removing their heads. So he tortured a couple of maidservants to find out if the picture was accurate. He found that indeed there was absolutely nothing against them, just this extravagant superstition. We need to be careful, he concluded: there are an awful lot of them.

The unknown writer to Diognetus, probably in the second century, says much the same; but just notice how up to date are the issues to which he draws attention. These Christians are no different in their country, language or customs. They marry and have children; it's just that they do not kill unwanted babies. They offer a shared table – but not a shared bed. They obey the law – and go beyond the law in their own lives! In fact, what the soul is to the body, Christians are to the world.[6]

In other words the core evangelistic question is not what we can learn from the salesmen but what must we be and do, that will make other people ask the questions to which Jesus Christ is the answer. This is the heart of evangelism, and it shifts our focus from sales talk to discipleship.

If people are coming slowly over years to Christ, influenced by authentic friendship and the quality of their Christian neighbours' lives, the church's priority must remain focused on these things. Brief campaigns and sales techniques in the name of the Church will never take the place of Christian nurture and service.

We are wise, therefore, if we concentrate our energies on the reality of our members' Christian lives and on encouraging them to be, not 'those out and out Christians who are never in' but good neighbours for its own sake. Nobody wants to be treated as a potential scalp in a soul-winner's belt. That would be, in the Jewish philosopher Martin Buber's phrase, an I-It relationship. Our friends and neighbours are not objects of whatever ambition we might have, even their salvation. They are people with feelings, made in God's image, infinitely valuable as such in their own right. 'I and Thou'[7] is the only authentic relation.

Every authentic Christian 'I', however, wishes those he is fond of to become as he is, but for his sufferings;[8] and it is good to consider acceptable bridges to that outcome.

All churches are mixtures of the genuine and non-genuine, even those who adhere to the Gathered Church Community concept in preference to the Reformed approach. If this be granted, then every congregation is in measure a mission field; and more so, the 'Prescopalians' (Presbyterian and Episcopalian) who assume a mixed church.

Evangelism in such circumstances will take place in part through the life of the church. Like the Saviour before him, the preacher will include the warning that not everyone who calls Jesus Lord will enter the kingdom of heaven.[9] As God's message is preached people will realise their need. The church at prayer will be aware that not all the members might be in the kingdom yet. Pastoral visitors will be ready to explore whether people are in the faith.[10] Indeed such enquiry is a proper part of the work of catechetical visiting such as Richard Baxter engaged in (see chapter 10).

One Scottish congregation has tried this in measure. They distribute a Christian basics booklet to those whom the minister or leader will be visiting soon, and opportunity is thereby made to go over the gospel and the individual's response in the course of a home visit. Wallace Benn, some time bishop of Lewes, followed Baxter's model more closely while vicar of St Peter's church, Harold Wood, in Essex. Members were invited systematically to his home for pastoral discussion; he reported in some detail of its effectiveness.[11]

John Finney, a leader in the Anglican Church's decade of evangelism, has investigated the effectiveness of different factors in evangelism. 80% of people who come to Christ from outside the Christian fold come through their friends; and they take an average of four years to do so.[12] We really need to depend on God and abandon impatience.

Of 550 people from every colour in the theological spectrum two thirds came quietly over a period of time, one third at a time of crisis of some sort. The story was one of people experiencing the goodness of God, as well as hearing the good news about God, from steady friends.

Peter Neilson, National Adviser in Evangelism in the Church of Scotland for eleven years from 1986 to 1997, thinks this is a major clue to the success of 'Alpha' courses all over Britain. The Alpha course is a ten week course of instruction in Christian basics, designed to be used with small groups, with a weekend away at the end of the course to give opportunity for concentrated time together. An outline is given, and a video presentation available, for each meeting. Emphasising the importance of adjusting its use to each local situation Neilson sees the critical ingredients in three 'F' words:

- *friends* who bring friends;
- *food*: copying our Lord Jesus in this, who did so much incisive spiritual work in the ambience of shared meals;
- *freshness* in both the content and the style of the video and printed materials,[13] and the lively expectancy of God actually changing people's lives.

I think also of the minister friend, concerned at the loss of teenagers in his church, who decided to try all-age style services geared with items suitable for people of different ages. For example he gets young people involved in role play that illustrates the theme of the sermon; a contemporary Good Samaritan playlet, say. This systematic attempt to cater for those whom he hopes will attend, has been followed by a very considerable increase in the number attending.

Much has been made of the failings of an infamous late evening service in England which turned out to be a platform for the vicar's earth mother theology and sexual gratification. Less publicised but more to be admired has been the Christian disco and chat show 9pm service of a Scottish congregation. They have a youth worker working on the streets among young people. By this means invitations to a service that speaks their language come from a relationship that already exists. Here is a church ready to meet its constituency culturally without compromising the gospel.

It is remarkable how Charles Simeon, lifelong lecturer and five times Dean of theology at King's College, Cambridge, stuck to such tenets despite the bitter divide it caused in his church for the first eleven years of his 65-year ministry.

Rural people were pouring from the impoverished countryside to fuel the Industrial Revolution. The well-to-do Cambridge residents and students hated these poor people who filled the crumbling hovels in the back streets of the city, and termed them riff-raff.

Simeon began his ministry by going from door to door through his parish, approaching people with the words, 'My name is Simeon. I have called to enquire if I can do anything for your welfare.' His friendliness so affected the poor peasants that they began to attend the church. Unfortunately, their smelly clothes and unwashed state offended the better-off members who paid rents for their pews.

They locked their pews so they were not available in the mornings, and hired a guest lecturer to preach to them on Sunday afternoons. Undaunted, Simeon bought timber out of his £49-a-year salary, and made portable benches for his Sunday morning congregation. Every week he would set them in the aisles, then open the doors and invite the poor to enter.

This went on for eleven years. In Simeon's twelfth year revival came, the wall of conflict came down and the congregation united. Simeon stayed there for a further fifty-four years.[14]

When our church in Edinburgh decided to appoint a full time social worker the appointment proved a powerful bond with the lives of the unchurched, especially among those in most obvious need. The clause we used in the process of gaining the consent of congregation and Presbytery was, 'The love of Jesus is more credible when it is visible as well as audible.'[15]

The point is put into typically neat form by Bill Hybels:

> **MI=HP+CP+CC**
> **M**aximum **I**mpact flows when **H**igh **P**otency (a deep relationship with God) is combined with **C**lose **P**roximity to people and **C**lear **C**ommunication.[16]

What of mass evangelism? I have come away from recent involvement in such a campaign among young people in the west of Scotland with a number of convictions. As one of the team running the Youth for Christ (YFC) youth evangelism event 'Our Turn Now' in the summer of 1995 in the Kelvin Hall, Glasgow, I sat among young people on the opening night, my ears blasted by mere sound and rhythm: for the first twenty minutes I did not hear one single word of the songs being performed (sung? ministered?).

Then came singing with some words audible, interviewing and a very enthusiastic, accessible-language, start-where-they-are talk by Tony Campolo: middle aged! but real, alive, contact-establishing. My principles of cognitive communication, however, had been trampled all over by the method of opening with 120 decibel cacophony.

During that evening, on the other hand, several thousand youngsters, many of them not committed Christians, had heard in a living way about Jesus ('living' in being agreeable with Scripture, in forging bridges with their own lives and in including definite moral-social challenge). Many of them would not have come, I suspect, had the opening singing group not been one of the publicised attractions.

I decided that I would rather do evangelism Youth For Christ's way than not do it in mine. It was moving to see the joy of Christian young people at leading their peers to Christ and the joy of their peers at coming to that point of commitment and decision.

I decided I was prepared to put up with the cacophony for the sake of seeing some kids in heaven, although I believe very firmly that it would be better, and perfectly possible, to lay on word-audible singing, with substantial content, that was just as alive and gripping.

The real involvement of congregations was minor and I am deeply convinced that such initiatives should not be taken until it is really possible to say that it is the work of the Christian church, of many denominations, in a whole area: really and unitedly wanting it, rather than just letting it happen for lack of the energy needed to discourage it.

This puts a great responsibility on those who believe in such work. By all means let them beaver away at its being widely and cordially wanted; but let them wait until it is. To our shame Christ's church is often more of a sleeping partner than a lively initiator and needs the catalytic effect of individuals, and para-church groups, with vision. Let them provide it, but let them not displace the role of Christ's church. Para-church organisations are not churches but the handmaids of the church.

My own summary of the mass evangelism question would therefore be that it must be kept very secondary to the primary evangelistic method, the vital development of a local congregation and the circles of human contact it represents. Let parachurch leaders initiate – and co-ordinate, if explicit consent is given them – the welling up of desire for a mass evangelistic campaign among many churches in a whole area; but let them await such widespread desire before acting.

William Abrahams in *The Logic of Evangelism* coheres the dialectic we have been exploring. People have tended to choose, he says, *either* converting *or* witnessing *or* discipling as the core issue. We should rather see them all as part of a process, a set of activities which have an eye to initiating people to:

- become part of the new community, the church.
- convince them of the truth of Christianity.
- provide them with moral vision.
- create a certain disposition within them ready for their encounter with God.

Abrahams adds two points to follow that encounter:

- receive and develop gifts from the Spirit.
- engage in specified spiritual disciplines.

Abrahams thus rejects the polarisation between nurture and evangelism, in favour of a whole continuum of God's activity. In fact the three agents in this dynamic of personal movement are God, the church and the evangelist.[17]

God is at work more pervasively than we allow when we either focus on a narrow technique or refuse to. A congregation's work of mercy, missionary support, special missionary endeavour: all die when engaged in merely for their own sake or ours, and can come alive at God's call and gracious anointing.

In developing natural, church-based evangelism, I suggest the best way to approach it is by following the 'management spiral' spelt out in chapter 11. A time of seeking God in prayer will be followed by stages of:

- Audit, establishing accurately the facts about one's catchment area: the natural boundaries, major meeting places, places of work, types of housing, age, sex and ethnic mix of the population, levels and types of employment. Caring involves counting! as every shepherd knows. Audit also involves our knowing the facts about ourselves: how much we can realistically achieve, our strengths and weaknesses.

- Brainstorm possible plans for action and choosing the one which best fits the congregation's resources and the needs and missionary opportunities in our area.
- Implement the chosen approach however simple, steadily monitoring it and periodically reviewing it.

It is effectiveness for which we long. The form the church's programme takes, must be decided by a prayerfully planning church: alive to God, to each other and to the hurting world around it. Might now be a suitable time to spend a while jotting on to paper some possible developments of that programme?

References

1. Source: *Scottish Church Census*, National Bible Society of Scotland, 1995.

2. R.C. Halverson, chaplain to the U.S. Senate, in the introduction to RPH, p. xiii, xiv.

3. O. Costas, *The Church and its Mission*, Wheaton, Tyndale, 1974, p. 89.

4. 1 Corinthians 14:24,25.

5. I acknowledge the sequence of thought in the article by Bryant Myers in *MARC Newsletter*, Bromley, MARC, No. 92-1, March 1992, p. 3, 4.

6. Epistle to Diognetus, vii, trans. in T. Dowley, ed., *History of Christianity*, Berkhamsted, Lion publishing, 1977, p. 69.

7. Martin Buber, *I and Thou*, Edinburgh, T&T Clarke, 1959.

8. Acts 26:28,29.

9. Matthew 7:15-23.

10. 2 Corinthians 13:5; Revelation 3:14-22.

11. W. Benn, *The Baxter Model*, Orthos booklet 13, Fellowship of Word and Spirit, Northwich, 1993. See also chapter 10 where there is fuller description of both Baxter's and Benn's work.

12. J. Finney, *Finding Faith Today*, Swindon, British and Foreign Bible Society, 1992, p. 25.

13. Many of us would be unhappy with some aspects of the Alpha course. Overall however its content is a simple, clear gospel introduction.

14. R. Bakke, *The Urban Christian*, Eastbourne, MARC, 2nd edn., 1989, p. 19,20.

15. J.R.W. Stott, in the TEAR Fund soundstrip, *Walk in his shoes*, Teddington, TEAR Fund, 1975. The accompanying booklet written by Stott, with the same title, was published by IVP.

16. Bill Hybels and Mark Mittleberg, *Becoming a Contagious Christian*, Amersham, Scripture Press, 1994.

17. W.D. Abrahams, 'The Logic of Evangelism', reviewed in *MARC Newsletter*, Eastbourne, MARC, No. 92-1, March 1992, p. 3, 4.

ORGANISATION

Chapter 13. Leadership

Chapter 14. Team Work

Chapter 15. Time Management

Chapter 16. Stress

CHAPTER 13

LEADERSHIP

The work, skills and styles of servant leadership

My servant David will be prince among them. I the Lord have spoken (Ezekiel 34:24).

Be shepherds, not lording it over those entrusted to you, but being examples to the flock (1 Peter 5:2,3).

A leader is a person with a magnet in his heart
and a compass in his head (Source unknown).

Many of the problems brought to me for exploration while Principal of a Bible College were matters of church leadership. This is not surprising in view of its difficulty and the surprisingly small teaching emphasis given in the New Testament to the leadership task.[1]

Why ever does the New Testament give so little instruction on this evidently momentous matter? It is an important question whose answer should have, I believe, a profound influence upon our whole approach to giving a lead in Christian work. We start from some first principles.

Christian leadership: a theological framework

Initiative comes from God, and God has a plan. He is going to bring everything in the universe into appropriate relationship to one head, Christ. That purpose includes the church making the gospel known to all nations, and herself being presented to Jesus Christ radiant and holy on the great day of judgement.

In carrying forward this plan God institutes pastor-teachers through whose lips he teaches his people and distributes talent among them. 'The saints,' says Calvin, 'are gathered into the society of Christ on the principle that whatever benefits God confers upon them, they should in turn share with one another.'[2]

Somehow there has to be established a connection between God's forward plan – the fact of it made known,[3] but its local detail obscure to us – and our practical Amen to it. The connection is that while God alone must lead and rule, he uses men and women to implement his will: not transferring to them his right and honour, yet doing his own work through them.[4]

Baptism, Eucharist and Ministry (BEM),[5] the so-called Lima document of the World Council of Churches, makes the same point. The church lives through the Holy Spirit, who sanctifies people and gives them particular gifts. In order to fulfil its mission the church needs people who are publicly and continually responsible for pointing to its fundamental dependence on Jesus Christ. Christ continues through the Holy Spirit to call people into the ordained ministry. As heralds and ambassadors they represent Christ and proclaim his message. As leaders and teachers they call people to submit to Christ's authority. As pastors they assemble and guide God's people.

The authority of the ordained minister, says BEM, is rooted in Jesus Christ who has inherited it from the Father (Matt. 28.18), and who confers it by the Holy Spirit through the act of ordination.[6] This act takes place within a community who by that act accord him public recognition. It is a consecration to service; his authority is authentic to the extent that it conforms to Christ's model of sacrificial love and service. Evangelicals might wish to say that the Church first recognises the anointing of the Holy Spirit on a life and then in ordination invokes its divine confirmation and continuance.

There are problematic aspects of BEM. It draws a distinction, between 'lay' and 'ordained' members, which BEM itself has difficulty defining and which certainly goes beyond scripture. Nonetheless the overall shape is biblical; it is a helpful confirmation of the underlying theology of leadership. The church is a community indwelt by the Holy Spirit; he anoints people for servant leadership, an anointing which the church recognises by ordination and respects by followership.

How God shows his regard for us when he takes us, each with a different part to play, to represent him! Christ, then, continues through the Holy Spirit to call people to, and equip them for, leadership.

Christian leadership: its tasks

At this point, uncertainty comes. What functions does Scripture ascribe to Christian leaders? Are they to 'direct' people in the normal managerial sense? There are biblical parameters on church polity, but is it in a pastor's job description, or a leadership team's, to formulate strategy? Who decides whether to have a building, engage in outreach activities and if so of what sort, build a retirement home for the elderly in the congregation?

Puzzlingly, our elders and betters are not much help to us at this point, although there is one vital principle to be gained from a brief survey of their contributions. All of them write so as to preserve Christ's authority for himself, and to protect the church from the leaders' usurping it. They deal, however, with the government and care of the church rather than its visionary leadership.

According to Calvin the power of the church is three-fold: doctrinal, juridical and legislative. As to doctrine the leadership is responsible to state what the church believes and to explain it. Jurisdiction centres around moral discipline. Legislation should primarily concern the proper conduct of worship with a view to the peace of the church.[7]

When it comes to identifying those responsible for presiding over its government, Calvin recognises only pastors and teachers as having any 'ordinary office in the church'.[8] He distinguishes between these two, although not very clearly: pastors are to proclaim the gospel and administer the sacraments, whereas teaching involves public discourse and private admonition.

Strategic organisational development (call it what you will; I mean, by that term, the whole prayerful, strategic, decision-taking process, whether simple or detailed) is simply not mentioned, even though so much of Calvin's life was dominated by precisely that question. It is hardly surprising that strategic missiological and organisational development have taken a back seat in the ecclesiology of those who have leaned heavily on Calvin.

Owen spells out eleven duties in the leadership task. It is interesting that only one could be regarded as 'giving a corporate lead'. The eleven are: to preach, pray, administer the sacraments, preserve the doctrine of the gospel, labour for conversions, comfort the tempted and weary, suffer with those who suffer, care for the poor and visit the sick, care for the rule of the church (see next paragraph), further fellowship between churches and live an exemplary life.

Rule in the church consists, for Owen, of three matters: to admit and exclude members; to direct the church to obey Christ's will; and to conduct the church's life and the church's meetings decently and in order. In the second of these Owen goes a little beyond Calvin.

Owen specifies in addition twelve duties of elders which I give because I find it a thought-provoking checklist for our practice: to oversee members' conduct, keep watch against divisions, warn members as to their duties, watch against their spiritual decline, visit the sick, advise deacons on the help of the poor, dispose of gifts for the poor, acquaint the pastor(s) of the state of the flock, consult with him about important things to be proposed to the church, protect its freedom, consult together about the church's duty and preservation and to maintain its peace and unity.[9]

The list is imaginative and there is a nod in the direction of strategic planning in the ninth duty: 'consult together about important things to be proposed to the church.' Owen does not specify, however, what these things might be and scarcely provides guidance on areas of responsibility and styles of leadership: matters which make so much difference to the morale and progress of a congregation.

BEM spells out a limited range of tasks for the ordained, defined by the functions of the threefold office:

- Bishops preach the Word, preside at the sacraments and administer discipline. They have pastoral oversight of an area and a responsibility for leadership in the church's mission and for inter-church relations.

- Presbyters minister the Word and sacraments and exercise pastoral care and discipline. They prepare members for Christian life and ministry.

- Deacons represent the church as servant, struggling with the myriad needs of societies and persons. They help read in worship and teaching, exercise a ministry of love and fulfil tasks of administration and 'governance'.

The report of the Assembly Council of the Church of Scotland to the General Assembly in 1990 proposed a sevenfold list of ministerial tasks which have value as a practical checklist: the ministry of Word and Sacrament; personal study and spiritual growth; pastoral work; mission to the parish; community involvement; service in the structures of the church; and organisation and administration.

Within those headings the following leadership tasks were identified: training; liaison; prayer; equipping the congregation (to share in pastoral care); oversight; encouraging congregational mission; and stimulating discussion on priorities.[10]

In its own quiet way there is a fair amount of leadership in the above list. Notice two dynamics in particular: to take a living interest in every department of the congregation's life, and to stimulate its planning and mission. It would be good to see, as the opening statement from which all duties flow, the responsibility of a church leadership team to provide the congregation with leadership, vision, oversight and Christian care. The emphasis would be bound to be given a more strategic note than the 'maintenance' ethos that so often pertains.

It is interesting that no 'success mentality' is prescribed for church leaders in the New Testament. Actually they are given hardly any leadership directions at all. Professor Howard Marshall has written, 'The New Testament generally is not greatly interested in leadership and ministry.' He points out that from the beginning there were persons who exercised oversight over other believers in the sense of spiritual care and discipline; and the distinction between local leaders and those involved in itinerant mission. Marshall goes on:

> The need for vision arises when we face the problem of 'What should the church do? Shall we change our location, establish a social centre ...?' Questions of this kind don't arise in the New Testament to any great extent. Nor does it ask who makes such decisions. There is no doubt that the church grows and spreads when it has people with 'vision', like Paul, who have a combination of personal qualities and divine guidance. There is little in the New Testament by way of theology of such people.... When we see people with such gifts of vision we should let them loose, while at the same time maintaining some kind of set-up to restrain them.
>
> The church was to test the spirits of the prophets; by analogy, it also needs to test the visions of the leaders without stifling the Spirit. If it can maintain the balance between freedom and constraint, it will have achieved its aim, but there is no set of simple rules to guide it in doing so.[11]

In other words, Marshall questions whether the New Testament supports the forward strategy responsibility I have proposed for church leaders. On the other hand, as he observes, the church grows and spreads whenever it has people with vision; and does not the command of our Lord, to preach the good news to every creature and to make disciples of all nations, require such people?

The task of Christian leading: its New Testament vocabulary

Consideration of the words used to describe the actions of the leadership team in the New Testament, points to such a responsibility.

Hegeomai, to lead, is used in Luke 22:26: 'The one who leads should be like one who serves.' Christian leaders will serve; but clearly they will lead. In Hebrews 13:7 and 23 the same verb is used. The lead involves speaking God's Word, living an exemplary life and watching over the congregation. The latter task involves at least monitoring the congregation's response to the preached Word as well as taking care of them.

Proistemi is to work as does a foreman or the player-manager of a football team, directing and presiding, conducting the affairs. In Romans 12:8, those who carry out this task are commanded to do so with zeal.

Epimeleomai, to take care and have the management of a situation, is used side by side with *proistemi* in 1 Timothy 3:5. Linked as it is with *proistemi*, management is the natural meaning of the word in this context.

Echein en hypotage, 'Keep under discipline', is used in conjunction with *proistemi* and *epimeleomai* in 1 Timothy 3:4,5. Ridderbos concludes, 'It can be gathered from this that the task of the presbyter-episkopos consists particularly in giving leadership to, and seeing that things go well in, the church.'[12]

Kopiao, to labour hard at something, is used both in a general way as in 1 Thessalonians 5:12 'respect those who labour among you, who are over you in the Lord and admonish you'; and specifically of the lead given in Christian teaching. 1 Timothy 5:17 mentions the honour (possibly, honorarium) due to elders who direct the affairs of the church well, particular those who labour in the Word and in teaching. 'It is to be inferred from this,' says Ridderbos, 'that the elders had the leadership of the church not only in terms of adminis-tration and church order, but also in a spiritual and essential sense.'[13]

Agrupneo means literally to keep oneself awake; it is used of the responsibility of church leaders to watch over and guard the congregation's lives as they give a lead (Heb. 13:17).

Noutheteo, to warn, guide and admonish, is a specific act of leadership much neglected and calling for courage and wisdom. In 1 Thessalonians 5:12 the church is commanded to respect this responsibility; the 'feel' of it is indicated two verses later where the same verb is used again: 'Warn those who are idle, encourage the timid, help the weak.'[14]

Poimaino, to shepherd. Comparing 1 Peter 5:1-4 with John 10:1-28 it is explicit that one responsibility of the shepherd is to give a lead, show the way: 'he leads them out, goes on ahead of them and his sheep follow because they know his voice.'[15] One only has to consider the strategic lead given by Jesus – knowing when it was time for a thing, sending the twelve out on mission, not yet going to Jerusalem, sticking to preaching despite the miracle hysteria – to see with what content he invests leadership.

From what we have seen so far it is clear that we leaders must give a lead, rather as the player-manager of a sports team might, staying alert and working hard to ensure that the church's life and ministry are conducted effectively.

Even those leaders who most eschew the language of strategic leadership can often be the most earnest and vigorous in exercising it. William Still, one of the great Church of Scotland leaders of the twentieth century, repeatedly called for the abandoning of church structures for the sake of the church as a family. It is noteworthy how clear his own aims were and how rigorously he excluded even minor planning which was in conflict with them. But he knew exactly how many people were in his parish, built a complete strategy around the results of that audit and regularly adapted the use of resources (people, time and plant) accordingly. This is but the exercise of strategic leadership.

What is the pastor whose gift is preaching, but who is weak on visionary leadership or organisational management, to do? Surely this is where the doctrine of the church comes in. Each Christian is given a manifestation of the Holy Spirit for the common good: given to each as God determines, leadership gifts included (1 Cor. 12:7-28). It is right both to expect and to pray that God will give the gifts needed for the life and demands of a congregation, whether to the pastor or to others. Leadership gifts that the minister lacks may be looked for in other members or potential members of the leadership team.

It is unrealistic however – as both the Bible and experience show – to expect corporate effort without a chairman or leader. There is plenty of corporate leadership in scripture, and a plural leadership is virtually prescribed in the New Testament, as we are about to see. But there is no evidence, from Old or New Testaments, of merely collegiate lead; always one person rises to the surface and actually takes the lead or is recognised as spokesman for the group decision. If the leadership team is accountable to God for *giving* the lead, the chairman or pastor is finally responsible for *ensuring* that it is given.

It is time, therefore, to consider what the New Testament says about these people.

The people who do the leading

For ordinary ongoing church leaders, the people who beyond the apostolic age occupy the leadership role in the Church, five main nouns are used.

The word *presbuteros* (elder) indicates that they should be mature Christians; *episkopos* (overseer or bishop) that they are to superintend or oversee the congregation's life. The two words are used interchangeably, the choice possibly made according to the emphasis intended in each context.

The usage of the words indicates a group of leaders in each church, with decision-making powers and responsibility to ensure care for needy Christians and to promulgate and defend the truth against the threat of false teachers. Their overseeing includes preaching and teaching so as to equip Christians for service, ruling on decisions, matters of discipline, good church relations, administration and the correction of error. The emphasis is consistently on the exercise of function rather than on status.

This non-status emphasis is confirmed by examination of the terms available to the New Testament writers but not used by them when teaching about the life of the church. They used some terms, for example, in describing secular officials, but eschewed them in writing of the Christian community. These include *archon* (ruler, prince, chief) which speaks of taking precedence, and *hegemon* (prince, governor): both words speak of standing, status and authority.

These words being part of the writers' linguistic currency, it is significant that they do not make use of them for the life of the church. Owen comments, 'Our Saviour will have nothing of lordship, dominance or pre-eminence in lordly power, in his church.'[16]

Küng points out that all the other words in secular Greek for civil and religious authorities are likewise avoided in connection with the ministers of the church. This is true not only of the basic word for hierarchy already mentioned (*arche, archon*), but also of the expression *hoi en telei*: those who wield power, an expression which speaks of 'the power of office'.[17]

The only time the word *poimen*, shepherd, is used, it is in conjunction with *didaskalos*, teacher. Pastor-teachers are the victory gift of the living Christ to the Church, to equip Christians for their works of service (Eph. 4:12). They are to give a lead through teaching and preaching scripture, keeping people growing in understanding and community.

The fifth word is *oikonomos*, steward or manager. 'The overseer is to be irreproachable as a manager of God's household.'[18] The steward is not so familiar a modern figure, but the Scottish factor who manages the estate on behalf of the laird is a good example of what is in mind. He is entrusted with running affairs in line with the owner's instructions; and while he has considerable freedom in day to day decisions, he is expected to reflect his master's mind and heart in his whole management style.

In the same way the church leader is responsible to take initiative and ensure the care and development of the church in harmony with the mind and heart of God as revealed in scripture, and he will give account of his stewardship in due time. Notice four lessons from this metaphor.

- Not to abdicate the responsibility to lead well. It will not do to plod along without giving thought to the church's best. 'He who manages, must do so with zeal and earnestness.'[19]

- The spirit of leadership is to be scriptural, not secular. The temptations here are both the obvious ones of dignity and status, and the subtle ones: secular models which produce visible results without the need of the Spirit. Scripture repeatedly warns us about them:

  'The Kings among the Gentiles lord it over them, and those who exercise authority over them call themselves Benefactors. But you are not to be like that. Instead, the greatest among you should be like the youngest, and the one who is leading like the one who serves.'

  'I have washed your feet. I have set you an example that you should do as I have done for you.'

  Peter spells it out in three parallel contrasts. We are to lead, not because we have to, but willingly and voluntarily; not greedy for money, but from a real desire to serve; not as lording it over, but being examples to the flock.

- A strong note is the wholeheartedness which Scripture associates with leadership. Paul was so concerned for the Church at Corinth that he had no peace of mind to take the opportunity in Asia Minor, and went to Macedonia to get news of them.[20] He toiled, went without sleep and felt daily the pressure of his concern for the church. When someone fell into sin, he burned with shame and distress (2 Cor. 11:27ff.). His prayer commitment to individuals and churches was constant night and day.[21]

- Another prominent feature of leadership in Scripture is a willingness to put one's head over the parapet and press for something in the teeth of opposition or difficulty. When Queen Athaliah destroyed all but one of the royal family, the priest Jehoiada said, 'The King's son *shall* reign, in line with God's promise.' Risking his own neck he arranged for Joash's coronation and Athaliah's execution (2 Chron. 23:3ff.). Far easier to go along with the then power in the land and stick to taking religious services; but Jehoiada courageously accepted two responsibilities of leadership: to protect God's revealed will from assault, and to be rid of that which assaulted and defiled it.

In all discipline one risks being considered harsh. Installing godliness, however, also requires our removing all that defiles.[22] William Still writes, 'If I have been able these years to do anything for the Lord, it has been because of that ruthlessness with evil which allows it no quarter.'[23]

Jesus' leadership in training the disciples bears scrutiny under the searchlight of the most modern leadership theory: the vision, planning, initiating, organising, directing, reviewing and developing of a work, totally in charge and yet giving each participant their autonomy and challenge. Our Lord was boss, yet quite unselfconsciously and to the development of his followers.[24]

The same was seen in the earliest days of the Church. Peter simply took the lead in the Jewish mission[25] as Paul did in the Gentile mission.[26] There was a ceaseless stream of energetic initiative; even their enemies complained they had turned the world upside down. Such leadership is vital for a church's progress; it is as simple as that.

We have seen what the Bible does and does not say about leaders. They are mature overseers but without overtones of status: they serve. That service is alert, hardworking, aimed at ensuring that things go as the Master, to whom they will render account, will want them to.

All leadership has its tone: aggressive or gentle, dictatorial or respectful. It is to these issues that we turn.

Christian leadership: its ethos

Christ-like leadership is spiritual. Its aims will be spiritual. Reicke comments on 1 Thessalonians 5:12, 'The task of the "those who are over you in the Lord" is in large measure their efforts for the eternal salvation of believers.'[27] Its methods will be spiritual. Paul comments, 'the weapons we fight with are not the weapons of the world. On the contrary, they have divine power to demolish strongholds. We demolish arguments and every pretension that sets itself up against the knowledge of God, and we take captive every thought to make it obedient to Christ.'[28] Its power is spiritual.

Paul was sensitive to the importance of competence in the delivery of his messages,[29] yet when making reference to the source of his effectiveness as a preacher he lays it exclusively at the door of the Holy Spirit: 'My message and my preaching were not with wise and persuasive words, but with a demonstration of the Spirit's power, so that your faith might not rest on men's wisdom, but on God's power.'[30]

Its practitioners are to be Spirit-filled people; the requirement is so fundamental that even in choosing men for the distribution of practical support the criterion was 'men known to be full of the Spirit and wisdom' (Acts 6:3).

Christ-like leadership is pastoral. Reicke on *proistemi* is again helpful. There are eight instances of the verb in the New Testament; in most cases it seems to have the sense of 'to lead, preside, direct, govern'; but the context shows in each case that one must take into account the sense 'to care for, to assist'. Exactly the same is true of *hegeomai* (to lead) and, of course, of *poimano*, to shepherd. The leaders are never running a business even when finance is being discussed; nor an amateur law court even when exercising discipline (although they will proceed as justly as the best law courts). They will ever conduct matters pastorally.

Christ-like leadership is biblical. The point is not as obvious as it seems. Some church leadership has become dominated by success to the exclusion of considerations that come higher in scripture. Not man's wisdom, nor denominational tradition, nor convenience but agreement with biblical principle is the way to honour God in our leading.

Christlike leadership is menial. I use 'menial' not in its derogatory sense but to emphasise that leaders are not to build a name for themselves nor to avoid the most menial of tasks but to *serve* their people. It can require a definite decision, to wash and bandage another's smelly feet. Let it be so: we are in the business of serving.

Christlike leadership is visionary, first, in *giving* people vision. The leaders I have been prepared to follow to death have shown me what the work is all about. They have believed anything is possible (or if they haven't, they have kept their introverted doubts to themselves); they have 'imagined' ways of having a go at a thing for Jesus.

Secondly, Christian leadership is visionary in being committed to expectancy as both an attitude (expect great things from God) and a way of approaching the whole future of our church (attempt great things for God). 'A vision is an attempt to articulate, as clearly and vividly as possible, the desired future state of the organisation.'[31]

Christlike leadership is sacrificial. It has no martyr spirit, no reluctance. 'Poor me' is absent from its vocabulary. If we think we are the one who is hard done by, we know nothing of Calvary love. Christian leadership says, with the Saviour, 'Doing God's will sustains me.' 'There is no limit we may place to our willingness to serve the flock,' says Eric Alexander, 'people should see in us absolute consecration to God's will: the spirit expressed in the words "I run to do your will."'[32]

Christian leadership: its form

Leadership in the church should be marked by *plurality*. As we have seen, words like 'elders' and 'overseers' (bishops) are plural words in the New Testament. A congregation is best led by a college or team of leaders, whatever title we give them.

Leadership in the church should be marked by *equality*. The New Testament knows no hierarchy. It goes to some lengths to avoid all thought of status or superiority and forbids all pulling of rank. Whatever the balance of duties between the different elders, they constituted one team of equals.

Leadership in the church should be marked by *diversity*. Some labour particularly in the Word and for the sowing of spiritual seed have a right of support from the church.[33] Some will be particularly wise in directing the affairs of the church, in a caring way: it is to be hoped that those who labour at preaching and teaching will be like that (1 Timothy 5:17).

Leadership in the church should be marked by *unity*. There was no doubt in the minds of the Council at Jerusalem that the requirement to be circumcised put the very gospel on the line (Acts 15:9-11). The place of the Jewish Law had the potential to split the early church; the leadership took the most vigorous steps to maintain unity. In other words, unity between Christians is to characterise in particular the leadership team.

Leadership in the church should be marked by *humility*. This fits Jesus' command that the greatest is to be as the youngest, and the leading one as serving.[34] As Michael Green points out, if we pause and consider the life of the Son of God as though it were not familiar to us, we have to be astounded. He deserved abject homage and the throne of the King of Kings; actually he turns up as a refugee, virtually anonymous, and after some local teaching and healing washes his friends' feet and suffers public execution. Our leadership model is the suffering servant[35] and his precept for greatness is to be the servant who humbles himself.[36] 'The way of the Christian leader,' says Henri Nouwen, 'is downward mobility.'[37]

Leadership in the church should be marked by *authority*. Let us deal with the limits of authority first. I have found no-one who expresses it better than Calvin did:

> The only way to build up the church is for the ministers themselves to endeavour to preserve Christ's authority for himself. Whatever authority and dignity the Spirit in Scripture accords to men, it is wholly given not to the men personally, but to the ministry to which they have been appointed; or (to speak more briefly) to the Word, whose ministry is entrusted to them.[38]

For Calvin the limits to authority are that it is used constructively, in the service of the people; to reserve Christ's authority for him alone; in matters of right belief and behaviour according to the scriptures, and of orderly running of the church; but not beyond that.

Given these essential limitations, we note that our Lord does indeed make over the exercise of authority to the church leadership. The model for its exercise being our Lord Jesus, it may not be manipulative or domineering; but nor is it to be abdicated.

Christian leadership styles[39]

Christian leaders do not always seem to be aware of the effect of their personal style. As Robert Burns observed,

> O wad some Pow'r the giftie gie us
> To see oursels as others see us!

The wise leader knows himself. For this purpose I include three classifications of leadership style in this section.

The first issue to be alert to is whether we are impulsive or planned in our leading. H.N. Maloney recognises three styles:

- Impulsive leaders live by reacting to what is happening. There is little planning ahead. They are quick to act and do not make time to think. Such leadership is feelings-based and tends to be characterised by defensiveness, empathy or both.
- Instinctive leaders fly by the seat of their pants, instinctively. They rely on their own giftedness and have an innate sense of how to build loyalty to themselves and their ideas. They know what is right and go for it. They are perceptive but often not very reflective.
- Intentional leaders 'function thoughtfully and with planning. They think of leadership as primarily a skill rather than a talent; they do not assume that their personalities are substitutes for training. They are open to being influenced by theories of group dynamics, problem solving and change. They are self-reflective, aware of their feelings, but believe that the best decisions are those that are made from a combination of vision, logic and emotions.'[40]

Secondly, do we lead from the front or follow everyone else's opinion – or, usually healthier, something in between? J.W. Alexander provides a second analysis by which to evaluate the way we relate to others as leaders.

- The dictator makes practically all the decisions for the church. A nod is sometimes given – sometimes more than a nod – in the direction of waiting on God and perceiving his will together; but the testimony of the followers is that this leader's discernment of the mind of the Spirit is the operative one. A dictatorial leader 'makes too many decisions, seeks too little counsel, delegates too little responsibility and spends too little time in committee meetings'.

- The consensus leader makes practically no decisions. He asks people their opinions on a given issue hoping the group will reach unanimity. He gives no firm lead, allows each successive opinion to dominate, has none of his own, minimally cuts through unnecessary verbiage or red herrings and inadequately summarises and clarifies. If unanimity cannot be reached, at least a high percentage of agreement is availed. A consensus leader makes too few decisions, seeks too much counsel, delegates too little responsibility and wastes too many hours in discussion.

- The participative-delegatory leader clarifies the question, seeks advice, invites members to participate in group discussion, balances his own and the group's decision-making, delegates to individuals the sub-decisions still to be made and uses committee time with careful stewardship.[41]

Clearly if my development of Alexander's categories is reasonable one is normally wise to lead a healthy and gifted team in a participative-delegation style. That might not be the case however with a leader who has stronger than average entrepreneurial and imagineering gifts in the context of a spiritually young congregation. Such a person might well give a more individual lead ('dictatorial') in the early stages.

Similarly, I have seen God blessing a time of quiet prayer with the leader facilitating a genuinely corporate decision, which is a kind of 'well-led consensus' leadership style. Alexander suggests that each group or leadership team should agree with its leader as to which style fits the members best; certainly the pastor or leadership chairman should be sensitive to the impact which a given style is likely to have on the church's life.

The third classification of leadership style examines the balance between a minister's concern for people and his concern for the task. Imagine a graph with concern for people along one axis, work concerns along the other; see figure 13.1:

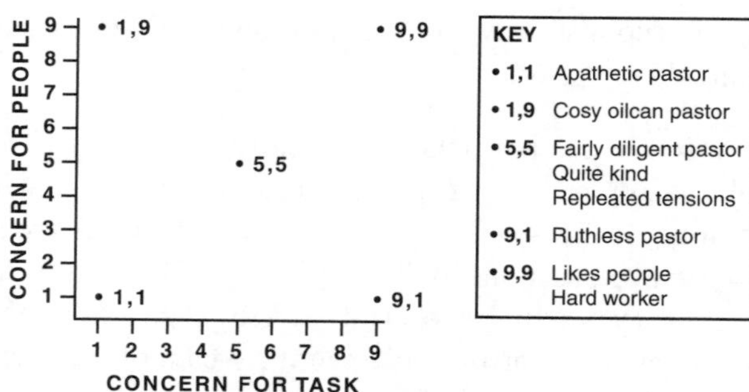

FIGURE 13.1[42]

The 9,1 pastor, ruthless, concerned for the task but not very much for the people, is busy and gets a lot done. A church, however, needs to be a hospital as well as an army: every authentic gospel ministry tends to be attended by the inadequate and the spiritually walking wounded. Jesus has a task for the Church but his emphasis is surely on people rather than on programmes as the means of its achievement.

It is Finney who uses the term 'oilcan ministry' of the 1,9 pastor, cosy but ineffective, who rushes round pouring oil on every squeak. This is the church whose stomachs and mouths tense up when anyone lays commitment on the line or suggests that the congregation actually gets something difficult done for the Saviour.

Ministers can similarly be found anywhere along the continuum from 3,3 (pretty lazy but awfully nice; the congregation's pet dog) to 7,7 (trying hard but rushed, anxious and too busy to be consulted about a problem).

Second best is good enough for the 5,5 pastor. They are not much good at saying no, so there tend to be too many efforts, on too many fronts, for the available resources. Everyone is catered for because they do not like to displease anyone, and campaigns are run on the 'occasional crisis' model rather than by a systematic process.

In theory the 5,5 position is comfortable. In fact it is exhausting, under-achieving and 'particularly difficult for the leader, who is the recipient of much hostility'.[43] Better to do a few things well.

How strong a leader must a pastor be? Omnicompetence is not a burden God lays on anyone. World-conquering visionary leadership is not God's expectation of every pastor in a leadership team. Acceptance of one's particular responsibilities is one thing; collapse because one is assuming someone else's proper contribution is quite another.

There are two approaches to this problem. First, a leadership group can be looked to, corporately, to identify and between them to provide what a particular congregation needs. Exercises exist to facilitate this division of labour.[44] Secondly, help can be given to ministers to develop in their identified areas of weakness and to provide them with the training to play their part well. Many a Christian follower has caused great pain by saying, 'Lead or get out of the way'[45] when quite possibly God was saying no such thing.

This is worth illustrating. The Baptist pastor Deans Buchanan writes of:

> a long and profound questioning of my calling, enforced on me by others. A dark night of the soul: when the iron in my soul weighed down the Spirit; when praise and prayer died on my lips; when fear of a broken future, and public failure, paralysed all action; when treading the winepress alone, I remember preaching, overwhelmed with feelings of unworthiness and hypocrisy.
>
> Two sayings, which I attributed to Luther. The first was for my self: 'I care not how far I fall, as long as I fall into the lap of God.' The second for my work (and my faith), the great encouragement to 'trust the bare Word of God', filled my soul: a broken man preached a pathetic sermon of a broken Christ from the unbreakable Word. Weeks later, when life began to flow again, I discovered that in the worst hour someone was utterly cured of a perfectionist attitude which was destroying health, life, work and service. The bare Word of God – at least I had still believed that – had done its work.'[46]

Let the other members of the leadership team be God's servants in this. Meanwhile let the pastor ask God's help in the unhesitating faith that God rewards those who earnestly seek him,[47] plan his own growth and simply do his best, leaving the issue of it all with God. God does not ask for more; he gives generously without finding fault.

Scripture commands the church to 'respect those who work hard among you, who are over you in the Lord and who admonish you. Hold them in the highest regard in love because of their work.'[48] The vital test is whether, by living in the biblical spirit of leadership, we have earned that regard.

For reflection

- The tasks of leadership, the people in leadership: is there any particular lesson that I can take from those sections for my own life?

■ Pause for a few minutes and reaffirm the great values of your leadership: sacrificial, menial, spiritual ...

■ How do you rate the plurality and equality of your congregation's exercise of leadership? Do you need to take any steps in the light of that evaluation?

■ Could you usefully make any adjustments to your leadership style in the light of Maloney's and Alexander's classifications, or thatof the management grid (p. 182)?

References

1. Writers who have drawn attention to this include J.D.G. Dunn, *Jesus and the Spirit*, London, SCM, 1975, p. 345-349; M. Harper, *Let My People Grow*, London, Hodder, 1977, 170f. quoting Dietrich Bonhoeffer's 'Life Together'.

2. INST., 4.1.3.

3. Ephesians 1:9-14.

4. My modification of INST., 4.3.1.

5. *Baptism, Eucharist and Ministry*, Geneva, WCC, 1982, Faith and Order Paper no.111. Hereafter BEM.

6. *Op. cit.*, Ministry section, II.B.19, p. 22.

7. INST., 4.10 throughout.

8. *Op. cit.*, 4.3.4.

9. J. Owen, 'The True Nature of a Gospel Church', *Collected Works*, Goold edition, vol. 16, 1968 reprint, Edinburgh, Banner of Truth, p. 30-143.

10. 'The Basic Tasks of the Ordained Minister,' Assembly Council Report, *Reports to the General Assembly of the Church of Scotland*, Edinburgh, 1990, p. 92ff.

11. I.H. Marshall, *The New Testament View of Christian Leadership*, paper presented at Scottish Evangelical Alliance Council, 1996, p. 8.

12. H. Ridderbos, *Paul: an Outline of his Theology*, London, SPCK, 1977, p. 458.

13. *Ibid.*

14. This threefold task is explored in S.M. Gilmour, 'Pastoral Care in the New Testament church', *NTS*, vol. 10, 1964, p. 393-398.

15. John 10:3, 4.

16. J. Owen, 'On the True Nature of a Gospel Church', *Works*, vol. 16, Edinburgh, Banner of Truth reprint, 1968, p. 32.

17. H. Küng, *The Church*, London, Burns and Oates, 1968, pp. 388-393 esp. 388f.

18. Titus 1:7; an expanded translation of *theou oikonomos* but quite

legitimate in view of 1 Timothy 3:5; Hebrews 3:2-6.

19. Romans 12:8.

20. 2 Corinthians 2:13.

21. 1 Thessalonians 1:2; 2 Timothy 1:3.

22. In 2 Kings 12:3 for example the narrator, having paid tribute to what Joash did achieve in his reform, records that he failed to remove the places of idolatry, the competitors for God in his people's lives.

23. W. Still, 'Elijah: leadership as exemplified in his life and work', unpublished address delivered at the Scottish Conference of the Teachers' Training Colleges Christian Unions, May 1971, no. 2, p. 43.

24. Luke 9:1-11; 10:1-21.

25. Acts 1:15; 2:14; 3:3ff, 12ff; 4:19; 5:3, 29; 10:46; 11:4.

26. Acts 13:16,46; 14:9; 16:3.

27. B. Reicke, TDNT, 6. 700-702, s.v. *proistemi* (transitive 'to set over'; intransitive 'to put oneself at the head' and therefore to govern or maintain). Reicke beautifully concludes 'In all these instances the verb has in the NT the primary senses of both 'to lead' and 'to care for,' and this agrees with the distinctive nature of office in the NT, since according to Luke 22:26, the one who is chief is to be as he who serves' (p. 702).

28. 2 Corinthians 10:3-5.

29. E.g. Acts 26:1-3.

30. 1 Corinthians 2:4f.

31. J.E. Means, *Effective Pastors for a New Century*, Grand Rapids, Baker, 1993, p. 143, quoting R.H. Kilmann *et al*, *Corporate Transformation*, San Francisco, Jossey Bass, 1988, p. 135.

32. E.J. Alexander, second talk on the eldership, St George's Tron Halls, Glasgow, 15 November 1986. He has written on the theme under the titles 'A Biblical View of the Eldership' and 'The Elder's Task' in *The Rutherford Journal of Church and Ministry*, vol. 4 nos. 1 & 2, Spring and Winter 1997.

33. 1 Corinthians 11:12.

34. Luke 22:26. Note in passing, with due deference to Collins (ch. 10, n. 37), that the contrast between leading and serving substantiates the traditional interpretation of *diakoneo* as humble, footwashing-style serving: vv. 25-27.

35. M. Green, *Called to Serve*, London, Hodder, 1964, p. 11-17.

36. Matthew 23:6-11.

37. H. Nouwen, *In the Name of Jesus: Reflections on Christian Leadership*, London, DLT, 1989, Sec. III.

38. INST., 4.8.1, 2.

39. S. Escobar, 'The Elements of Style in Crafting New International Mission Leaders', *Evangelical Missions Quarterly*, Jan. 1992, p. 6-15, explores five parameters of leadership style.

40. H.N. Maloney, 'Impulsive, Intuitional, Intentional: Three Styles of Leadership', *CTA newsletter*, no. 60, July 1992, Church Westcote, Clinical

Theology Association, p. 1-3.

41. J.W. Alexander, *Managing Our Work*, Downers Grove, IVP, second edition, 1975, p. 83-88.

42. This 'management grid' was proposed by R.R. Blake and J. Mouton, *Advanced Management Office Executive*, Houston, Gulf Pub. Co., 1962; *The Managerial Grid*, Houston, Gulf, 1967 and *The New Managerial Grid*, Houston, Gulf, 1978. It appears in Adair, p. 31 and is nicely discussed in J. Finney, *Understanding Leadership*, London, Daybreak, 1989, pp.16-21.

43. Finney, 1989, p. 20.

44. For example, in *What makes Churches Grow? A Basic Course on Church Growth*, London, British and Foreign Bible Society, 2nd edition, 1979, unit 4, pp. 10-13.

45. L. Gilbert, 'Lead or Get Out of the Way', article in *Leadership*, 1996, p. 126. Another great medicine for such times is C.H. Spurgeon, 'The Blind Eye and the Deaf Ear', chapter 22 in *Lectures to My Students*, Marshall Morgan and Scott, London, 1954, p. 321-355. I quote a paragraph on page 240.

46. D. Buchanan, 'Ministry and Suffering in the Life of Paul': article in *Ministry Today*, Journal of the Richard Baxter Institute for Ministry, Chelmsford, Issue 8, October 1996, p. 6-26.

47. Hebrews 11:6; James 1:5-8.

48. 1 Thessalonians 5:12, 13.

CHAPTER FOURTEEN

TEAM WORK

The stages and dynamics of corporate cohesion

How good and pleasant it is when brothers live together in unity! It is like precious oil poured on the head. It is as if the dew of Hermon were falling on Mount Zion. For there the Lord bestows his blessing, even life for evermore (Psalm 133).

Not many clergy are equally adept at social analysis and strategy, helpful counsel, faithful preaching and institutional administration. Different members of the body will usually serve different ones of these functions (D.L. Bartlett, *Ministry in the New Testament*, p. 198).

If ever a group existed for team life and fails to be itself without it, the church is that group. Every single picture of what it means to be a believer in the New Testament is a corporate picture. We constitute a body under one head, a nation under one king, a flock under one shepherd, a building under one coping stone.

Even the New Testament word for Christians, the Greek word *hagioi*, saints, is a plural word. It occurs in the singular just once, at the end of a letter when Paul says 'greet every saint in the fellowship'. Apart from that – a corporate greeting in itself – the word is 'Christians', plural, on every single occasion. The New Testament would not recognise an independent, freelance Christian; it is a contradiction in terms.

The team-ness of the church is the second fundamental blessing of the gospel. When Jesus Christ gives us new life, he makes us into a new community. He is our peace, who has made alienated people one, actually destroying, by the virtue of his death and resurrection, the barriers between them![1]

It follows, as light comes with the rising sun, that church life is a team event; and to the extent that it fails to be a team, it fails to be the church and is just another human club aping the real thing. No wonder such churches attract no-one; and no wonder the real thing is so attractive, for we are made to be together. It was a spy sent out by the emperor Hadrian who reported back wistfully, 'Behold, how they love one another!'

We are not only made to work together; we are commanded to. The reigning Christ gave pastor-teachers to prepare God's people for works of service: from him the whole body, joined and held together by every supporting member, grows and builds itself up in love as each part does its work.[2] In the final prayer before his execution our Lord prayed that we would be one in union with God so that the world might believe.[3]

Authentic ministry does not monopolise ministry; it multiplies it.[4] The New Testament is peppered with calls to stand side by side contending as one man for the faith,[5] to sink differences for the sake of working together.[6] Dynamic and warm-hearted team-ness is, hand in hand with doctrinal truth and practical holiness, the chief distinguishing mark of New Testament Christianity.

That is easier to say, however, than to live by. I think of the pastor, feeling his unworthiness, who asked a fellow church leader just before the service to pray for him: and was roundly told that that was no part of his duties. I think of the gifted officebearers who long to lighten their minister's overwork with appropriate support they are well able to give – and whose offers of help are shunned.

I think of the pastor friend who could not leave his house to go visiting, afternoon after afternoon, so devastated was he by reaction to his ministry: and of his church secretary, angry that he was lazy and did not love his people.

It is interesting that Bartlett's study of ministry in the New Testament specifically examines conflict resolution in successive New Testament writers.[7] We may draw comfort from the fact that it featured as a problem in its own right from the birth of the church.

The point does not need labouring. Team-ness is not additional to, but part of, the gospel. Yet the full team-ness of gospel work is one of the hardest aspects of Christian service to achieve, and its distortion is far and away the chief source of loneliness and resentment in Christian workers. Steps can, however, be taken to make discord less likely, to make corporate action go well and to resolve things when it doesn't.

The task of this chapter, therefore, is to set guidelines for a biblical and practical approach to achieving good teamwork. The behavioural sciences have clarified much about the skills that contribute to it and we can learn from their findings.

The number and the roles of teams in congregations vary hugely between churches. A church committed to simplicity of structure might have only a leadership team and a financial board, both meeting quite rarely. Other churches will have many more: worship, Christian education, parish mission, social action and a dozen others. The same principles, however, enhance their functioning.

Hind suggests eight skills which help at all stages of team work:

- Presenting yourself to others, e.g. by dress and appearance;
- Being open, e.g. not withholding information;
- Being sensitive to others' needs and feelings;
- Giving space for others to contribute;
- Accepting criticism and not taking it personally;
- Working with confidence;
- Working to the best of our abilities;
- Acknowledging (or, accepting responsibility for taking) the role of the leader.[8]

According to the New Testament, Christian service should be characterised by plurality and diversity (cp chapter 13). One of the joys of having the preached Word used by God is to see people develop and to see ideas and enthusiasm coming forward into the team life of a church. Let such team-ness be part of our expectation, something we encourage.

Choosing our team members

We often have little choice over the selection of people with whom to work. Doubtless that is healthy: we can choose our friends but are given our families, and it is the same with the church family. Quite often however we need to add to a team or appoint one for special work. What principles guide us?

Jesus chose a rich mixture of people to be his twelve disciples; and not one, as far as we can see, on 'worldly' criteria: no religious professionals, no managing directors. At no time in the ministry is it more vital to be close to the Lord than when selecting teams, especially those individuals who will be in leadership.

Choosing teams and leaders is a gift. It was said of Michelangelo that he could look at a rough rock and discern the figure that was in it, ready to be made apparent in all its glory by his sculpting; that is how to be thinking of our members as we plan the formation or enlargement of teams.

There are times when one can narrow the choice. For certain purposes I classified a church by 'VCL' (visible commitment level), i.e. by their attendance at the life of the church, giving a rating of A to D. The 'As' were those who already had some identified role: elder, youth leader, pastoral visitor. The 'Bs' were others who attended at least three times a month. The 'Cs' were the less regulars; 'Ds' we rarely saw!

The list was primarily fuel for pastoral understanding and prayer but it had real value when forming committees or teams. A key officebearer – church secretary or treasurer, say – would be sought among the 'As', applying the kind of criteria Scripture lays down in passages like 1 Timothy 3:1ff.[9]

When we ran an audit of the parish for the purpose of planning outreach, however, the audit team (except for the chairman) was chosen from 'Bs'. People with genuine commitment but minimal responsibility in the church grew in knowledge and understanding of the area for which we were responsible to God. Many grew in other ways too; and we had spared the 'As' who were already too busy in the church from being emotionally blackmailed into yet another task. Some individuals are particularly gifted in discerning what people are capable of becoming in Christ; a gift to draw on at times of selection.

Natural strengths and weaknesses should be considered but must not be determinative. One person is a marvellous visionary and sees the picture both whole and optimistically; another is a nuts and bolts person, excellent and conscientious at a given task but a drag on a strategic planning committee. But it's back to Michelangelo (see above): we do well to be humble and open to what a person is becoming in Christ, whose appointments often cut clean across the obvious criteria.

The choice of David out of all Jesse's sons, to be the future king (1 Sam. 16:6-13) is packed with insights on this; I have seen great blessing accrue to a church from jettisoning practically every sensible criterion in favour of an uneducated and inappropriately skilled person on whom there was the stamp of God's anointing.

Group structure

For all that most churches run simple committee or mission team arrangements, it is worth choosing a committee structure that services the group's task: for different structures have different strengths. One church team might be best structured in a way that supports a person's entitlement to give a firm lead, while another – a house group run on a rota basis, for example – might prefer a structure that actually minimises 'lead' in favour of shared coordination.

The structure of a group, in fact, helps to explain each member's role and sets patterns for communication. It clarifies where authority lies, and its extent. It establishes lines of responsibility.[10] The sort of issue that can be at stake in a congregation is – to whom is an elder responsible for the discharge of his duty to visit his district: to the pastor, or to the session clerk or church secretary? If it be answered 'to the leadership team' there is still the issue, who is the more appropriate person to monitor such diligence, or to whom should a member turn if they seek a change of elder for some reason?

Confusion and hurt feelings can often be avoided by drawing up clear lines of accountability. It pays, therefore, to be aware of the different possibilities. I am drawing from Cormack's nomenclature and a selection of his options.[11]

In a *line* structure there is one senior person to whom all the others report directly. The advantage of the structure is its simplicity; there is no doubt who is in charge and decisions can be fast. The corresponding disadvantage is perhaps over-dependence on one person.

A modification is the *cabinet* structure; this was how Jesus related to the twelve disciples. He related directly to all twelve but communicated more with, and was closer to, an inner group among the twelve. The dangers are that such an approach can be invidious and divisive; but the cabinet structure does reflect what actually happens very frequently, for it is unrealistic to expect a leader of a large group to consult equally with all. It also prepares the cabinet for leadership either in the future or in the leader's absence.

In a *staff* structure the leader remains responsible for the whole group, but 'staff' or advisers, perhaps a secretary and vice-chairman, provide support to the leader and sometimes training to the team. A typical church example might be when a minister remains leader of the permanent group of officebearers but an assistant pastor or youth worker is appointed. The focus is on the support they give. The structure requires good relationships between leader and staff.

The focus in *functional* structures is on task achievement. The chairman has several vice-chairmen, each responsible for a team with an assigned task: finance, music, education, pastoral care. The structure is efficient; the risks are competition between resources (shall I go to the choir or the prayer meeting) and isolation of the leader.

In a *matrix* structure there are no leaders. The focus is away from seniority and on to team equality. One of the team might act as coordinator or each person does so in turn. An example would be a Bible study group where each person takes turn in leading; or I think of a period when four of us, pastors, met monthly in total confidentiality in each other's manse in turn. The equal and opposite dangers in the matrix structure are lack of planning because no-one is responsible, and domination by the strongest personality.

On the *core group* model a small inner group are driving a work but either call on others to join them for specific tasks (strategic planning; financial monitoring) or buy in the services of other individuals or groups to achieve given tasks – perhaps regular cleaning, catering or financial reporting. A church example would be a small group of elders running an independent evangelical church, sharing the chairmanship and overseeing the different works – outreach team, children's work, pastoral care.

Any group is only as good as its members, but it can greatly ease functioning if the kind of structure one intends is clear to all. The ever-present danger is individuals making a kingdom for themselves, even in the kingdom of God (don't we know it). The price of freedom from this is eternal vigilance, clear communication and unfortunately, on occasion, action by the rest to reserve the kingship for Jesus. Above all, 'the organisational form must support the life of Christ's body, not simply help to maintain an institution.'[12]

Monitoring the team's performance is dealt with under the management cycle in chapter twelve.

Delegation

The more I read on management theory, the more impressive is Jesus' delegation evidenced in Luke 9:1ff. and 10:1ff., the sending out of the twelve and then the seventy-two. It is clear that our Lord had planned well in advance. Then he gave them authority and power, delegated the task, instructed them clearly and gave guidance on how to respond when they were accepted or rejected while on mission. Do we do as well when sending workers to their tasks?

When the workers returned the debriefing is immensely moving.

The seventy-two reported back; Jesus improved the occasion by explaining the tremendous significance of their success ('I saw Satan fall'), along with further instruction, warning, prayer and closing encouragement – as the management manuals would say, motivation.[13]

Good delegation 'enhances the quality of the work, the capabilities and commitments of the employees, and the efficiency and power of the manager. Few other management practices can make such a claim.'[14] Delegation for us involves volunteers as often as employees but its eight guiding principles still hold:

- Delegate clearly and completely. Is the person to gather information or make decisions? How often to report back? Satisfying what criteria so he can know how well he is doing? What level of initiative – in ascending order, is he to wait for instructions, make recommendations, act and then report or just run the show?

- Allow participation: both parties take part in deciding which assignment is delegated and how it should be accomplished.

- Give authority commensurate with responsibility.

- Work within the team structure: through our sub-leaders rather than by-passing them, and with all the relevant people informed. If the organist or treasurer says, 'I didn't know you'd given one of the choir the job of choosing and buying the next hymn book', we've failed to keep the right people informed and probably transgressed their areas of reference.

- Give adequate support: and reward in public, criticise in private.

- Make a practice of it. Do it because it's a good thing to do, not just to be rescued in a crisis. Delegate pleasant and unpleasant tasks alike, and to appropriate people.

- Avoid upward delegation. Subordinates sometimes give the leader the job back, either obviously ('I've done this bit – back to you now') or subtly: they ask how to solve the problem and hold the leader accountable for the result. They have become the manager, and the leader is worse off than when he started. Instead, ask 'What do you think?', return the task again, support the diffident, stand by the delegation.

To delegate acceptably, however, also calls for practical sense and good relationships. Garratt's overview of the skill is:

- make any introductory remarks
- describe the assignment
- set objectives
- indicate performance standards
- allow questions
- check understanding
- indicate authority/responsibility
- use examples or illustrations
- indicate review and follow up procedure[15]

Remember to thank them; to specify the level of initiative expected;[16] and, in formal delegation of sizeable tasks, to make a written note of the arrangement and give a copy to the person.

The abounding Christian team always has a leader who keeps, and teaches, our primary loyalty to Jesus Christ. He is also loyal to the church. He seeks his people's growth and fulfilment, crucifying every temptation to an ego trip or the abuse of power and influence. To modify Cormack's model for high morale:

- The *leader* shares the challenge, sets the example and communicates faith in God.
- The *team members* give of their best, emulate the leader and believe in God, in themselves and in each other.[17]

Stages in the development of a team[18]

Every congregation with a history of having a full time pastor is familiar with the ministerial honeymoon phenomenon. For the first year the pastor can't do anything wrong, for the second he can't do anything right. Then, steadily, both parties learn to see each other's strengths and weaknesses in perspective and establish a *modus vivendi*, usually charitable and affectionate.

This pattern in fact fits a sequence of four stages which groups tend to go through in their development. Forewarned is forearmed: the stages are worth knowing about. Tuckman has proposed titles for the four stages: forming, storming, norming and performing.[19] At each stage there is a characteristic style of relationship between members of the team, in which there is something to achieve if the group is to work well together; and each of these developments calls for identifiable skills.

In Stage 1, 'forming', members of the group find out what ways of behaving are acceptable ('testing'), present themselves to and adapt to each other and the group's work. Each adjusts to those more shy or more forceful than himself and decides how assertive to be if the group starts going in a direction with which he is uncomfortable.

Quite early on, one or more individuals tend to come to the fore; the others feel safe to rely on ('dependence') the lead they are giving. 'We have found the Messiah.... Here is a true Israelite.... How do you know me?... I saw you under the fig tree ... you are the Son of God':[20] these are testing and dependence exchanges. We see their equivalent in church groups.

The group's *task* in stage 1 is that of orientation to its work, deciding what information is needed, perhaps what values are guiding such choices, learning the ground rules of the work. In the Gospels we see Jesus indicating that fishermen will become fishers of men in order to further God's reign. Here are ground rules underlying their task as future Apostles. Every church with a new pastor, every house group and summer mission team, goes through such a stage and will do its whole work better if it achieves this orientation maturely.

I therefore want to write in some detail about the *skills and attitudes* which facilitate a positive experience of stage 1 in both the team's relationships (what the behaviourists term 'group structure') and its addressing its work.

At stage 1 in particular the sociable use of relationship building can be of inestimable benefit. Be definite and pleasant from the first minute when greeting people. Smile! Look at the colour of the person's eyes because we want to meet them and know more about them. Initiate conversations, ask open questions and then really listen to the replies because we esteem the person.[21] Pleasantly and positively assert our viewpoint on initial discussion rather than being either aggressive, dominating or mouselike. All these make for a *team* experience.

A word about our ability to behave in such ways. C.S. Lewis writes somewhere of living 'as if' in the Christian life. We might be feeling terrified of taking a lead in a service but if that is our role we have to act 'as if' in order to do it well. This is not hypocrisy but faith, for it is rooted in the 'since you have been called by God' of our work.

Vulnerable personalities often need this courage of faith in a team setting, relating to others not on the basis of their feelings about themselves (which are both fluctuating and fairly irrelevant) but 'living as if'. The Christian psychiatrist Ruth Fowke comments:

> There is a way for weakness to become strength. This happens when that weakness, whatever it may be, is consciously accepted and given over to Jesus Christ. This giving must be a deliberate act, undertaken with expectation of its efficacy. Many people find it helpful to pray audibly about this, because they then have to be quite definite about their intentions and their requests. Having committed the weakness, and the worry about it, to Christ, one must not expect to sit back and feel different. It is only as one gets on with living, and does the difficult things, that strength to do them comes. The power of God only becomes available as one draws upon it in the time of need; it is not given in advance.[22]

Stage 2: 'storming'. The honeymoon of the group does not last; nor should it. On any team that cares about the shared work there will be differences of opinion on how to go about it ('intragroup conflict'). We see it as couples adjust to marriage, especially older couples who have firm opinions and have learned independence; it surfaces when a church mission team becomes tired and different opinions are aired; congregations express it as new music or some other change is introduced.[23] Difference of opinion can be strong and team members hostile towards one another or to the leader as they express their viewpoint. Thus we see Judas complaining, 'that could have been sold and the money given to the poor', or Peter taking Jesus aside and saying, 'Never, Lord, that will never happen to you!' No wonder Tuckman called this the storming stage.

The *task* to do well in stage two is the emotional response to the demands of the team's work, as illustrated by Judas and Peter above. They were expressing the discrepancy between their personal orientation and that demanded by the task. Thus a leadership group might vote for parish visitation but stare glumly at the floor or individually resist commitment when it comes to volunteering for tasks.

The *skills and attitudes* which facilitate this second phase of a group's development deserve more space than is possible in this chapter, for conflict resolution is a major theme in the New Testament[24] and can occupy more emotional space than any other single element in Christian leadership. Hind sagely comments, 'at this stage of the process we should use our higher level personal skills'.[25] He identifies negotiation, critical thinking and assertive communication skills. Textbooks have been written on each of these and it is only possible to outline those aspects of these which I have found firmly practical. They centre round conflict resolution and involve skill in assertion, non-assertion (passivity) and aggression.

A comment, first, about the word assertion. It can be used in a bad sense. Our Lord eschewed self-assertion; our salvation depended on his doing so. In that sense we are called to follow him.[26] It can also be used, however, in a good sense. It is widely so used as a technical term, with a defined meaning, in treatments of conflict resolution. It is in this latter sense that it is briefly defined, and used, in the ensuing paragraphs.

We all find it difficult to disagree without sensitivity about hurting people's feelings, and difficult to accept criticism reasonably and without feeling hurt. The phase two situation, therefore, in which the defining feature is disagreement or even conflict, is a critical area for a team's functioning. *Assertiveness at Work* by K. and K. Back[27] is a fine study of the skills that enable us to work neither aggressively nor non-assertively but assertively.

They define aggression as standing up for our view in such a way that we violate the rights or dismiss the beliefs of others. Non-assertion involves not standing up for our point of view, or doing so in such a way that others can easily disregard them, e.g. in apologetic or self-effacing ways. Assertion is standing up for our own rights [28] in such a way that we do not violate another person's; expressing our opinions in direct and appropriate ways.

Take an example. You as pastor have been asked to spend more time on visiting members in their homes. Our response would be aggressive if we said, 'What! This parish is killing me with overwork already. There's no way I can do more visiting.' A non-assertive response would be, 'Yes, I know it's my fault, there just don't seem to be enough hours in a day. I'm useless.' An assertive response could be: 'I do appreciate that members like to be visited by the minister. However, I don't see that I can add to my current prioritised visiting schedule with my workload as it is at present. Shall we discuss a team approach to this?'

Aggressive contributions stir up conflict by emphasising disagreement and down-playing agreement. They dismiss others' opinions, take an entrenched position, put down alternative views. Aggressive contributors see things in black and white; can't be wrong; won't accept others' right to disagree with them.[29]

Non-assertive contributions underplay their own value and are abandoned as soon as they are examined or questioned. Non-assertive contributors gloss over disagreements and express their viewpoints apologetically if at all. They see disagreement as conflict, and avoid conflict at all costs because it hurts. They fear to upset others by disagreeing and fear the loss of face involved in being wrong. They feel they have no right to disagree. Often the result is that intelligently perceived problems are not considered and decisions are taken to which not everyone is committed.

Assertive contributions involve agreeing and disagreeing openly and stating our viewpoint firmly and clearly[30] without putting ourself or others down. K. and K. Back suggest that 'I' statements can help the clear, yet constructive, statement of doubt or difference: 'I see a difficulty in that; can we get round it?' or 'I don't agree that everyone need be exhausted if we run a bookstall, because....' Assertive contributors accept people's having different opinions, and that it is desirable to state them. They do not assume that disagreements need lead to conflict; they recognise that opinions might be not right and wrong, merely different.

We see examples of firm assertion in Galatians chapter two, e.g. Paul's private visit to those recognised as leaders of the Church. It evidently involved open statement of the issues (circumcision, v. 4f, and recognition of each other's respective mission fields, 6-10), full acceptance of each other's right to a definitive viewpoint, esteem of each other in the process of stating differences (implied, e.g. v. 7), recognition of the other party's position, decision about a win-win way forward and a brotherly handshake on the deal as its conditions were negotiated (v. 9, 10).

It seems there was no pouting, no secretive forming of cabals to manipulate the decision-making; they focused on the issues not the personalities, worked to discern the hand of God (v. 7) and resolved the affair around the principles of the gospel (v. 5) and its implications (v. 10).

If assertiveness (as thus defined) is the best spirit in which to approach disagreement, there are times when happy difference of opinion becomes painful conflict. David Cormack suggests ten operating principles for resolving it, all with their origins in the Bible:

- The initiative is ours, whether we are in the right or the wrong: Matthew 5:23,24 and 18:15.
- Act now: 1 John 2:11.
- Keep our own (inner) peace: John 14:27.
- Share our peace: 2 Corinthians 5:19.
- Confess our part: Romans 7:21, 24.
- Renounce conflict: Luke 17:3,4.
- Forgive those who act against us (Matt. 6:12) rather than deny that there is anger, smile as though it does not hurt or fake as though all is forgotten.
- Keep the conflict contained: stick to the original issues and the original parties involved: Proverbs 17:9.
- Listen.
- Focus on our own faults: 2 Corinthians 12:20, 'You may not find me as you want me to be.'[31]

How shall we use these operating principles? Cormack suggests three stages corresponding to the phases of conflict. Conflict escalates by the processes of separation, divergence and destruction; reconciliation by those of disengagement, convergence and integration.

In disengagement we stop fighting back and pursuing our own aims at any cost. In convergence we come together, not just in attitude but in physical meeting, and share the facts, our feelings, our visions of how things could be. At the integration stage, unity is now a joint goal and both sides are working together, each as the other's keeper. Cormack suggests repentance, confession and forgiveness are the costly steps in achieving unity: 'Who will start the bidding?'[32]

Hurt feelings and people insisting on their own way are such regular features of pastors' pain that I feel justified in having spelt out some assertiveness and conflict-resolving skills in detail. For an excellent treatment of the issue, Whetten and Cameron, pp. 400-428, is highly recommended.[33]

Hurt feelings, of course, are not always appropriate! David Cormack lists some common irrational beliefs; among them:

- It is necessary for an adult to have the love, approval and respect of all those around them.
- It is bad when things are not entirely how I would like them to be.
- The future is determined by the past.

- Things are getting better if only we don't interfere. So don't rock the boat.[34]

Part of God's purpose in allowing the storming phases of a church's life, surely, is to grow our maturity in such things. He is more concerned for our holiness than our happiness (although there is no joy like that of deepening holiness).

To whatever extent we need the negotiating skills, however, a measure of 'storming' is a regular stage, often healthy and not infrequently repeated, in the maturing of a group to excellence in cooperation and achievement.

The New Testament does not lead us to expect that the result will always be the team continuing. Paul and Barnabas had such a sharp disagreement over whether to take John Mark on the second missionary journey (he had dropped out half way through the first), that they parted company.[35] The whole experience must have caused them and the church great pain; and yet in God's goodness the result was two missionary journeys in place of one. This included John Mark's development under Barnabas the 'Son of encouragement', so much so that at the end of Paul's life Mark was one of those who was a significant help to him.[36] God over-ruled it to lead to 'wider and fuller service'.[37] This serves to remind us that even alienation and separation need not be disqualifying, such a patient and redeeming God have we.

Stage 3: 'norming'. In the third stage in a group's maturity, members adjust together and the group develops cohesion. People accept each other, warts and all. The expression of family-ness gives the church or team a feeling of unity and identity, morale develops and enthusiasm bubbles up: the sense that something significant is going on here.

The *task* facing the team for its development of maturity is one of open, confident exchange of 'relevant interpretations',[38] working with real insight and sharing in the church's or group's work. Team members grow in their own opinions, their contribution and their commitment to both the work and each other. The group develops its own procedures and members set themselves to productive work.

The *skills and attitudes* of this 'settling into productive working together mode' include: sheer enthusiasm; esteem and concern for the others in the team; support of those who are going through a bad patch; encouragement of the diffident; allowing equal opportunity to everyone to contribute. This latter can involve real self-restraint by those who contribute most, especially if they are extroverts with skills appropriate to the team's work. To hold back when we know the right answer or best next step, simply to give someone space to make a contribution we could possibly have made better, calls for real thoughtfulness!

Sensitivity is therefore an asset, as is the capacity to give and accept criticism kindly and constructively.[39] It is the attitude that we are sharing in this together; that it is important, momentous and exciting work, that we are privileged to be working with these particular people and like them so much; and a sacrificial willingness that has no reluctance about it. It is such appetite, for this task, with these people, that most brings glow to 'norming'.

Stage 4, the 'performing' stage is Tuckman's title for a team getting on with the work. The structure of the group has ceased to be an issue and the group's energies can be invested in the work. Stage 4 is characterised by the emergence of solutions and a good job being done.

What *skills and attitudes* help us really contribute to a team's performance? I would highlight the following.

Take an interest, and show an interest: get involved. That way, if we are quiet, we are more likely to have something to say when asked. Read the minutes, make enthusiastic suggestions to fellow team members, do your homework.

Think of others in the team. Wonder how they are, ask after them, notice when they are looking tired. Express appreciation of their contribution. During a discussion, if we see that flash of an eye or raising of an eyebrow that indicates an idea, ask if they have any comment to make. If we are talkative or confident, ration our contribution to give others space.

Assume the best and give others the benefit of the doubt. Once when I was shaking hands at the church door a member turned right away from me and I felt sure I must have done something to offend her. I phoned her to find out. Nothing of the sort, she had simply been tugged from behind just as we had started to greet each other. In relationships, behave with warm confidence on the assumption that all is well. We shall be helping to make and keep it that way.

Be a team player: not independent but cooperative and willing.

Subjugate self to the team's life: we are all a bit odd and the defining feature of maturity is when our continuing weaknesses do not hinder performance or spoil relationships. Is not this the delivery in practice of our daily spiritual death and resurrection?[40]

The importance of monitoring a team's performance, and instruments for doing so, are included in chapter 11 and its appendices.[41]

There is a balance worth being aware of in this regard, between getting the work done, maintaining the team's spirit and developing the individuals within it.[42] Usually called the three-circles model, it assumes that the needs of all three are interdependent – to neglect one, jeopardises them all. See figure 14.1:

FIGURE 14.1 Three circles model of team work balance

Thus if a team fails to achieve its task, both team morale and the fulfilment of the individuals will suffer. To ignore or undervalue an individual is de-motivating, impairing both team-building and the achievement of the task; and a spirit of disaffection and distrust in a team also affect its performance and the individuals involved.

A wise pastor, therefore, will be alert to nourish all three: the unique individuality of the members, the coherence of the team and the quality of work done.

Team work is a delicate instrument but has boundless possibilities for the glory of God and the salvation of men and women. 'How good and pleasant it is when brothers live together in unity! It is like precious oil poured on the head. It is as if the dew of Hermon were falling on Mount Zion. For there the Lord bestows his blessing, even life for evermore.'

Concluding exercise

- 'Forming, storming, norming, performing': do any of my church committees or groups need special attention based on the stage they are going through?

- How good a balance of team spirit, task achievement, and individual development am I achieving? Does any of these need more, or less, of my time just now?

References

1 Ephesians 2:12-21.

2. Ephesians 4:7-16.

3. John 17:20-23.

4. E.g. Exodus 18:17-23; Luke 9:1-6; 10:1-24; Ephesians 4:11f.; 2 Timothy 2:2.

5. E.g. Philippians 1:27.

6. E.g. Philippians 4:2,3.

7. D.L. Bartlett, *Ministry in the New Testament*, Minneapolis, Fortress, 1993. Unfortunately he draws on a partial canon, omitting several sections of the New Testament that are vital for any New Testament doctrine of ministry. This reduces the value of his contribution very considerably.

8. D. Hind, *Transferable Personal Skills*, Sunderland, Business Education, 1989, p. 223-227; compare P. Beasley-Murray, *Dynamic Leadership*, Eastbourne, MARC, 1990, p. 53.

9. See chapter 13.

10. D. Cormack, *Team Spirit*, Eastbourne, MARC, Second edition, 1990, p. 60.

11. Cormack, 1990, p. 59-74; compare also King, 1987, p. 97-112.

12. L.O. Richards, *Church Leadership*, Grand Rapids, Zondervan, 1980, p. 284.

13. Luke 10:17-24.

14. Whetton and Cameron, p. 113. There are as many delegation checklists as books and seminars on the subject. What follows is based on Whetton

and Cameron with guidelines learnt elsewhere from both theory and practice.

15. S. Garratt, *Manage Your Time*, London, Fontana, 1985, p. 108.

16. Whetten and Cameron spell this out in more detail: p. 116-118.

17. Cormack, 1990, p. 139-145.

18. For this section of the chapter I use the terms group, team, congregation and church interchangeably.

19. B.W. Tuckman, 'Developmental Sequence in Small Groups', *Psychological Bulletin, 1965,* Vol. 63, No. 6, p. 384-399.

20. John 1:41, 47, 48, 49.

21. Hind, p. 235.

22. R. Fowke, *Coping with Crises*, London, Hodder & Stoughton, 1968, p. 15.

23. C. Ashton, *Church on the Threshold*, London, Daybreak, 1991, p. 79-81 outlines wise approaches to this and to different views on re-baptism.

24. It is interesting that D.L. Bartlett, *Ministry in the New Testament*, Minneapolis, Fortress, 1993, identifies conflict resolution as one of the four dynamics to examine in each major section of the New Testament corpus, amounting to 15% (24 pages out of 156) of his examination of the material. It deserves all the skill we can bring it. Unfortunately Bartlett's treatment is weak, amounting only to the question, where authority lies; but it is a significant indicator of the prominence of the issue even in the pristine Church.

25. Hind, p. 236.

26. Philippians 2:3-11; 1 Peter 2:18-25.

27. K. Back and K. Back, *Assertiveness at Work*, Maidenhead, McGraw-Hill, second edn., 1991.

28. In a sense Christians have abandoned their rights but here 'rights' is used in the valid sense of something to which we are entitled; or others are, from us.

29. Back, p. 51.

30. Back, p. 52.

31. Cormack, 1990, p. 91-98.

32. Cormack, 1990, p. 99-102.

33. Whetten and Cameron, p. 400-428. Table 7.2 on p. 403 ('A comparison of five conflict management approaches') is quite brilliant.

34. Cormack, *Peacing Together*, Eastbourne, MARC 1989, p. 178.

35. Acts 13:13; 15:36-40.

36. 2 Timothy 4:11.

37. G.M. Philip, *Congregational Record* of Sandyford Henderson Memorial Church, Glasgow, Bible Reading note, 8-10 August, 1994, on Acts 15:36-41.

38. Tuckman, p. 387.

39. Giving and accepting criticism are higher order interpersonal skills which deserve study. Space precludes it here but Back (p. 88-96), Whetten

and Cameron (p. 412-419) and J. Whitehead, *Business Skills for Secretaries*, Kingston upon Thames, Croner, 1992, p. 68-71, are all helpful.

40. Galatians 2:20; 1 Corinthians 15:31.

41. Cormack, 1990, p. 160.

42. J. Adair, *Effective Leadership*, London, Pan, revised edition, 1988, p. 33-48.

CHAPTER FIFTEEN

TIME MANAGEMENT

'Too busy to prepare well'

This is the day the LORD has made (Psalm 118:24).

'Dear woman, why do you involve me?' Jesus replied.
'My time has not yet come' (John 2:4).

Everything should be done in a fitting and orderly way
(1 Corinthians 14:40).

The Norfolk woodcutter was told he would work far faster and more efficiently if he sharpened his saw. 'Aarr,' he replied, 'Oi aren't got toime to.' Have you time to read this chapter?

A friend of mine was one of three ministers simultaneously in a Glasgow hospital ward recovering from heart attacks. All agreed that what had put them there had been largely administrative. The excessive amount of work to be done, and the resultant chaotic desk, had ended up paralysing their use of time. The guilt they felt, had led to pastoral visiting of a quality that they knew didn't minister to people. The stress had produced loss of sleep, overeating, hypertension and finally myocardial infarction. They were lucky to be alive.

In his or her lifetime the average western professional will spend three years in wasteful meetings, four years being interrupted, five years waiting in queues, six years eating and seven years in the bathroom. One year is spent looking for things, eight months spent opening advertising mail and six months waiting at red lights.[1]

An analysis of the modern pastor's task well illustrates the 'too busy to prepare well' problem. One such lists the following: the demands of pastoral visits, elders' meetings, financial board, 92 sermons and 36 Bible studies per year each averaging about three hours' preparation, the monthly Parish magazine, outside speaking engagements, weddings, funerals, baptism visits, keeping up with reading, priority visits (especially the elderly) and intercessory prayer for church and parish ...

... and in addition: four local area committees, a committee in Edinburgh, school chaplaincy. Hospital and eventide home visiting occupied three afternoons a week. Occasional radio broadcasting, trusteeship on two independent Christian Trusts and two secular social care committees.[2]

What results is the constant tyranny of the urgent. It is one thing to plan our work; it is another to work our plan, especially when the Christian pastor observes from the life of his Master that the interruptions *are* the work.[3] We should not be surprised that the modern pastor finds himself too busy to prepare well.

Role ambiguity is another major element in the problem. Is it part of a housing scheme pastor's calling to help when non-member parishioners come with housing problems, debt problems and a hundred other ills that flesh is heir to? Some people expect us to be regularly at the Men's Club, Women's Guild, all four uniformed organisations, keeping in touch with the nursery group; but are they right?

Not that all the problem lies outside us. The pastor John Ortberg writes perceptively of sloth, 'the last taboo'.[4] Sloth is not doing nothing; it is the failure to do what should be done when it needs to be done, 'like the Kamikaze pilot who flew seventeen missions'. Some workaholics can be guilty of it. A human sloth avoids the unpleasant task, lets things run their course, allows the daily pressures to push aside planning. Ortberg suggests ways of diagnosing the presence of laziness; but before I list them, I would want to add that genuine burnout paints a similar picture. If, therefore, the result of reading the list is severe nausea and dizziness, move right on to the next chapter.

Ortberg watches for tell-tale signs. His desk and office get messier, he runs late, he stops doing things his wife appreciates ('say, keeping the grass under three feet high') yet has energy for that game of basketball, there is little time for celebration. He experiences 'an odd combination of hurry and wastefulness. I rush in the morning, telling my wife I have no time for breakfast, no time to see the kids off to school; too much to do. Later in the morning, I read the sports section or make an unnecessary phone call.'

Finally, he has a sense of dis-ease at the end of the day: 'I just don't feel right about what I've done or been that day.'[5]

We know the factors that lead to the late start, the long coffee break, the ignoble art of pottering. We have no visible boss, no time card to click, no apparent sanction if we are indulgent. There are more commendable ones also: irregular and unpredictable hours, constant availability, there *is* too much to do: and it is right and godly to look after ourselves.

Now, you for whom I am especially writing this chapter, you are one of the least lazy and most 'get it done' people I know. In fact I'm not sure I know any lazy pastors, although they no doubt exist. At present I'm identifying the elements that conspire to produce the problem, 'too busy to prepare well'. If the cap doesn't fit – please don't wear it! I've no desire to burden anyone. This chapter is an attempt to *dis*-burden, to help make productive order out of frantic chaos by way of a framework for addressing it.

I am not offering a stress-free life. Within limits stress is desirable and improves performance. Strategies that worked last year completely fail this. There are many stresses in the lives of Christian workers and they become more debilitating in each successive decade. All I can offer is to accept these realities and outline a coping strategy.

Three friends with business backgrounds, now in the ministry, filled in time log sheets for me for three weeks along with descriptions of typical and ideal weeks, and made comments on the exercise. The chief problems were: no such thing as a typical week; how quickly a week gets eaten up; how hard it is to do all the visits, even the essential ones, and spend as long as one would like in the study; daily devotions are abandoned or shortened on busy mornings; 'doing this for you has made me realise how full the minister's life is and how tolerant my dear wife is.' One wrote:

> Administration is the problem. There is so much, and it takes so much time. I need to do 6 or 7 hours a week to keep up. That is the first hour of the day (post etc.) plus another 3-hour period. But my 'standard' does not allow for this so I do it when I can. It's very hard work to keep to plan – so easy to get waylaid.
>
> General weariness is my main enemy, especially in the evenings. I always intend to do more admin in the evening, but I'm usually too tired. Time for 'general reading' never realised.

These are pastors who get an unusually large amount done with better than average efficiency. The two who work in cities are pouring a gallon into a pint pot; the (very) rural one, by his testimony, less so.

As I read their accounts, the main difference is predictability. The rural minister wrote 'during the three weeks in question there were no emergencies of any sort'. This might qualify for the Guinness Book of Records but reflects the quantitative difference between city and some country ministry. The scene can be very different in multiple-church rural arrangements.

We have seen components to the problem: gallon into pint pot,[6] unpredictabilities, time-stealers both internal and external, sloth, role ambiguity and the terrible triplets poor planning, perfectionism and procrastination (of whom more later). What of the impact of all this?

A great deal depends on what we make of busyness, planning and organisation. As we have seen from Ortberg, putting too little into the day can be as destructive as overload. The under-pressurised person becomes tired quickly, lethargic, unfulfilled. Guilt over genuinely low performance is enervating, demoralising and breeds shifty superficiality into our relationships. True stress brings anxiety, tension, forgetfulness and often the kind of overwork cycle outlined in chapter three: hence the systems approach to stress and balance in chapter sixteen, which deals also with critical stress and burnout.

Optimum pressure, on the other hand, is desirable and good for us if taken in the right spirit. It increases our response to life, our creativity and our energy. It gets our adrenaline working, brings out our best performance and improves our relationships, our self-esteem, our confidence and our effectiveness.

The critical point is the stress threshold beyond which the graph goes into decline. It is wise to know our own limits, for each of us has his own unique threshold; ways of recognising it are offered in the third section of the chapter. The chief keys to best performance are found in the skills of time management, especially good planning, good organisation and delivery; to these we now turn.

Time: a theological framework

Psalm 118:24 should be not only a fact, but our *aim* in our use of time: this is the day *the Lord* has made. Our target is that our use of time this day reflects a genuine authoring by God. The Puritan Jeremiah Burroughs laid down an excellent principle:

> Be sure of your call to every business you go about. Though it is the least business, be sure of your call to it. Then, whatever you meet with, you may quiet your heart with this: I know I am where God would have me. Nothing in the world will quiet the heart so much as this: when I meet with any cross, I know I am where God would have me, in my place and calling: I am about the work that God has set me.[7]

Clearly that involves considering in advance what God has called us to, confident that it will be the happiest and most fulfilling use of our time.

A similar principle reaches us from Ephesians 5:16, translated variously as 'redeem the time' and 'make the most of every opportunity'. The verb is *exagorazo*. The agora was the market place where you went to buy goods and slaves. *Exagorazo* is to make your selection from the options available. In Ephesians 5:16 what is available is *ton kairon*: the time, but time of a certain sort (for there are two words for time in Greek): today's time seen as opportunity, pregnant with the possibility of fulfilment or regretful loss.

If we combine the words we are given this thought. We seek to ensure, as seen so astonishingly in our Lord's life, God's authoring of our time so that we can say with some confidence, 'This day, the way it is panning out, is the day that *the Lord* has made; I will rejoice and be glad in it.' It is to this task that we turn.

Time management is both an art and a science and has a profuse literature. Any number of courses in it are available from both Christian and secular organisations, usually for considerable sums of money. The fact that companies and even individuals are prepared to pay them indicates how dominating a problem it is.

I state the three basic steps as **Plan, Organise and Obey**. If you are reading this chapter in an emergency – go straight to Organise! But it would be regrettable if you did not return to Plan, in order to turn the crisis into a process, soon.

1. Plan

Plenty of people are efficient; far fewer are effective. The efficient person does things right. The effective person does the right things. The major cause of pottering is failing to identify rigorously, in advance, what to do.

In order to know what to do we need to have a list from which to choose. In order for that list to be appropriate it should reflect both the unavoidable demands on our time and our goals in life – both the 'I ought' and the 'I'd like' – and both the vocational and the personal.

That is demanding. The only way I know of making a list that reflects all of these balances is to approach it systematically, grouping our innumerable activities into related areas so that we can make sense of them, see them at a glance, evaluate the balance between them. I shall term these our Key areas.[8]

Clarify your vision. A major source of stress is the uncomfortable feeling that there is no marriage between our actual use of time and important but non-urgent goals we feel we should be achieving.

The solution is to draw up our list of key areas of activity both deductively and inductively i.e. from above and from below. We should list both our lives' great objectives so as to deduce key areas from first principle, and our myriad actual tasks so as to classify them into logical groupings. Take an example of each approach.

Starting *deductively* we might infer from first principles that our reason for existing – to glorify and enjoy God – implies certain key areas: to know him better; to become 'one approved, a workman who does not need to be ashamed and who correctly handles the word of truth';[9] to be a good spouse and parent; to steward the family finances.

Starting *inductively* and leading into the key areas from below tends to produce a different list: a salutary discovery. It might in fact be quite difficult to draw up the list without writing items down as we go along for a week or two. Then we find ourselves writing funeral visits, school talk, sermon preparation (last), vestry hour, letter for the parish magazine, church committee ... and we start to group them logically. We group the car log, recording of visits, writing to missionaries and the post into Administration. Visits to organisations, lunch club and school we call Chaplaincies. Funerals, systematic visiting, baptism preparation and hospital visits we might name Pastoral Work; and so on.

In order to check the lists for adequacy, it can be helpful to recognise the four sources of a typical 'To Do' list. The pastor's equivalent of 'boss-imposed' is perhaps a combination of God and our denominational affiliation. Then there is the 'system-imposed': committees, family commitments. The 'subordinate-imposed' would be those arising from any assistance we might have and their equivalent: the organist likes the hymn list by Thursday, an elder thinks we should visit Mrs MacSoandSo. Finally there are the 'self-imposed' goals: the self-development, that theological reading project.[10]

We now have two lists of Key areas of our lives, reached deductively and inductively respectively. The next task is to marry these into one list of 5-7 Key areas for work and 2-3 personal areas. Here is one illustrative list:

WORK

1. Preparation: sermons, Bible study, planning, schools.
2. Staff and officebearer relationships.
3. Administration.

4. Pastoral Work including prayer.
5. Committees: congregational, wider.
6. Chaplaincies and organisations.
7. Projects: reading, writing, fabric.

PERSONAL

8. Family and friends.
9. Personal development.[11]

There is a sound physiological basis to limiting the number of Key areas to this absolute maximum. The subconscious mind can tick away at this number of areas without our help and without our panic; but multiply them, or leave them as a myriad unrelated tasks, and the subconscious process of evaluation and development is significantly impaired.

Every facet of our life now belongs in one of 8 or 9 drawers, chosen by us to reflect both what we would like to do and consider important, and what we must do in order to satisfy external demands. We now have a manageable base from which to ensure that we attend to those matters which we consider important but which keep being strangled by the urgent; and that we do not forget follow-up.

Now to get our goals into our diaries. Each of our Key areas will contain a number of goals or activities. My suggestion is that you acquire a looseleaf binder, either commercially produced or plain. Dividers separate our nine Key areas. Each goal or significant activity has a page. Break down each into the steps needed to complete it. Columns for ticking make it easy to see at a glance which ones we have transferred to our overall 'To Do' list and which have been completed.

Make one 'To Do' list, the bridge between our dreaming and our diary. Mine is just a cheap note book. It is fed from our Key areas, our mail, from every input that requires a response. It is the meeting point of our proactive and reactive living. Take every scrap of paper on which you have reminders, add the items to the 'To Do' list and throw away the scraps. Never again use odd scraps of paper. The list contains at least two columns for completion: the priority rating of each task, and the time required to complete it.

A way to estimate the time required for a project is to do one hour of it, see how far we have got and multiply up. Very large tasks should be broken into manageable portions.

Prioritise your tasks. Prioritising is achieved by considering the importance and the urgency of a task, a process which is best kept simple:

> Grade 1: High urgency, high importance work
> Grade 2: Low urgency, high importance work
> Grade 3: High urgency, low importance work
> Grade 4: Low urgency, low importance work

An additional sorting, if in doubt, can be achieved by asking what the consequences will be if a task is not completed. If the consequences are serious, we have a grade 1 task.

We now have only one list to obey. It contains what we want and what others want from us. It is intelligently and rationally priority graded. Now for the diary.

2. Organise

Diarise our work. Hopefully your diary has a month per page; it should have at least a week. We shall have marked the commitments it already contains. We need the overview of the week so as to plan ahead. Plan to complete preparation for speaking at least a day in advance. It reduces panic; it is much easier to see gaps in argument and disjunctions in order of thought if there is a time gap between preparation and the final perusal of notes; and in pastoral work other things enter in and to have one's week planned with leeway makes the emergencies less disruptive.

At this stage we have a weekly plan in overview, three sessions (morning, afternoon, evening) for each of seven days, with some entries already in place by virtue of prior arrangement: times of services and known meetings together with preparation and standard 'time off' pencilled in. Now is the time for the 'To Do' list; but first, a word about Prime Time.

We might be larks who function best early in the morning or owls who do best by working on late into the night but all of us have periods of the day when we work best. For most of us this starts about thirty minutes after getting up in the morning as our automatic inner systems prime us for the day: blood sugar rises and so on. The best time to do Grade 1 tasks is during this prime time, in 40-50 minute all-out stretches followed by a five minute total break before starting again.

There is a physiological basis to this pattern. The brain works at maximum output for about forty-five minutes and then needs a pause before a second burst. A good time to do a group of smaller, Grade 2 or 3 tasks is after two or three such spells. Most brains are no longer in prime time by then, and the variety of turning from left brain hemisphere activity (analytic, linguistic, rational, linear) to right hemisphere – artistic, intuitive, synthetic, creative – actually enhances our overall performance in both spheres.[12]

Here we are, therefore, with the coming week's overview partly timetabled and a 'To Do' list. It might be possible immediately to allocate high priority, sizeable tasks to available prime time. The best option however, in my opinion, is a daily (or weekly) 'To Do' list; and the best time to draw it up is during the last few minutes of work the previous working day. Make this a habit. There is nothing quite like getting into the study, at the hour one's head and heart approve, knowing what Grade 1 task to get down to and with a five minute reward available in 50 minutes if we spend the time well.

Unlike the overall 'To Do' list which is one long list, it is best to draw up the day's or week's 'To Do' list in categories. In parish ministry I find a week's list helpful and use six categories: Preparation/Writing, Letters, Phones, 'To Town For', Visits, and Team meeting. Now grade the tasks, visibly and vigorously. For a happy life,

- Guard your prime time and use it for sizeable grade 1 tasks.
- Start with grade 1, not grade 3 tasks.
- Do one thing at a time. The conscious brain can only concentrate on one thing at a time. If something else occurs to you – jot it down on today's 'To Do' list or diary page (same thing in my case) and return to it later.
- Do first, the task you least want to do

There is an additional benefit from writing the week's plan in categories (letters, phones...). It is then easy at the end of a sustained task – a fifty minute prime time slot, say – to survey the quick tasks and choose one appropriate for the time available. In line with the final bullet point above, choose the one we most want to avoid.

3. Obey

Time management is not about planning; it is about results. Make the break from goals to action. It feels terrible to butterfly from one half-completed task to another and end the day unsatisfied. The Jerusalem Bible has a powerful translation of Proverbs 12:24:

> For the diligent hand, authority;
> For the slack hand, forced labour.

There is a lot in that verse; perhaps the thought in it lay behind Paul's decision:

> Therefore I do not run like a man running aimlessly; I do not fight like a man beating the air. No, I beat my body and make it my slave lest, after preaching to others, I be disqualified for the prize.[13]

I do not know any other way of getting the task done than simply obeying, especially for the first four minutes so as to get me going, the 'To Do' list that in a wiser moment I have set myself; and not to stop until I have completed that day's proper agenda. There is great satisfaction in ticking or crossing off each activity as we complete it.

Try to list, each day, only what is achievable today. Anything not completed can be transferred to tomorrow, but the ability to devise a realistic, ambitious daily plan is a valuable part of good planning and organisation. There is one final stage which helps in this, and to it we now turn.

Analyse our time. This powerful, encouraging and constructive exercise can be designed so as not to occupy very much time. Its benefits make its costs better than acceptable. The basic idea is to have a record – either annually for two weeks, or on a more frequent basis – of where our time actually, honestly, accurately goes.

The research evidence is that there is a salutary difference between the way people think they allocate their time, and how they actually do. They discover this through keeping and analysing a log of their use of time. This one- or two-week exercise is strongly recommended. Of the time logs we have seen and used, the instrument in the appendix to this chapter is superior enough to the others to warrant explanation (see chapter appendix for time log chart).

The day's activities are already divided into our chosen Key Areas, so it is easy to total the time spent in each Key Area and check that over a period we are balancing our expenditure of time across our different life goals. Pick the dominant activity for each 15 minute time slot. At the end of the day give each row a ruthless priority coding in the column provided. Then we can see at a glance whether we are trying too hard (all grade 1 work), being a good steward of time or being self-indulgent (too many grade 3 and grade 4 tasks).

Don't give up. In my experience it takes at least a week to get into the habit of keeping a time log; but the benefits in self-understanding, accurate evaluation and progress in stewardship of time make it very worthwhile.

Paperwork

The three 'D' words that cover this are Dump, Delegate and Deal. Note the order. If we start by dumping as much as possible (in the case of hoarders, a little more than that), we save a lot of paper shifting, paper-losing, procrastination and guilt.

Paperwork, 1: dump it. Don't worry about knowing everything. When mail comes, immediately throw away everything we might be able to do without. Mackenzie writes of the manager whose request for another filing cabinet was refused. His boss said, 'The reason is that I see no evidence that you are attempting to control the amount of paper you are saving. I'd like you to purge your files by tossing out everything you're not *sure* you will need at some point. Let me know the results, and whether you still need the extra filing space.' In the ten years since, he has never needed more than one filing cabinet.[14]

Purge your files annually. You'll find some useful material you had forgotten, in addition to the pleasure and efficiency of travelling lighter.

Paperwork, 2: delegate it. Delegation was covered in chapter fourteen. Carried out well, it is the exercise of Christian fellowship: participation in God's work together, the appropriate division of labour bringing wide benefit.

Paperwork, 3: deal with it. As far as is possible, no item should cross our desk more than once: the great killer of good paperwork is dealing with items repeatedly and indecisively. First we give it a quick look, then we put it aside for proper attention later and look at the next item. The answer is to find an approach that ensures we deal effectively with paperwork when we first see it.

When *receiving* paper work, we do not have to handle it immediately. It can be put into an 'IN' tray and postponed till after prime time. When *handling* paperwork, do not put an item down until we have done something definite with it. Make a decision first time. If it will take some reading and now is not the time – note it in the 'To Do' list and file it according to subject. Then it is out of sight, in place and will automatically be appropriately dealt with by the 'To Do' list's priority grading exercise. If it should be passed on, start the process, whether in the 'Out' tray or church pigeon hole. A rapid way to answer a business letter is to write a reply on the original, indicate 'handwritten for rapid response', keep a copy only if necessary (the time log will record it otherwise) and return it in the same envelope.

Anniversary Reminder System
It means a great deal to a bereaved person or an eighty year old that we remember their special anniversary; especially, one year after bereavement. Choose your system:

- on computers most Organisers have a system for bringing up anniversaries.
- 5 x 3 inch cards, kept Jan-Dec. Monthly dividers ease quick reference.
- an old Desk Diary, one page per day.

This is something to check at the end of work, the working day before each start of week. That way, we remember to buy the card in time.

'Desk Secretary'
This is the traditional name for the file in our cabinet, or concertina file by our desk, in which we keep date orientated commitments: future speaking and writing engagements filed by their 'start' date, mail that requires action but not immediately. Some people have 1-31 (for the current month) and Jan-Dec. I find it easier simply to keep it in date order, with just enough dividers to make finding easy.

Filing
The arrangement fits our Key Areas. This reduces to one the number of ways we classify the different sides of our life. The first file is the through the year 'Desk Secretary', and the last is A-Z for reference. If our Key Areas looseleaf book is organised the same way with *when*, *what* and *reference* sections, we really do run our life by one integrated method.

Filing is best done in bursts rather than item by item, so we have implied at least three trays: IN, containing material for immediate or almost immediate attention; FILING, with the growing pile of material to file; and OUT, containing letters to be posted and items to be taken to people. There is no easy way of running a filing system but the capacity to retrieve information and do tasks in appropriate order makes the effort cost effective. The best principle is to KISS: Keep it simple, stupid. 'Efficiency is intelligent laziness' (Nick Mercer).

Desk

Only contains one item of business: that which we are working on just now. The phone, and the in/filing/out trays, are far enough away – preferably on a table just behind us or beside the desk – not to constitute a temptation during prime time working. The 'To Do' lists should be just within reach.

Getting started

Do not do this during prime time: it is such fun, and requires courage rather than brain, so do it by appointment late morning or afternoon. Take the large pile of papers you keep shuffling through for the right one, and put the whole lot on your empty desk. Look at each sheet. If you know you'll do nothing about it – throw it out. If you don't know for sure that you have to do something about it – throw it out. If it needs attention – add the information to your master 'To Do' list and then file the paper: for if it has a place in your life, it belongs either in one of your Key Areas, or in your dates file (Desk Secretary), or in the A-Z reference section.

We now have a master list of what needs to be done, and we know where to find all the materials we need to do it. All that remains is when to do it, and that is achieved by the urgent/important prioritisation process followed by diarisation.

Time stealers

It would be best if you stop reading at this point and spend 2-3 minutes writing down what, in your life, produces waste and loss of time.

Whole books have been written on this one subject.[15] For many pastors there is a common theme. The very facts of too much to do and role ambiguity produce indecision, pottering, management by crisis and attempting too much. Telephone interruptions, drop-in visitors, procrastination: all have their place, but all have their appropriate coping strategy also.

As I pen these words I have just programmed an alarm to buzz me at 11.02. To do so, took less than two seconds. Today I started late. The temptation would have been to have coffee at the usual time, about 10.45. I therefore intercepted laziness and delayed my mid-morning reward for work done. That both encouraged my best, and prolonged it to a length my head approved but my laziness might not otherwise have achieved. Also involved was the prior choice between two competing, valid priorities on the use of this particular slot in time.

Then there are the subtler time-stealers. Telephoning when we think of it instead of banking our calls so as to do them in a group outside prime time. Failing to identify in advance what to cover: unstructured telephone calls waste time. Inability to say no. Interruptions from drop-in visitors. Reading too much through perfectionism. In fact the chief culprits worldwide are the three 'Ps': Poor planning, Procrastination and Perfectionism. We have spent time on the planning; a word on each of the others.

Perfectionism. Doing the best we reasonably can, is one thing. Perfection is another, and is impossible. It is permissible to do things well enough. In fact for the over-perfectionist pastor the best motto might be a cheerful, 'If it's worth doing, it's worth doing badly.' Edmund Burke observed, nobody made a greater mistake than he who did nothing because he could only do a little.

Procrastination. This problem is about us. We own it. The key to it lies in this chapter: by planning, making the decision what to do and when; then obeying our own orders. The vague is always more threatening than the classified, so if there are tasks we are avoiding, we have to make an appointment with ourselves and:

- Choose the worst first.
- Just make a start on it: we can do *any* task for five minutes.
- Write down the consequences of not doing it.
- Take no coffee, visit no bathroom and beg our spouse to give us no food or drink until we can show them, say, the outline or first draft.

The attitude we bring

George Whitefield's diary records that he was on his knees weeping over having wasted thirty minutes in a day. David Livingstone, who started work at ten years old, worked in a cotton mill from six in the morning until eight at night. But he used his 'leisure' hours with such determination that he mastered Latin before he was sixteen and was qualified in theology and medicine by the time he was twenty-seven. John Wesley's phenomenal achievement is closely tied to his refusal to waste even five minutes.

No doubt some of the great men had the balance wrong; but was not their urgency over others' salvation, their awareness of mortality, a truer reflection of the God's heart than most of ours? 'William James affirmed that the great use of one's life is to spend it for something that will outlast it: for the value of life is computed not by its duration but by its donation. Not how long we live, but how fully and how well.'[16]

It was Abraham Lincoln who said that a person is about as happy as he makes up his mind to be. For sixteen years in my previous church I could have enjoyed the honour of serving wonderful people and of offering them Jesus more, and could have agonised over how well or badly I was doing it very much less. Difficulties are opportunities for growth. Sub-pathological pressure is given us by God to develop our skills, improve our performance, raise our adrenaline. There is a very significant connection between our use of time and Hebrews 12:11, especially its last eight words:

> No discipline seems pleasant at the time, but painful. Later on, however, it produces a harvest of righteousness and peace *for those who have been trained by it.*

We are suggesting that 'too busy to prepare well' is something not so much to resent as to accept, for which we develop a coping strategy. It is up to us whether to approach it in a martyr spirit as a burden, or sacrificially as a privilege.

PMA – a positive mental attitude – is a thoroughly biblical approach: the courage, in faith, to hang on and be thankful. The time does come for some of us however to be signed off for a period and to learn new patterns of stress management. To this we now turn.

Reflection

- Draw up a skill assessment exercise based on the chapter, then complete it with respect to your own time use. Identify one adjustment to your time management that is called for in the light of your answer, and implement it for two weeks. Here are three items to get you started:

1. I make a daily 'To Do' list.
2. I concentrate on only one important task at a time.

3. I allow myself to worry about things at only one particular time during the day, not all the time.

References

1. Michael Fortino, 'Time Flies when you're not having fun.' Quoted in *LandMARC*, Eastbourne, MARC, 1989, page number not noted.

2. T. Swanston, Congregational Record of West Parish Church, Inverness, January and March 1984.

3. Matthew 9:19f.; 14:13f.; 19:13f..

4. J. Ortberg, 'The Last Taboo: today's unforgivable sin that no leader dare confess', *Leadership*, Spring 1994, p. 80- 85.

5. Ortberg, p. 81, 82.

6. The term is discussed in 'The Basic Tasks of the Ordained Minister', Assembly Council Report, *Reports to the General Assembly of the Church of Scotland*, Edinburgh, 1990, p. 92.

7. J. Burroughs, *The Rare Jewel of Christian Contentment*, Edinburgh, Banner of Truth reprint, 1964 (first published 1648), p. 217.

8. I use the term proposed in the literature of *Time Manager International*, Henley-in-Arden, to whom acknowledgement is made.

9. 2 Timothy 2:15.

10. I am indebted to a day seminar run by *CareerTrack International*, Milton Keynes, for this classification of sources of the 'To Do' list.

11. Every book I have and every seminar attended on time management recommend this exercise. It is hugely helpful. In addition the best time log analysis involves the use of such a list. Do it!

12. P. Russell, *The Brain Book*, London, Routledge and Kegan Paul, 1979, p. 48-63.

13. 1 Corinthians 9:26f.

14. A. Mackenzie, *The Time Trap*, New York, Amacom, 1990, p. 149.

15. A. Mackenzie, *The Time Trap*, New York, Amacom, 1990, is written round the twenty biggest time wasters and how to cure them.

16. J.O. Sanders, *Spiritual Leadership*, London, MMS, 1967, p. 85.

APPENDIX TO CHAPTER 15

In this illustration, the Key Areas used are the same as those in the text of the chapter.

	key areas										
	preparation	officebearers	administration	pastoral work	committees	chaplaincy	projects	family and friends	personal development	*description of task*	priority
7.00-7.15											
7.15-7.30											
7.30-7.45											
7.45-8.00											
8.00-8.15											
8.15-8.30											
through the day in 15-minute slots											
evening											
TOTAL TIME SPENT IN EACH KEY AREA											

CHAPTER 16

STRESS

'To be honest, Peter, at times I feel too tired to be excited.'
Letter from a friend in Christian work.

Elijah came to a broom tree, sat down under it and prayed that he might die. 'I have had enough, Lord,' he said. 'Take my life; I am no better than my ancestors.' Then he lay down under the tree and fell asleep (1 Kings 19:4,5).

'O, what I owe to the furnace, the file and the hammer of my Lord!' (Samuel Rutherford).

Even Bill Hybels of Willowcreek Community Church in South Barrington, Illinois, renowned worldwide for his drive, tells of an occasion when he suddenly started weeping because of not having catered for his emotions.[1] If it can happen to Bill Hybels, it can happen to anyone.[2] If you have been too busy for a while and are tired, watch out for the warning signs:

- something going wrong that would not previously have phased you, feels like the last straw and makes you lose your temper or come very close to it.

- you become more susceptible to temptation, especially the besetting ones from your past.

- you are losing your sense of proportion and life isn't fun any more.

- sleeplessness, vague guilt, deep misery that a good night's sleep does not resolve, obsession with difficulties, constant self-denigration.

- you lose your pleasant interest in people and become introverted, self-critical and lethargic. You don't really care how other people's lives are going.

- just one more request for help makes you feel that you are carrying the whole universe on your shoulders and cannot bear it any longer.
- low-flying aircraft seem to have it in for you personally.
- you have become indecisive, unable to accept responsibility. The response 'I don't know' has become your trademark.
- your previously resilient mind has lost its bounce and creativity.

The pastor with a score of three out of that nine would be well advised to take action along the lines of the coping strategies suggested in this chapter.[3] Stress and exhaustion undoubtedly jeopardise our capacity to minister.

I have made use of a secular model in describing the causes and effects of stress and ways of preventing and managing it.[4] Whetten and Cameron identify three basic elements in their framework for understanding stress. First, there are its causes: the stressors. These produce effects in us: our reactions. Finally we all have different capacities in the face of stress: our resiliency. See figure 16-1.

FIGURE 16.1: Experiencing Stress[5]

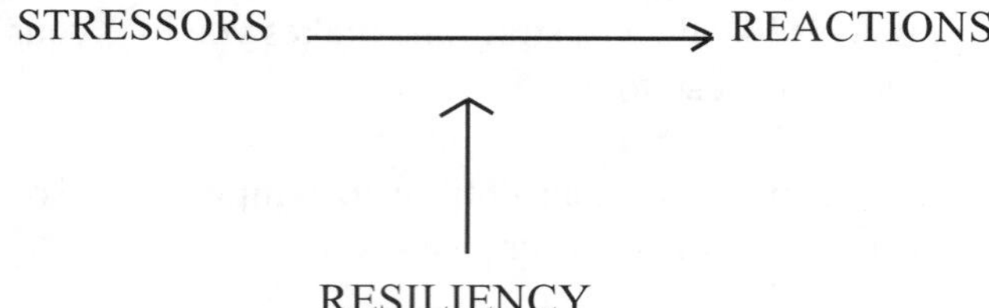

Just to see the diagram suggests the three angles from which to address stress. In the immediate we learn to deal with our reactions and emotions: these are reactive strategies and short term. Over a period it is possible to build our resiliency by developing specific skills: this is a proactive strategy and mid term. In the long term, to enact a different lifestyle may be desirable, and for some people medically necessary: increased delegation, taking up a creative hobby, even a change of church. These are enactive strategies.

We can now develop our diagram; see figure 16-2.

Factor worked on:	The stressor	Our resiliency	Our reactions
Approach:	Eliminate or reduce the stressor	Develop our resiliency	Learn coping mechanisms
Type of approach:	Enactive	Proactive	Reactive
Is this a short or long term approach?	Long term	Mid term	Short term
Effect:	Permanent	Growing	Immediate
Time required to take effect:	Takes a long time	Moderate time and continues	Short time, then repeat

FIGURE 16.2: Table of Stress Managing Strategies[6]

Whetten and Cameron claim that the best strategies are those that eliminate the stressors altogether.[7] If the greatest good for Christians were to experience no stress, that would be true. In sending stressful situations, however, God is often calling for a response from us for the sake of our growth and his larger purpose.

We need to bear in mind, moreover, that to run away from one situation can simply lead to repeating its mistakes and pains in the next. The outcome might be more like diminished responsiveness and final breakdown than progress. Let us therefore identify some causes of stress commonly experienced by Christian workers and explore how to address them.

THE STRESSORS: eliminate, reduce and manage them

The list which follows centres on Christian workers in Western society. Space forbids consideration of the daily danger of crime, kidnapping, rape, robbery, violence and starvation to which missionaries in some overseas situations are exposed.[8] Similarly omitted are the background stressors of childhood physical, psychological and sexual abuse and their impact on performance, self-esteem and relationships. These have been recognised in chapter three and warrant dedicated treatment outside the scope of this book.

I use the acronym WASPS to summarise my categories of stressors. May it encourage us to remember that we can, at least partially, draw the sting they carry.

W: Workload stress. Many pastors have too much to do. They end up with the gnawing sense that even the essentials, let alone the desirable tasks and the space for reflection and development, are not being covered.

It is idle to pretend that this stressor is easy to resolve. Its elimination is not normally an option. Chapter 15 covered the main lines along which to address it: especially delegation and time management.

A: Anticipatory stress. We anticipate failure, embarrassment, the rejection of our ministry, other job-related threats.

A vivid personal nightmare (literally) over years has been of being in the pulpit, totally unprepared and performing abysmally or disgracefully with a number of esteemed visiting clergy in the congregation. The relief of waking to find it a dream is phenomenal; I hope I shall never be in the position of waking only to find that it isn't. Clearly I experience anticipatory stress over preaching!

Anticipatory stress is not likely to be eliminable but can be reduced by good time management. Severe or chronic stress calls for making plans about the anticipated stressor. Overseas missionary candidates prepare for culture shock, for example, by learning as much as possible about cross cultural adjustment and about their destination in particular. It is also addressed by approaching the anticipated threat as a friend rather than as an enemy.[9]

S: Spiritual stress. Our spiritual life has the enmity of Satan and his forces: 'the sovereignties and powers who originate the darkness in this world, the spiritual army of evil in the heavens.'[10] James Denney writes of the 'omnipresent, steady, persistent pressure, the sleepless malignity, of the evil forces that beset men's life'.[11]

Elimination of Satan, of course, is not part of our task. Even after losing the battle for Jesus' soul through the terrible initial temptations in his ministry the evil one waited on, biding his time and sifting his friends.[12] While we cannot eliminate Satan and his minions, however, we can take steps to reduce him as a stressor. Spiritual battling is briefly covered in chapter four.

We can eliminate, however, some spiritual stress. Concerning temptation our Lord says, 'If your eye offends you – cut it out; if your hand – cut it off.'[13] *Leadership* magazine, for example, ran a moving article from a pastor who by going to peep-shows addicted himself to lust. The result was nearly the loss of his marriage and ministry despite a thousand prayers for release; and finally, the mercy of God, which at the time of writing had given him a dawning delight in Jesus Christ and in his wife again.[14]

For others, it will be the dominance of TV, or too much escapist reading; or adultery, covetousness, alcohol, a hobby indulged in to the jeopardising of fellowship with Christ. Elimination of spiritual stress involves instant rejection and constant resistance of temptation plus, if it is a real problem, making yourself accountable to a trusted friend to report every failure.

The other, perhaps the major, spiritual stress is simply the sense of responsibility to God for our ministry: the pressure to preach well, pastor lovingly, 'be a good minister'. I don't see how it can be other than a greater pressure than that required in being a good lawyer or decorator, doctor or roadsweeper. It is more exclusively God's work and we fear to let him down, a fear explored in chapter 3.

> Who is equal to such a task? Our competence comes from God: he has made us competent to serve the new covenant, not of the letter but of the Spirit.[15]

and

> Go in this your strength: have not I called you?[16]

P: People stress. I listened recently to a group of younger ministers from all over Scotland. Their expressed concerns strongly reflected this category of stress. Encounter stresses generally arise from conflicts either about people's respective roles, or where disagreement exists, over how to solve a problem; or individuals just fail to get along well.[17]

> An organist insisted that the final decision on choice of hymn tunes lay with him, not with the new pastor. There were probably several dynamics at stake: a play for power in the new situation, his avowed policy of getting his own way, testing the new pastor's mettle, and the need to gain reassurance by asserting himself.

It is possible to make a real dent in the stress of personal encounter. All of its elements are skills in which we can train: communication, being sensitive to other's feelings, developing friendships, being firm but not aggressive when disagreeing, giving verbal 'strokes' that encourage the diffident and show appreciation for effort.

S: Situational stress. The stresses in Christian workers' situations are many. Situation stresses include job fit, aspects of our local situation, lack of success and the impact of life change. The best approach is, by reflecting, to identify our own situational stressors, accept them and brainstorm strategies for responding.

Those strategies might be to enact situational change, either major (seek a new situation) or minor. The latter might include work redesign, delegation or finding means for reducing the impact of a particular stress. For example, unremitting availability can be eased by use of an answerphone for our day off and family mealtimes. Our task is to identify the possible coping strategies and choose the best fit in our circumstances.

The industrial psychologists have established that there is no such thing as a perfectly round peg in a perfectly round hole when it comes to matching people to jobs. It is the same in ministry. There is always some lack of job-fit between a pastor and a church, and that can vary over time as the situation alters. It can be addressed by team work and by further training or mentoring. If the sense of misfit is severe it might be best to recognise that God's call to a given church is not necessarily for life.

Richard Baxter comments:

> What should a minister do who finds he has lost the affections of his people? To this I answer, if they be so vile as people, that they hate him not for any weakness or misconduct of his but merely for endeavouring their good, and would hate any other that should do his duty: then must he with patience and meekness continue to 'instruct those who oppose themselves, in the hope that God will give them repentance.'
>
> If it is on account of any weakness of his, or difference on minor matters, or prejudice against him personally, let him try to remove the prejudice. If they cannot accept his personality and ministry, let him leave them and try whether another man might not be fitter for them, and he fitter for another people.[18]

Another people, only – or another work altogether? The Lutheran church in America reported, 'All callings which, in the order of creation, contribute to community are equally holy. It is not therefore a degradation or a sign of unfaithfulness, if a man leaves the ministry for another calling. What is decisive, and may be disgraceful, is his reason for doing so. But equally disgraceful may be his reason for coveting the prerogatives of the ministry (cf. Simon Magus). In either case a man must feel himself called of God to that specific function.'[19]

I include these two quotations because in some circumstances the need to eliminate stressors should leave us free to seek another charge or even to perceive another calling with a clear conscience, after due prayer and consultation.

The reduction of situational stress need not normally involve so drastic a change.

> A severe building problem proved a stress to two successive pastors and beyond the combined capacity of congregation and denomination to resolve. It was eliminated as a stressor when a member found a civil engineer willing to make it his problem.

A final category of stress arising from our situation is too important to omit: dramatic life change. Two doctors measured the impact of this. They rated the death of husband, wife or child at 100 units. Marital breakdown, personal injury, loss of job, significant change in the family or one's finances and other factors were each given their own stress scores.[20]

50% of people with scores of 150-300, and 80% with scores over 300, become seriously ill anything up to 12 months later. Clearly these are findings for which we must cater when devising our management of stress; at the very least, by limiting stress (as far as possible) at times of major change in our lives.

To summarise this section: we have seen the WASPS that cause pastors stress. To draw their sting requires us to eliminate or reduce them as causes of stress, primarily by strategies as straightforward as time management, staying on top spiritually, good relationships and work re-design.

Stress management starts with prevention. It does not however stop there.

RESILIENCY: develop it

Intuitively, when work demands more of our time we abandon such balance as time with the children and music, and give more and more time to work. Resiliency however, and the likelihood of our lives ministering, do not work like that. It is important to recognise that the development of resiliency is counter-intuitive. We don't slip into resiliency; we work towards it by intercepting inertia and taking steps towards balance.

A wise pastor includes space for the physical, intellectual, family, cultural and social sides to life as well as to work, for balance improves our resilience. For the sake of younger pastors I would point out that you only get one shot at your children's childhood. The circus may be back next year, but childhood won't.[21]

A friend visited his adult son. As they were preparing to go out to a Christian commitment his wife said, 'Go and watch him play football today, Dad.' What, instead of church? Finally he agreed.

On the way to the ground the son stopped the car and said, 'Dad, in all the years I've played football – school, school team, youth team and now works team – this is the first time you've ever come and watched me.' The father's church activities had always come first. He had used the excuse, 'There will be another time for football; today I should be at the church meeting.' But the other time had never come.

God help us live balanced lives.

Rhythms of rest and work

In a little booklet of rare power William Still invites us on theological grounds to live and work restfully.[22] It is Satan's desire, says Still, that we lose our heads and hearts in fevered, self-destructive activity. Actually, we need rest: to submit ourselves to God, in order that the divine life may be poured progressively into every part of our being. This is negative in that it requires us to cease from self so that the Almighty may fill us with life-giving grace; yet positive, replete with the vibrant blessings of God.

God himself is eternal, completely satisfied with his own perfections in triune harmony and love, restfully working. He saves sinners into a corresponding rest, resting in him for salvation. He offers us peace, purchased by Christ; it remains for us to experience this gift. Resting of this sort is energising: for not activity, but rest, is the basis of energy.

We enjoy this restful work, first, by alternating rest and work. We can learn, by practice, the length of rest and work periods that are good for us individually. For example take 10-30 minutes to relax during each day. In that time, rest in the finished work of a gracious God.

Just as God rested, he wants man to.[23] Put your head down, your feet up, relax from the head downwards; if necessary, with medical help. Persist in this (unless you are one of those for whom this is wrong advice), draw in stray thoughts, breathe properly. Give thought to justification, in which we accept all that Christ has done for us, and to sanctification, in which we appropriate a new world, a new nature and a new master. If we dwell on these, we shall approach worries differently. Rest is our first priority, for *everything* depends on him not on us.[24]

We also enjoy restful work by simultaneous rest and work. We aim for controlled relaxation in our active lives, by leaning on the Lord and his salvation as we labour.

Tension is paralysing! We remember better when our minds are relaxed. There is a parallel here with physical expertise. A pianist learns to use his weight rather than his strength as he varies the volume of his play; a sawyer, the weight of saw and good technique rather than tense pressure.

So in our work, we strive to enter the rest (Heb. 4:11) of releasing competing cares for the one activity of mind, soul and body to which we are set, so that our minds begin to relax. We'll hardly know ourselves. Others too may not recognise us, we're so peaceful, cheerful and easy to get on with! – and, by the same token, we shall see others too in the best possible light. The result will be loving co-operation, a combination of relaxed control and activity which synchronise rest and work.

We are physical as well as spiritual beings. The evidence is overwhelming that those in good physical condition cope with stress better than others. We shall therefore ensure a healthy mixed diet, regular demanding exercise (not less than half an hour three times a week) and a day off.

We are also psychological beings. Interestingly, the kind of 30 minute deep relaxation described above has been shown to inhibit the negative effects of stress. It is a progressively learned skill: its benefits increase with regular use.

In the articles on the helping personality mentioned in chapter three the Australian psychologist Hugh Eadie described three practices for developing our resilience: training in self-awareness, a willingness to be helped, and allowing ourselves adequate opportunity for relaxation and for activities which bring personal satisfaction.[25]

We are also social beings. Build a support network. Take on a mentor relationship from a senior person you respect who is happy to do so and likely to benefit in turn from your contribution. Build task teams so that you and others are working together. Give time to take your spouse out, to develop friendships, to be with your family.

A sense of humour. It has been said that to an Englishman things might be serious but are never hopeless; to an Irishman things might be hopeless but are never serious. Many of us need to remember to see things in perspective and see the funny side of life.

OUR REACTIONS: learn the short term strategies for managing them. We have explored the elimination of stressors and the development of our resiliency. Stress gets through nonetheless and it can help to know immediate, short term coping mechanisms.

Spiritually, practise running to Jesus: preserve that inner citadel no-one else can reach where you learn to let him love you. There remember how valuable you are to him:

> He will take great delight in you; he shall be silent in his love, he will rejoice over you with singing.
>
> He shall see the fruit of the travail of his soul, and be satisfied.[26]

Physiologically, under stress we find the heart rate increasing, sweating, headaches. Relaxation techniques, time spent on peaceful mind pictures, deep abdominal breathing and taking time off can all help.

Psychologically, we can experience shock and loss of confidence and our performance of tasks can be or seem in jeopardy. Rehearsal (talking through stressful situations)[27] and reframing ('I've solved similar problems to this before. The alternatives available to me are....')[28] are two constructive mechanisms for resolving these.

We have seen a systems approach to stress and balance. Stresses can be reduced, our resiliency developed and our reactions coped with by learnt responses. Stress need not normally overwhelm us. If it does, however, medical help is appropriate. A rough guide as to when to seek such help is when our functioning is affected.

'Rest in the finished work of a gracious God.' Surely it is good so to shape our lives that we can keep going year after year.

Concluding exercises

- Score yourself on the stress assessment list on the first page of the chapter.

- Now might be a good time to draw the pie chart of our life activities (note 21). Then:

- Shade in the portion of each section that represents the time you give it.

- Write down one thing you can do to improve your life balance in the areas that need it.

- Because the intent of this exercise is not to add pressure to your life but to improve its balance, identify what you will stop doing to effect that.

- To make this a practical exercise and not just theory, do something today from the fourth and fifth bullet points.[29]

References

1. Bill Hybels, 'Reading Your Gauges', *Leadership*, Spring 1991, p. 32-38.

2. The stress process associated with the helping personality was explored in chapter 3. Compare R. Gledhill, 'Vicars Sacrifice Marital Joy on the Altar of Work', *The Times*, Wed. 27 March 1996.

3. J.B. Cairns, *Keeping Fit for Ministry*, Edinburgh, St Andrew Press, 1989, offers a commonsensical, balanced overview.

4. D.A. Whetten and K.S. Cameron, *Developing Management Skills*, New York, Harper Collins, 1991, p. 92-157.

5. *Ibid.*, p. 102.

6. Modified from Whetten and Cameron, p. 102.

7. Whetten and Cameron, p. 103.

8. R. Grant, 'Trauma in Missionary Life', *Missiology*, vol. XXIII, No. I January 1995, p. 71-83 deals movingly with the recognition of these and an approach to their management. S. Chalmers, *Pastoral Care of Missionaries*, Research Dissertation in Christian Mission, Glasgow Bible College, 1993, contains a recent bibliography in the field and an overview of strategies. M. Jones, ed., *Caring for the Missionary into the 21st Century*, Duns, Care for Mission publication, 1993, contains five wise papers.

9. James 1:2-4, J.B. Philips translation.

10. Ephesians 6:12, Jerusalem Bible translation.

11. J. Denney on 2 Corinthians 4:4.

12. Respectively Matthew 4:11, Luke 4:13 and Luke 22:31.

13. Matthew 5:29, 30.

14. Name withheld, 'The War Within', *Leadership*, Fall 1992, p. 96-112.

15. 2 Corinthians 2:14-3:6.

16. Judges 6:14.

17. Whetten and Cameron, p. 105 quoting W.C. Hamner and D.W. Organ, *Organisational Behaviour*, Dallas, Business Publications, 1978.

18. RP, p. 233; RPH, p. 122f.

19. 'Report on the Commission on the Doctrine of the Ministry', *Minutes*, The United Lutheran Church in America, 1952, p. 553f, quoted in J.W. Doberstein, ed, *The Minister's Prayer Book*, London, Collins, 1986, p. 182.

20. Two recent Christian books in which the scale is given and explored are: G. Davies, *Stress*, Eastbourne, Kingsway, 1988, p. 62-71; and P. Meadows, *Pressure Points*, Eastbourne, Kingsway, 2nd edition, 1993, p. 21-24.

21. The phrase is an echo from a very moving article 'The Day at the Beach' by Arthur Gordon, © 1959 by Arthur Gordon, first published in *Reader's Digest*, reprinted in Whetten and Cameron pp. 140-143. Whetten and Cameron offer a pie chart of life activities as a way of evaluating our balance: pp. 123-125.

22. W. Still, *Rhythms of Rest and Work*, 44 page booklet, Gilcomston South Church, Aberdeen. No date.

23. Psalm 95:11; Isaiah 30:15; 32:16-20; Matthew 11:28-30.

24. I remember Prof. Alex Cheyne saying to a group of us tired ministers at a conference, 'Relax: perhaps the essential things have been done already.'

25. H. Eadie, 'The Health of Scottish Clergymen', *Contact*, Vol. 48, 1972, p. 3-18.

26. Zephaniah 3:17; Isaiah 53:11.

27. Modified from Back and Back; various sections.

28. Whetten and Cameron, p. 138.

29. Modified from Whetten and Cameron p. 150f.

EPILOGUE

Chapter 17. Perseverance and Reward

CHAPTER SEVENTEEN

PERSEVERANCE AND REWARD

Going on going on

Well done, thou good and faithful servant (Matthew 25:21, 23).

Deliver me, O God, from a slothful mind, from all lukewarmness, and all dejection of spirit. I know these can only deaden my love to Thee. Mercifully free my heart from them, and give me a lively, zealous, active and cheerful spirit; that I may vigorously perform whatever thou commandest, thankfully suffer whatever thou choosest for me, and be ever ardent in all things with thy holy love (John Wesley).

In 1981/82 the journal *Leadership* conducted a large survey of pastors. They distributed 1,000 questionnaires, received 300 returns and reported, 'It appears that the thread running through each of the most frequently indicated significant problems had to do with expectations. Half felt their own unrealistic expectations were a major cause.... As a result of such expectations, many pastors overextend themselves by trying to "be and do it all" in order not to let themselves or others down.'[1]

What then of our approach to *going on* going on?

Value God's grace. I have a feeling that we too easily take salvation for granted and find peace and joy only from other, subsequent, secondary things. That's rather like the lovely and totally true to life occasion that Ron Dunn records, about the time he took his children to a funfair early in his ministry when the family finances were lean. It was a Saturday and he still had to prepare for Sunday.

They left at 6am, drove 100 miles and gave everything they'd got: swings, stalls, roundabouts, horrid food, the lot. At 9pm he was outvoted: the kids refused to go home 'so early'. About 1am on the way home one of the children started crying because they had forgotten to buy her a balloon. Dunn says his temper just flipped its lid; we can imagine it. $100 spent on trivia, he'd given his all and his best – and she grumbled and wept!

The Israelites behaved like that. They had cried to God for years about oppression and slavery in Egypt. Years and prayers later, they were no sooner given what they longed for – and that by God's mighty hand and outstretched arm – than they started moaning and scarcely stopped for forty years. We'd have done the same.

Actually we do the same. We were, to use Paul's neat and appalling summary, Christless, stateless, friendless, hopeless and godless,[2] sinful and lifeless.[3] In response God bankrupted heaven and handed over the Son of his love; *he* in turn gave up every comfort and honour for the life of a refugee and homeless wandering preacher, only to end up executed on a hangman's gibbet in public disgrace for us. And then we let our gratitude and pleasure be determined by mere details like the volume of blessing he is visibly giving through us in the short term.

It's appalling. If we valued things appropriately we should be so thrilled to be forgiven, so astounded that God justifies sinners, that every difficulty and disgrace for the Saviour's sake would be a trifle compared with the surpassing worth of knowing Christ Jesus our Lord.

The same revaluation can apply, if we let it, to the painful issue of the 'performance gap' between our standards and our actual living and serving. We need not live 'working towards acceptance' and driven by need. We may live on God's bounty, working from acceptance and kindled by grace. These are different universes. In the one we have grounds for pride or shame, depending on *our* performance. In the other we have grounds for gratitude, depending on Christ's.

One is slavery; the other, freedom. One is characterised by the faith of a servant; the other, that of a son or daughter. 'So many of us live lives of quiet dissatisfaction because we do not measure up to the standards we've set for ourselves,' observes Gordon MacDonald.[4] Let's enjoy living on God's free bounty, undeserved and yet poured out: in other words, grace. We shall be more peaceful and happier people, better adverts for the gospel, less strained, more gracious and forgiving ourselves.

Stick to the priorities. It takes patience and faith to concentrate on developing the preached Word, supportive prayer and integrity of meaningful pastoral work when there is not much or rapid evidence of its bearing fruit. The temptation is to rush around trying anything and everything to supplement this core. We do not suppose that these are the only legitimate congregational activities, but we appeal to Christian leaders to concentrate on them, to let nothing divert us from them and to put up with criticism for limiting our use of time on other things for the sake of their priority.

It is proper to say, with our betters, 'It would not be right for us to neglect the ministry of the word to wait on tables ... we will turn this responsibility over to these people and will concentrate on prayer and the ministry of the word.'

This is not to denigrate waiting on tables. It is, however, to insist that the only way to do justice to our priorities is to give them the space they need; and therefore to leave good things undone without feeling guilty.

Do not compare yourself with others. Competition, envy and their resultant demoralisation are the plagues of happy ministry. Measuring ourselves against others' achievements or personality are a sure recipe for misery. God knew what he was doing when he made you. It was you he meant to make. If he'd wanted to make you somebody else, he would have done so! On the success of others and concerning their coping better than we do, our Lord would say to us, 'What is that to you? You follow me.'

Do not look for thanks. Count yourself privileged to have something to do for Jesus. I know why we long for appreciation and preferably recognition too. We feel bad about ourselves. We feel we need reassuring that we are doing all right. It isn't true – we don't need reassuring at all. Let's be honest, that is self-indulgence.

There was a powerful cartoon in a journal for Christian leaders. Back home after the morning service, the minister was saying to his wife, 'How do you think the sermon went, dear?' (private thought: 'that was a real sparkler'). His wife is replying, 'It was really great, dear' (private thought: 'what a lousy, dull sermon'). Don't look for thanks.

An unknown author wrote, 'Never indulge in self-reflective acts of any kind, whether of self-congratulation or self-despair. Forget the things that are behind, the moment they are past, leaving them with God.' I suspect that is overstating the case. Our Lord commands us to examine ourselves[5] and it would be irresponsible not to make some assessment of the service we render him, if only for the sake of seeing if we could not somehow serve him better. We must ensure, however, that such monitoring is objective rather than introspective or self-congratulatory – or even self-denigrating. Forget the things that are behind.

Jesus told a parable about this in Luke 17:7-10. The servant coming in from the field doesn't wait to be served by the master. He gets the master's supper, puts on his waiter's clothes and serves him; after that he can eat. Would the master thank the servant for doing what he was told? No way; that was his duty. 'So you also, when you have done everything you were told to do, should say, "We are unworthy servants; we have only done our duty." '

Accept hardship, difficulty, discouragement and criticism: do not resent them. They are not enemies being nasty to us even though those who cause them might be. They are friends sent by God to develop our courage, stickability, cheerful perseverance and fellowship with our Lord Jesus.[6]

Remember Spurgeon's humour and courage:

> When I was preaching at the Surrey Gardens, an unknown censor of great ability used to send me a weekly list of my mispronunciations and other slips of speech. He never signed his name, and that was my only cause of complaint against him, for he left me in a debt which I could not acknowledge. I take this opportunity of confessing my obligations to him, for with genial temper, and an evident desire to benefit me, he marked down most relentlessly everything which he supposed me to have said incorrectly.
>
> Concerning some of these corrections he was in error himself, but for the most part he was right, and his remarks enabled me to perceive and avoid many mistakes. I looked for his weekly memoranda with much interest, and I trust I am all the better for them. He remarked on one occasion that I too often quoted the line, 'Nothing in my hands I bring,' and, he added, 'we are sufficiently informed of the vacuity of your hands.'
>
> A sensible friend who will unsparingly criticise you from week to week will be a far greater blessing to you than a thousand undiscriminating admirers if you have sense enough to bear his treatment, and grace enough to be thankful for it.[7]

Have confidence in God. He *is* still working everything in conformity with his purposes. He is *still* working all things together for the good of those who love him: every single thing that happens to us is a contributor from him to our salvation and our real good. He is still quite excellent at his job. He is still in the business of building and disciplining his church and is the God with whom we have to do. Calvin's definition of faith stands:

> A firm and certain knowledge of God's benevolence towards us, founded upon the truth of the freely given promise in Christ, both revealed to our minds and sealed upon our hearts through the Holy Spirit.[8]

If we know that God is well disposed towards us we shall go on unremittingly asking and expecting him to use our life and ministry, however much or little effect we see.

Always taking the (accurate) view that only God can do God's work we shall live in a spirit of dependence and expectation, and 'act as if.' By that I mean, that since people's destinies hang upon their response to the preached word we shall preach in that kind of a spirit: conveying by our demeanour, our tone of voice, our choice of language – by everything, that this preached word is a momentous encounter with the living God to whom we shall render account, that he is working in the process of it and that much is at stake. And this not just in our preaching but in the whole range of our ministry.

This does *not* call for lugubrious heaviness or lack of humour and humanity. I do think, however, that faith in God calls for passion and wholeheartedness: earnestness rather than casualness, the hard effort of rousing ourselves up to do our best rather than accepting second best or ease, precisely because we expect God to work and we owe him those things which are our responsibility in that shared task. It helps our people if our confidence in God is evident.

Enjoy ministering. Surely nothing is quite so dishonouring to God as a spirit of reluctant martyrdom about being in Christian work. Martyrdom?! Paul considered everything as loss compared to the surpassing greatness of *knowing* Christ Jesus, and it is greater still to be serving him as our life's employment. Compared with this, said Eric Alexander, I would not stoop to being President of the USA.[9]

In a certain church I was at a low ebb, going through a time of criticism from members, trying to avoid the things which caused offence. A friend visited; he had grown up in the Scottish highlands near peat bogs. 'Once when I was a wee boy,' he said, 'I was crossing an area of bog. Desperately I tried to avoid the boggy areas. My father told me, "Don't avoid the bog; fix your gaze on the clumps of firm grass and jump to them." ' I got the point.

We are in the kind of position Moses' mother found herself in. She had given up her son to the mercies of the river Nile rather than murder him at the royal command. Can we imagine the heartache? Then Pharaoh's daughter brought him to her (smart girl, Miriam) and Jochebed found herself breastfeeding that dear boychild after all: being paid to do that which was dearest to her heart. Is that not how it is with us in Christian service?

One of the vows taken by Church of Scotland ministers at their ordination captures this spirit of enjoyment. 'Do you engage faithfully, diligently *and cheerfully* to discharge the duties of your ministry, seeking in all things the kingdom of God?'

What is our vision? We want God to be glorified on earth. We aim to present our people to God perfect in Christ. We are back where we started in chapter one. We want, for God, the honour he deserves as God, King and redeemer. This is what we are for.

Quite soon now we shall be meeting him. Do we not want to be able to look into those piercing, approving eyes and hear the words, 'Well done, thou good and faithful servant'?

'It is enough that I live and die for Christ, who is to all his followers a gain both in life and death' (John Calvin: last letter to William Farel).[10]

References

1. C. Ellison, 'Where Does it Hurt?', *Leadership*, Spring 1982, p. 100.

2. Ephesians 2:12.

3. Ephesians 2:1-5.

4. G. MacDonald, 'What I want to be when I grow up', *Leadership*, Fall 1992, p. 70.

5. 2 Corinthians 13:5,6; Romans 12:3.

6. John 15:20; Romans 5:3-5; James 1:2-4; 1 Peter 1:6-9.

7. C.H. Spurgeon, *Lectures to My Students*, p. 331f: chapter XXII, entitled 'The Blind Eye and The Deaf Ear.' A powerful lecture.

8. INST., 3.2.7.

9. E.J. Alexander, unpublished talks on the Eldership, St George's Tron Church Halls, Glasgow, 15 November 1986. Edited versions, without this quotation, were written up as a series of four articles on the Eldership in *The Rutherford Journal of Church and Ministry*, vols. 3 and 4, Spring and Winter 1996 and 1997.

10. J. Calvin, *Letters of John Calvin*, reprint selected from Bonnet Edition first published 1855-57, Edinburgh, Banner of Truth, 1980, p. 246.

BIBLIOGRAPHY

Abraham, W.J. *The Logic of Evangelism*, London, Hodder, 1989.

Adair, J. *Effective Leadership*, London, Pan, revised edition, 1988.

Alexander, E.J. *St George's Tron Parish Church magazine*, Glasgow, Summer 1981.

'A Biblical View of the Eldership', *The Rutherford Journal of Church and Ministry*, vol. 4.1, Spring 1997.

'The Elder's Task', *The Rutherford Journal of Church and Ministry,* vol. 4.2, Winter 1997.

Alexander, J.W. *Managing our Work*, Downers Grove, IVP, 2nd edition 1975.

Allen, M. 'Fruitful Marks of Authentic Christian Ministry', in *Captive to the Word*, Burning Bush Publications, no place stated, n.d.

Ashton, C. *Church on the Threshold*, London, Daybreak, 1991.

Atkinson, D. 'Counselling as Covenant', *Lingdale Papers* no. 11, Clinical Theology Association, Oxford, 1989.

Augustine on John 6.51, Tractate 6, para 13 in NPNF 7.172.

Back, K.& K. Back. *Assertiveness at Work*, Maidenhead, McGraw-Hill, second edn. 1991.

R. Bakke, *The Urban Christian*, Eastbourne, MARC, 2nd edn 1989.

Baptism, Eucharist and Ministry, Geneva, WCC, 1982, Faith and Order Paper no.111.

Barker, M. 'The Call to the Ministry', *The Rutherford Journal of Church and Ministry*, vol. 2.2, Winter 1995.

'Ministers' Expectations', *The Rutherford Journal of Church and Ministry,* vol. 3.1, Spring 1996.

'The Minister and the Fellowship', *The Rutherford Journal of Church and Ministry*, vol. 3.2, Winter 1996.

'The Minister as a Member of the Fellowship', *The Rutherford Journal of Church and Ministry*, vol. 4.1, Spring 1997.

Barrs, J. article 'Shepherding Movement', in *New Dictionary of Theology*, ed. Ferguson, *et al*, Leicester, IVP, 1988.

Bartlett, D.L. *Ministry in the New Testament*, Minneapolis, Fortress, 1993.

Baxter, Richard. *The Reformed Pastor*, Houston edn, Basingstoke, Pickering and Inglis, 1983.

The Reformed Pastor, Banner of Truth edn, Edinburgh, 1989 reprint.

Beasley-Murray, P. *Dynamic Leadership*, Eastbourne, MARC, 1990.

Benn, W. 'The Baxter model: guidelines for pastoring today', *Orthos booklets* no.13, Fellowship of Word and Spirit, Northwich, 1993.

Bennet, D.G. 'Therapeutic love – an Incarnational Interpretation of counselling', *Lingdale papers* No. 1, Clinical Theology Association, Oxford, 1985.

B.F.B.S., *What makes Churches Grow?* A Basic Course on Church Growth, London, British and Foreign Bible Society, 2nd edition, 1979.

Blake, R.R. and J. Mouton, *Advanced Management Office Executive,* Houston, Gulf Pub. Co., 1962.

The Managerial Grid, Houston, Gulf Pub. Co., 1967.

The New Managerial Grid, Houston, Gulf Pub. Co., 1978.

Bona, John Cardinal. *A Treatise of Spiritual Life*, trans. DA Donovan, New York, Pustet, 1901.

Bridge, D. *How to Spot a Church Split Before it Happens*, Eastbourne, MARC, 1989.

Browne, Stanley G. *Medical Missions: Regaining the Initiative*, London, CMF, 1978.

Bruce, F.F. *The Speeches in Acts*, London, Tyndale Press monograph, date not noted.

Buber, M. *I and Thou*, Edinburgh, T&T Clarke, 1959.

Buchanan, D. 'Ministry and Suffering in the Life of Paul', *Ministry Today*, Issue 8, October 1996.

Bunyan, J. *Grace Abounding* and *The Pilgrim's Progress*, London, OUP, 1966.

Burroughs, Jeremiah. *The Rare Jewel of Christian Contentment*, Edinburgh, Banner of Truth reprint, 1964, (first published 1648).

Cairns, J.B. *Keeping Fit for Ministry*, Edinburgh, St Andrew Press, 1989.

Calvin, J. Commentary on Romans 8.13-18.

Institutes of the Christian religion. McNeill edition, London (SCM) and Philadelphia (Westminster), 1967: Library of Christian Classics Vols XX and XXI.

Letters of John Calvin, selected from Bonnet Edition first published 1855-57, Edinburgh, Banner of Truth, 1980.

Cameron, J.K., ed. *The First Book of Discipline,* Edinburgh, St Andrew Press, 1972.

Campbell, A.V. *Rediscovering Pastoral Care*, London, SCM, 1986.

Chalke, S. *Making a Team Work*, Eastbourne, Kingsway, 1995.

Chalmers, S. *Pastoral Care of Missionaries*, Research Dissertation in Christian Mission, Glasgow Bible College, 1993.

Chrysostom, John. *On the Priesthood* Bk 6.§12. NPNF First Series, Vol. 9, Grand Rapids, Eerdmans reprint, 1978.

Church of Scotland, *Reports to the General Assembly 1990*, Assembly Council Report 'The Basic Tasks of the Ordained Minister'.

Clements, Roy. *The Strength of Weakness*, Fearn, Christian Focus Publications 1994.

Clowney, E.P. *Resource of Divine Guidance*, paper given at Westminster Theological Seminary, Philadelphia, n.d.

Collins, J.N. *Diakonia: Reinterpreting the Ancient Sources*, Oxford, OUP, 1990.

Cormack, D. *Peacing Together*, Eastbourne, MARC (Mission Advanced Research and Communication Centre), 1989. *Team Spirit*, Eastbourne, MARC, Second edition, 1990.

Costas, O. *The Church and its Mission*, Wheaton, Tyndale, 1974.

Cox, C.J. and C.L. Cooper. *High Flyers*, Oxford, Blackwell, 1988.

Davies, G. *Stress*, Eastbourne Kingsway 1988.

Davis, Ken. *Secrets of Dynamic Communication*, Grand Rapids, Zondervan, 1991.

Deffenbacher, J.L. 'A cognitive-behavioural response and a modest proposal', *Counselling Psychologist*, vol. 13, p. 261-269.

Diognetus, letter to: possibly second century; quoted in Dowley, T., ed., *History of Christianity*, Berkhamsted, Lion publishing, 1977.

Doberstein, J.W., ed. *The Minister's Prayer Book*, London, Collins, 1986.

Dunn, J.D.G. *Jesus and the Spirit*, London, SCM, 1975.

Eadie, H.A. 'The Health of Scottish Clergymen', *Contact*, 41, Winter 1972, pp.2-22, with comments by Karl S.G. Greenlaw pp.23,24.

'Stress and the Clergyman', *Contact,* 42, Spring 1973, pp. 22-35.

'The Helping Personality', *Contact*, 49, Summer 1975, pp. 2-17.

Egan, G. *The Skilled Helper*, Pacific Grove, Brooks-Cole, 1990.

Ellison, C. *Where Does it Hurt?*, Leadership, Spring 1982.

Escobar, S. 'Elements of Style in Crafting New International Mission Leaders', *Evangelical Missions Quarterly*, Jan 1992.

Finney, J. *Understanding Leadership*, London, Daybreak, 1989.

Finding Faith Today, Swindon, British and Foreign Bible Society, 1992.

Finlayson, R.A. *The Cross in the Experience of Our Lord*, Fearn, Christian Focus Publications, 1993 reprint.

Forsyth, P.T. *Positive Preaching and the Modern Mind*, London, Hodder and Stoughton, 1907.

Fortino, Michael. 'Time Flies when you're Not Having Fun', source unknown.

Fowke, R. *Coping with Crises*, London, Hodder & Stoughton, 1968.

Francis, L.J. and R. Rodger. 'The Personality Profile of Anglican Clergymen', *Contact*, 113, 1994, pp.27-32.

Garratt, Sally. *Manage Your Time*, London, Fontana, 1985.

Gibbs, E. *Urban Church Growth*, Nottingham, Grove Books, 1977.

Gilbert, L. 'Lead or Get Out of the Way', *Leadership*, 1996.

Gilmour, S.M. 'Pastoral Care in the NT church', *NTS*, Vol.10, 1964.

Gledhill, R. 'Vicars Sacrifice Marital Joy on the Altar of Work', *The Times*, Wed. 27 March 1996.

Goh, P. 'Mission Agencies and the Management of Change', *EMA* Personnel Secretaries Group presentation on 30.11.95.

Goudge, E. *The Dean's Watch*, London, Hodder and Stoughton, 1960.

Grant, R. 'Trauma in Missionary Life', in *Missiology*, Vol. XXIII, No. I January 1995, p. 71-83.

Green, M. *Called to Serve*, London, Hodder, 1964.

Gregory the Great, *Pastoral Rule*, Book II, in NFNF, 2nd series, Vol 12.

Gregory of Naziansus, *Oration 2* In Defence of his Flight to Pontus, NPNF 2nd Series Vol.7, p.204ff.

Griffiths,M. *Get Your church involved in missions*, Sevenoaks, OMF, 1974.
A Task Unfinished, Crowborough, MARC/OMF, 1996.

Halverson, R.C. Introduction to Richard Baxter, *The Reformed Pastor*, Houston edn, Basingstoke, Pickering and Inglis, 1983.

Hamner and Organ, *Organisational Behaviour*, Dallas, Business Publications, 1978.

Haney, W.V. *Communication and Interpersonal Relations*, Homewood, Illinois, Irvin, 1979.

Harper, M. *Let My People Grow*, London, Hodder, 1977.

Harris, R. et al, eds., *Theological Wordbook of the Old Testament*, Chicago, Moody Press, 1980.

Harrison, R. *Organisation Culture and Quality of Service*, AMED, 1987.

Heppe, H. *Reformed Dogmatics*, Michigan, Baker, 1950.

Hind. D. *Transferable Personal Skills*, Sunderland, Business Education, 1989.

Hurding, R. *Roots and Shoots*, London, Hodder, 1985.

Hybels, Bill and Mark Mittleberg, *Becoming a Contagious Christian*, Amersham, Scripture Press, 1994.

Hybels, Bill. 'Reading Your Gauges', *Leadership*, Spring 1991, pp.32-38.

Jacobs, M. *Still Small Voice*, London, SPCK, 1982.

Jay, A. 'How to run a Meeting', *Harvard Business Review*, Mar-Apr 1976, pp.43-57.

Johnson, G. & K. Scholes. *Exploring Corporate Strategy*, New York, Prentice Hall, 1989.

Johnson, T.L. *Leading in Worship*: a source book for Presbyterian students and ministers, Oak Ridge TN, Covenant Foundation, 1996.

Sermon entitled 'Outlook', *Independent Presbyterian Church*, Savannah, GA, 23 Feb 1992.

Jones, G. & R. Jones. *Naturally Gifted*, London, SU, 1991.

Jones, M., ed. *Caring for the Missionary into the 21st Century*, Duns, Care for Mission publication, 1993.

Kidner, D. *Psalms 1-72*, Leicester, Tyndale OT commentaries, 1973.

Killick, H. 'Choosing Hymns', in *Rutherford Journal* Vol.3 No.2, Winter 1996, pp.11-14.

Kilmann, R.H. et al. *Corporate Transformation*, San Francisco, JosseyBass, 1988.

King, Philip. *Leadership Explosion*, London, Hodder, 1987.

King, Patricia. *Performance Planning and Appraisal*, New York, McGraw-Hill, 1989.

Kraybill, R. 'Ten commandments of meeting facilitation', in *Mediation and Facilitation Training Manual*, Akron Pennsylvania, Mennonite Conciliation Service, 3rd edn. 1995.

Küng, Hans, *The Church*, London, Burns and Oates, 1968.

Lawrence, Brother. *The Practice of the Presence of God*, London, Epworth, n.d.

Leadership. 'Turning Vision into Reality': an interview with Ken Blanchard, Spring 1996.

'The War Within', Name withheld, Fall 1992, p. 96-112.

Lloyd-Jones, D.M. *Preaching and Preachers*, London, Hodder, 1971.

MacDonald, Gordon. 'What I Want to be When I Grow Up', *Leadership*, Fall 1992, p.70.

McGrath and Kravitz. 'Group Research', *Annual Review of Psychology*, vol. 33, 1982, p. 195-230.

Mackenzie, A. *The Time Trap*, New York, Amacom, 1990.

Maloney, H.N. *Impulsive, Intuitional, Intentional: Three Styles of Leadership*, Church Westcote, Oxford: CTA newsletter 60, July 1992.

Marshall, I.H. *The New Testament View of Christian Leadership*, paper presented at Scottish Evangelical Alliance council, 1996.

Meadows, P. *Pressure Points*, Eastbourne Kingsway, 2nd edition, 1993.

Means, J.E. *Effective Pastors for a New Century*, Grand Rapids, Baker, 1993.

Michel, O. article s.v. *oikodomein*, in TDNT 5.141.

Moore, Carl. M. *Group Techniques for Idea Building*, Newbury Park, California, Sage, 1987.

Motyer, A. *Ordination for What?* Fellowship of Word and Spirit, Disley, Cheshire, n.d.

Murray, I.H. *Jonathan Edwards*, Edinburgh, Banner of Truth Press, 1987.

Myers, B. *MARC Newsletter*, Bromley, MARC, No.92-1, March 1992.

National Bible Society of Scotland, *Scottish Church Census*, 1995.

Nouwen, H. *In the Name of Jesus*: reflections on Christian leadership, London, DLT, 1989.

Ortberg, J. 'The Last Taboo: today's unforgivable sin that no leader dare confess', *Leadership*, Spring 1994, p. 80-85.

Ortiz, Juan Carlos. *Disciple*, Lakeland, 1971.

Owen, John. 'On Communion with the Trinity', *Works*, Vol. 2 , Edinburgh, Banner of Truth reprint 1968.

'On the True Nature of a Gospel Church', *Works*, Vol.16, Edinburgh, Banner of Truth reprint, 1968.

Packer, J.I. *Aspects of Authority*, Orthos Papers, number 9, Disley, Cheshire, n.d.

'The Practice of Evangelism', *The St Andrews 73 Report* on the Conference on Evangelism in Scotland, 1973, privately circulated.

'Introduction: Why Preach?' in *Preaching*, ed. S.T. Logan, Welwyn, Evangelical Press, 1986.

Peterson, E. *Working the Angles*, Grand Rapids, Eerdmans, 1987.

Philip, G.M. Bible Reading note on Acts 15:36-41, in *Congregational Record of Sandyford Henderson Memorial Church*, Glasgow, 8-10 Aug. 1994.

Philip, J. pastoral letter, *Congregational Record of Holyood Abbey Parish Church*, Edinburgh, April 1974.

Pinnock, C. 'The Work of the Holy Spirit in Hermeneutics', *Journal of Pentecostal Theology*, Vol.2, 1993, pp.3-23.

Reicke, B. *TDNT* 6.702 s.v. proistemi.

Richards, L.O. *Church Leadership*, Grand Rapids, Zondervan, 1980.

Ridderbos, H. *Paul: an Outline of his Theology*, London, SPCK, 1977.

Rogers, Carl R. *On Becoming a Person*, Boston, Houghton Mifflin, 1961.

Russell, P. *The Brain Book*, London, Routledge and Kegan Paul, 1979.

Sanders, J.O. *Spiritual Leadership*, London, MMS, 1967.

Schillebeeckx, E. *The Church with a Human Face*, London, SCM, 1985.

Sharpe, E. 'Personality Disorders and Candidate Selection', *Voluntary Agencies Medical Advisors (VAMA) Newsletter*, April 1996, pp.3-12.

Shorter Catechism, The. Edinburgh, Blackwood, 1966.

Spurgeon, C.H. *Lectures to my Students*, Marshall Morgan and Scott, London, 1954.

Still, W. 'Anointed Preaching', unpublished address to Crieff fellowship of ministers, January 1994.

pastoral letter, *Congregational Record of Gilcomston South Parish Church*, Aberdeen, February 1989.

Dying to Live, Fearn, Christian Focus Publications, 1991.

'Elijah: leadership as exemplified in his life and work,' unpublished address delivered at the Scottish Conference of the Teachers' Training Colleges Christian Unions, May 1971.

Letters of William Still, ed. S.B. Ferguson, Edinburgh, Banner of Truth Press, 1984.

Rhythms of Rest and Work, Aberdeen, Gilcomston South Church. n.d..

The Work of the Pastor, Aberdeen, Gilcomston South Church, 1976.

Towards Spiritual Maturity, Christian Focus Publications, 1992.

Stott, J.R.W. *Walk in His Shoes*, London, IVP, 1975.

Strachan, H. 'The Personal Passion for Christ', in *The Quiet Time*, edited by J.D.C. Anderson, London, IVF Press, 1957.

Swanston, T. pastoral letters, *Congregational Record of West Parish Church*, Inverness, January and March 1984.

Taylor, Dr and Mrs H. *Biography of James Hudson Taylor*, London, Hodder and Stoughton, 1973.

Taylor, M. *Learning to Care*, London, SPCK, 1983.

Thompson, J.G.S.S. art. on prayer in J. D. Douglas, ed., *New Bible Dictionary*, London, IVP, 1962, p.1020.

Tidball, D. J. *Skilful Shepherds*, Leicester, IVP, 1986.

Torrance, J.B. 'The place of Jesus Christ in worship', in Ray S. Anderson, ed., *Theological Foundations for Ministry*, Edinburgh, T&T Clark, 1979, p.348.

Torrance, T. *Expository Studies in St John's Miracles*, Edinburgh, James Clarke, 1938.

Torrance, T.F. quoted in R. Anderson *On Being Human*, Eerdmans, Grand Rapids, 1982.

Truax, C.B. and R.R. Carkhuff, *Towards Effective Counselling and Psychotherapy*, New York, Aldine, 1967.

Tuckman, B.W. 'Developmental Sequence in Small Groups', *Psychological Bulletin*, 1965, Vol.63, No.6, pp.384-399.

Warfield, B.B. 'On the Biblical Notion of Renewal', in *Biblical and Theological Studies*, Philadelphia, PRPC (Presbyterian and Reformed Publishing Company), 1952, p. 351-374.

'The Emotional Life of our Lord', *The Person and work of Christ*, PRPC, 1950.

Watson, David. *Discipleship*, London, Hodder & Stoughton, 1981.

Westminster Directory for the public worship of God, 1645.

Whetten, D.A. and K.S. Cameron. *Developing Management Skills*, New York, Harper Collins, 2nd ed. 1991.

White, C.P. 'The Church: A Caring Community', *Scottish Tyndale Bulletin*, 1977.

Sandyford Henderson Memorial Church Congregational Record, Glasgow, Pastoral letters of Sep and Nov 1998 and Nov 1999.

Whitehead, J. *Business Skills for Secretaries*, Kingston upon Thames, Croner, 1992.

Williamson, G.I. *The Shorter Catechism*, Presbyterian and Reformed Publishing Co., Nutley, NJ, 1972.

Wright, F. *The Pastoral Nature of the Ministry*, London, SCM, 1980.

Ziglar, Z. *Confessions*, New York, Pelican, 1978.

SCRIPTURE INDEX

Acts, cont

Romans

1 Corinthians

2 Corinthians

Galatians

Ephesians

PERSONS INDEX

SUBJECT INDEX

STUDY GUIDE

I am grateful to Operation Mobilisation in India and to Logos Ministries for this Study Guide which is used, in conjunction with an Indian edition of *The Effective Pastor*, in their leadership training. Ihave made a small number of changes to the guide

CPW
January 2002

Chapter 1 – Our Vision

1 What is the main danger that people face when they are involved in ministry?
2 Explain the benefits of maintaining our vision for God's work (50 words)
3 What is the ultimate purpose or reason for Christian work?
4 How can we resolve the tension between God's call and feelings of inadequacy?
5 Reflect on a time when you may have been busy for God but neglected to spend time with Him. What practical steps can you take in order to ensure that this will not happen again?

Chapter 2 – Our Present

1 Why are there only a few specific skills mentioned in the New Testament for those entering ministry?
2 What are the biblical qualifications for ministry?
3 Outline the things which will keep a Christian worker spiritually alive and vibrant.
4 How can we determine an authentic call to ministry?
5 List some of the dangers or obstacles one might face when entering Christian service or the ministry.
6 List some of the gifts or areas of ministry people have recognised and affirmed in you. Does this match with what you believe is your ministry? What action can you take in response to what you have learned from this?

Essay Project 1

Choose one of the following essay projects:

1 Outline the New Testament qualifications for Christian ministry and discuss its relevance today.
2 The New Testament does not give a job description for Christian ministry but a character reference. Outline the effects and implications this should have on a person's life and ministry.

Chapter 3 – Our Past

1 What is the main personality 'type' of a person who goes into Christian work? Discuss why being this personality type is both a strength and a weakness.
2 List the steps that are described as the 'guilt cycle'. Explain each one and show how they can manifest themselves in the life of a Christian worker.
3 List some of the physical symptoms of stress which can manifest themselves in a Christian worker.
4 Why is it that many Christian workers have a guilt-producing self image?
5 Is there a solution to the problem of the guilt cycle? Give reasons for your answer and discuss the implications it will have on a person's life.

Essay Project 2

1 Outline the destructive cycle that a Christian worker can get locked into because of their helping personality. Give suggestions as to how this cycle can be overcome spiritually and in a practical way.

Chapter 4 – Our Walk

1 Do you think a person's devotional life is private? Should Christians be instructed as to how they conduct themselves in this area?
2 Is it possible that a person in Christian service can go through

the motions of ministry activity, but not really be walking with Christ? If your answer is 'yes', give reasons for your answer and explain how this situation can be rectified.

3 What are the benefits of having a healthy devotional life?

4 Outline the biblical perspective which supports the importance of having a devotional life. Give scripture references to substantiate your answer.

5a List the main elements of a devotional life.

5b Do you need to adjust your life in any way so that you can further develop your devotional life? Give details.

6 How does the Lord's Prayer help structure our prayer life?

7 What are the two main dangers associated with fasting?

8 What practical advice may be considered useful in relation to fasting?

9 Have you discovered any changes that you need to make in your life as a result of studying this chapter?

Essay Project 3

What does the Bible say about spiritual warfare? What, if anything, can we learn from our own experience and that of others?

Chapter 5 – Preaching the Word

1 How would you describe the place of preaching in Christian ministry?

2 Explain how the importance of preaching is emphasised in the New Testament. Give scripture references.

3 In what way can preaching be described as a 'bridge'? What scripture can be used to illustrate this task?

4 Outline the essential elements which determine whether our preaching is biblical.

5 Give a definition of the ministry term "preaching".

6 Make a list of guidelines which will assist a person when seeking to prepare a message.

7 Should preachers review their sermons, method and style of preaching? Give reasons for your answer.

Chapter 6 – Public Worship

1 What are the Hebrew and Greek words for worship and what do they mean?
2 What should our attitude be when we meet together in church to worship God?
3 How would you reply to a person who says, 'I don't get much out of going to church, nor do I like the worship'?
4 What components should we expect to find in the context of worship and to what do they contribute?
5 Is there a need for structure in worship? Give reasons for your answer and state why you have come to this conclusion.
6 Outline the three basic stages of worship and the benefits that come through approaching God in this way.

Essay Project 4

Is there a place for inter-faith worship? How would you defend your position when discussing this with others?

Chapter 7 – A Praying People

1 Outline the differences between prayer in the Old Testament and prayer in the New Testament.
2 Explain why corporate prayer is vitally important in the life of the church.
3 Some people think that there is simply too much to pray for. How can a leader address this issue from a practical point of view.
4 Why do some ministers feel inadequate in relation to leading people to pray?

Essay Project 5

Outline the importance of prayer and explain the practical steps that a church leader can take in order to motivate more people to be involved in the prayer life of the church.

Chapter 8 – Caring

1. Why is Christian caring different from any other form of caring?
2. What can prevent a pastor or Christian worker from becoming discouraged in the routine of pastoral life?
3. Summarise the Christian distinctives in pastoral care.
4. List the Christian values which are most essential in pastoral care. Explain their importance.
5. List the vital elements which are outlined in Ezekiel 34 and explain the responsibilities of pastoral care.
6. What New Testament models are relevant to the task of pastoral care and how do they help us?
7. Take ten minutes to consider the following question and write your response somewhere that you can refer to later (e.g. a diary):
   What is the effect of my influence on people? Is it to nourish, gather, protect, heal and lead in a Christ-like way?

Essay Project 6

Discuss how the various models of pastoral care in the New Testament are relevant to your local situation.

Chapter 9 – Listening

1. How might you describe the account of the conversation between Jesus and the woman at the well?
2. What principles does JI Packer suggest can be identified in Jesus' method of dealing with people?
3. In what way can you answer the criticism that it is inappropriate to be structured in our approach to listening?
4. Outline what is suggested as the three stages in a fruitful listening approach.
5. How might you describe the aim of a model of listening?
6. Describe the benefits that a purposeful approach to listening might bring.
7. What is the task of the listener in spiritual direction?
8. Describe the three qualities that research has indicated makes for effective listening and explain why these are important.

9 For personal reflection: ask yourself whether you allow the Holy Spirit to be the real spiritual doctor in your work with people. Spend a few minutes to pray and respond as God leads.

Chapter 10 – Discipling

1 How would you describe the goal of Christian discipleship? What Bible texts may help us in this regard?
2 List and explain the various elements in the building process of edification.
3 What does the command of Christ to disciple all the nations involve?
4 What features do the gospels themselves include in the nature of discipleship?
5 What does the rest of the New Testament inform us are various elements of discipling?
6 Briefly outline the model of discipleship:
a) within the early church
b) given by Richard Baxter
c) given by David Watson's writings
7 Keeping in mind New Testament teaching, what principles of pastoral care can we learn from these models?
8 Consider how your church might personally benefit from the models of discipleship. List any changes that you think may need to take place.

Chapter 11 – Strategising

1a 'Ministry is not as simple as giving oneself to preaching, praying and caring'. How does the author justify this statement?
1b Do you agree with this? How does it relate to your experience? Explain your answer.
2 How does the author define "strategic management" and its aims?
3 What major lesson can we learn from Paul in the area of strategy?
4 Describe the six qualities that will enable the Christian leader to move the work of God forward.
5 What are some of the advantages of approaching our work strategically?

6 What considerations might we take into account to reduce tensions when planning change?

Essay Project 7

Write an overview of the management spiral as described by the author discussing each of the stages, the procedure for starting these components and the necessary tasks before, during and after a meeting.

Chapter 12 – Evangelising

1 'The New Testament does not define evangelism as a department of the church .... Rather it is the normal outcome of a spiritually strong community'. How does this contrast with some church growth schools of thought and what does the New Testament seem to suggest?

2a What does the author consider to be the most effective form of evangelism?

2b Where do we see this illustrated in the New Testament records and in history?

3 Describe the model presented by William Abraham concerning the approach to evangelism.

4 How does the author link a church-based evangelism to the management spiral to help our evangelistic approach?

Essay Project 8

Outline the serious situation concerning the decline of the church in the UK and suggest how some of these issues might begin to be tackled. How does the loss of young people from the church in the UK as described by the author make you feel? (see pages 155-164).

Chapter 13 – Leadership

1 'A community indwelt by the Holy Spirit; he anoints people for servant leadership ... which the church recognises by ordination'. Is this an adequate theology of leadership? Discuss.

2 List the eleven tasks that Owen defines as duties in the leadership.

3 How does Owen further define the task of ruling the church?
4 The author talks about the importance of leaders having vision. Do you think this is adequately represented in your situation? Give reasons for your answer.
5 Summarise what we might learn from the words used to describe the actions of Christian leadership.
6 How might a pastor who has a gift for preaching but is weak on leadership take encouragement from this author?
7 Detail the main words used to describe leadership and explain their function in the church.
8 List the qualities that naturally follow from the image of the leader as a steward.

Essay Project 9

1 Write a detailed description of the eight words surveyed by the author to describe the tasks of Christian leadership and observe in your own ministry which of these need to be strengthened and why.
2 Outline the various styles of Christian leadership. Reflect on where you are personally and list your strengths and weaknesses. What aspects of your approach to leadership may have to change? Make a plan to implement your findings.

Chapter 14 – Team Work

1 Is it accurate to state that the church exists as a "team"? Give reasons for your answer.
2 '..The teamness of gospel work is one of the hardest aspects of Christian service to achieve.' To what extent do you agree with this answer? Draw on biblical sources for guidance.
3 List the eight skills which have been noted to help all stages of team work.
4 Give an overview of the various possible structures for organising a team and consider the strengths or weaknesses of each.
5 'Good delegation enhances the quality of the work.' Outline the underlying principles of delegation.

Essay Project 10

Outline the stages in the development of a team and relate it to your own experience. Where can you see these in action in the groups of which you are part?

Chapter 15 – Time Management

1 What does the author conclude to be some of the reasons why his ministerial friends are in hospital with heart problems?
2 List some of the complicating factors for Christian leaders that makes them susceptible to sloth.
3 'Within limits, stress is desirable and improves performance.' Do you agree with the author? Reflect on your own experience, and that of colleagues, and explain your answer.
4 List some scriptures that can guide us in our thoughts concerning time management and briefly outline the insights that they give us.
5 What advice can we give to those who find paperwork a pressure in ministry?
6 Describe the time-stealing items that are common to leaders and outline strategies for dealing with them.

Chapter 16 – Stress

1a What are some of the warning signs that indicate we may be too busy and are suffering from stress?
1b Do you agree with the author when he states that scoring three out of the above list means we are in danger of jeopardising our capacity to minister? Defend your answer using personal examples.
2 Outline the three basic elements in the framework for understanding stress and explain how recognising these will assist us in ministry.
3 Is it appropriate to suggest that the best remedy for stress is to eliminate it altogether?
4 What is the acronym used to summarise the categories of the stressor and what do they stand for?
5 Outline the helpful advice the author gives in relation to a leader having balance.

6 From a theological perspective what advice does the Bible give in relation to stress?
7 According to the Australian psychologist Eadie, what are the three practices which can develop our resilience?

Epilogue – Perseverance and Reward

1 How does the truth of God's grace help us persevere in ministry?
2 Explain why there is a temptation in ministry to be sidetracked from the essential priorities.
3 What is the inevitable result of comparing ourselves to others? Give scripture references that may encourage us.
4 Initially we may think that difficult people will hinder our ministry, but what positive contribution can they in effect make to our lives and work?
5 'Have confidence in God'. How does the author expand on this statement as a basic principle for endurance?
6 Have you ever had a time when you did not 'engage faithfully, diligently and cheerfully … (in) the duties of your ministry'? Why was this? How did you resolve the situation?

The Little Book of things you should know about Ministry

Reid Ferguson

There are some astonishing gaps in the information with which church leaders are expected to guide their congregation. Some things are never said that would be of great usefulness if brought to the fore, discussed honestly and learnt from. How much pain, heartaches and mistakes would be prevented if the topics in this book were explored.

These short and thought provoking chapters will enable you to think through the issues involved in leading a congregation in your own context and enable you to serve your flock with greater success.

'Reid Ferguson blends common sense and uncommonly mature biblical wisdom in this helpful handbook for church leaders. He is refreshingly candid, consistently thought-provoking, and eminently practical.'

Phillip R. Johnson
Executive Director, Grace to You Ministries

'When we are dispirited; when we feel unappreciated, opposed or unsupported; the wisest responses can be considered from these pages. Read a chapter every week!'

C Peter White, Sandyford Henderson Memorial Church

'This may be a little book but it deals with massive issues. Reid Ferguson clearly knows ministry inside out, he knows people with all their fears and foibles but more importantly he knows God. I have no doubt that this book will help to raise the bar as we are inspired to love Christ more.'

David Meredith, Culloden Free Church, Inverness, Scotland

Reid Ferguson is a native of Rochester NY. A third generation minister, he has been at the independent, Evangelical Church of Fairport, Rochester, for 27 years, 6 of which have been Senior Pastor.

ISBN 1 85792 7869

Christian Focus Publications
publishes books for all ages

Our mission statement -

STAYING FAITHFUL
In dependence upon God we seek to help make his infallible word, the Bible, relevant. Our aim is to ensure that the Lord Jesus Christ is presented as the only hope to obtain forgiveness of sin, live a useful life and look forward to heaven with him.

REACHING OUT
Christ's last command requires us to reach out to our world with his gospel. We seek to help fulfill that by publishing books that point people towards Jesus and for them to develop a Christ-like maturity. We aim to equip all levels of readers for life, work ministry and mission.

Books in our adult range are published in three imprints.

Christian Heritage contains classic writings from the past.

Mentor focuses on books written at a level suitable for Bible College and seminary students, pastors, and other serious readers; the imprint includes commentaries, doctrinal studies, examination of current issues, and church history.

Christian Focus contains popular works including biographies, commentaries, basic doctrine, and Christian living. Our children's books are also published in this imprint.

For a free catalogue of all our titles, please write to

Christian Focus Publications, Ltd
Geanies House, Fearn,
Ross-shire, IV20 1TW, Scotland, United Kingdom
info@christianfocus.com

For details of our titles visit us on our website
www.christianfocus.com